WORKING WITH
WARRIORS

WORKING WITH
WARRIORS

DENNIS MARTIN

MILO BOOKS LTD

Published in October 2008 by Milo Books

ISBN 978 1 903854 79 2

Typeset by Jayne Walsh

Printed in Great Britain by
Cox & Wyman Ltd, Reading, Berkshire

MILO BOOKS LTD
The Old Weighbridge
Station Road
Wrea Green
Lancs PR4 2PH
United Kingdom
www.milobooks.com

This book is dedicated to the memory of my parents:
Henry George Martin
and
Sarah Martin
And with love to my family:
Sheila, Eric, Steven

ABOUT THE AUTHOR

Dennis Martin spent his entire adult life involved in frontline security, working on the nightclub doors in Liverpool, protecting VIPs all over the world, then training bodyguards and other security professionals.

He is also a widely published writer, with articles appearing in *Black Belt*, *Soldier of Fortune*, *SWAT*, *Combat Handguns*, *Mars and Minerva* and *Combat*. His regular 'On Guard' column in *Fighting Arts International* is widely accepted as being the impetus behind reality-based self-protection.

Dennis is still heavily involved in self-protection training and can be contacted at DenCQB@yahoo.co.uk

CONTENTS

FOREWORD

THESE DAYS, 'reality training' has become a buzz phrase, almost a fashion accessory, in the realm of combat martial arts, and the internet has spawned an army of pseudo-warriors whose only contact with this reality has patently been via the computer keyboard. The 'titans' of the World Wide Web, each wanting to stake their claim as potentate, are all fighting and arguing over a crown that, in my eyes, is already in situ. It was taken decades ago, ironically by a man that would likely not claim it; in fact he'd probably be embarrassed to think that he was even in the running.

As a young martial arts aspirant, I lived and breathed combative training. It was all I thought about, all I talked about and pretty much all I did. I drove everyone insane with my fervour. Even when I was balancing four kids, two jobs (and one angry wife), I still managed to train every day, often twice a day, year in, year out, with no seasons, no holidays and no days off for good behaviour. It was hard and often brutal training, the old-fashioned, honest KUGB (Karate Union of Great Britain) stuff where bulbous knuckles and broken noses met and danced on hard-wood dojo floors across the world.

What sustained me through that unforgiving period of forge training was a treat that landed on my welcome mat once a month: my copy of Terry O'Neill's *Fighting Arts International* (*FAI*). I can still remember the excitement of perusing the glossary for my column of choice when I came home from work (sweeping floors in a factory). There were three or four martial arts magazines on the market at that time, but they were all a diluted facsimile by comparison. And of course (cup of tea in hand, feet up, telly off) the first section I turned to and the column that I savoured most was always Dennis Martin's.

Don't get me wrong, this magazine – originally conceived by Den, Terry and the late Steve Cattle - was both sophisticated and cosmopolitan, it offered variety and quality as staple, and a plethora of choice to drool over. Terry is a martial arts polymath so there was something in *Fighting Arts International* to satisfy every taste. But it was Den's words that always got first reading in my abode, and it was Den's ideas that inspired me to walk my own warrior path.

Ironically, as a completely unknown second dan in the KUGB, I approached *FAI* with my very first article (entitled 'Confrontation, Desensitization'), which as it turned out became the keystone to my future career as a writer. *FAI* published me and encouraged me to expand not just my martial armoury but also my literary canon. And for that I will be eternally grateful.

Of course, later, many years on, after my ten-year sojourn as a nightclub doorman, after the release of my book *Watch My Back* and after teaming up with the erudite (old, and way too powerful) Peter Consterdine, I (along with the 'old man') was often seen by many as the pioneer of reality training in Britain, but I knew better. Den was there first, too early for the majority (though right on cue for me and the small few) and definitely way ahead of his time, but he was there and he was writing it and doing and teaching it 'like it is' when my belt was brown and my first encounter on the pavement arena was five years ahead, in a future I had yet to conceive, let alone live.

So, as you can imagine, when Peter and I started the British Combat Association, Den was top of the list of people that we invited to teach on our instructor's course. Dennis Martin was, and still remains the most popular trainer on our programme, and for me personally – despite the message-board titans with their hard-sounding reality web addresses – he is the most impressive and credible instructor of real self-defence in the world today. No contest. And when you read this book, and experience his amazing lineage, you will understand why.

And let me tell you, if you had even suggested, way back then, when Terry O'Neill and Dennis Martin were my martial arts deities, that in years to come I'd not only be good friends with them both but that Dennis Martin would invite me to write the Foreword to his first book, I might have suspected that you and your marbles had parted company. I certainly doubt that I'd have believed you. But here I am, and I have to say that it is genuinely a great honour. This book will be the most prized of my vast collection. I know that you are going to love and be amazed by it too. Den's has been (and continues to be) a startling and enlightening life, one that you will wish you'd lived, but will be grateful by the last line on the last page that you did – but only through the safety of these pages.

Geoff Thompson, Coventry, 2008

Geoff Thompson is the bestselling author of *Watch My Back* and over twenty other books on self-protection and training. He is also a BAFTA award-winning screenwriter. His books and DVDs are available through www. GeoffThompson.com

INTRODUCTION

WRITING A BOOK such as this causes you to reflect on the various critical, pivotal moments that shape the entire course of your life. The prime pivotal point came for me in April 1965, when I attended a karate demonstration, the first of its kind, presented by a group of visiting Japanese experts at St George's Hall in Liverpool.

When performing the solo, formal *kata* exercises, these masters moved like independently-sprung tigers, dropping into low straddle-stances, legs like spring-steel, leaping high into the air, then punctuating the flow with staccato kicks, piston-like punches and scything chops. Working with partners on the sparring drills, they still delivered their strikes with fearsome impact. Each shot was pulled a fraction of an inch short of lethal contact, and this blend of ferocity and control was curiously compelling. If anyone deserved the title 'heavy hitters' it was this troupe of Japanese gentlemen. I had never seen anything like it, and it changed my life forever.

I quickly joined the local karate club, and began a journey that eventually took me into frontline security on nightclub doors, into VIP close protection all over the world, and into the training of military, police security and civilian personnel in close-quarter combatives.

Along the way I met and became friends with several staunch men, notably Terry O'Neill and Gary Spiers. Terry, rated by *Black Belt* magazine as topping the list of 'The Toughest Men on Planet Earth', has been the most influential person in my life. Gary, known in Japan as Kuma-san ('Mister Bear') because of his size, had vast experience of professional violence on three continents. Liverpool doormen are not easily impressed, but Gary became a legend to us.

In this book I have tried to tell the story of what it has been like working with such men. Some of the tales may seem far-fetched, but, as far as time and memory permit, everything in the book is true. I know. I was there.

A visiting Japanese master demonstrates karate at St George's Hall, Liverpool, in April 1965.

CHAPTER 1

THE BEGINNER

MY INTRODUCTION TO the world of martial arts came at, of all places, a local fete. I went along and, amid the tombolas and stalls selling home-made jam, I saw a demonstration of judo by some men in what appeared to be white pyjamas. I was intrigued.

Being an avid young reader, I started seeking judo manuals from the public library and looked for a club to learn at. It wasn't easy. In 1962, information about martial arts was hard to find. I was fifteen years old and still attending West Derby High School and one day while walking down Quarry Road on my way back to school after lunch, I noticed a small plaque on a doorway, announcing the Mersey Judo Club. The following Saturday I joined their children's class, then after a while started attending the adults classes too. I enjoyed judo and visited several clubs, including the Liverpool Transport group in Green Lane, and Pilkingtons in St Helens.

Like most teens at the time I enjoyed going to see Merseybeat groups, mainly at the Cavern Club. I was regular at lunchtime sessions while still at school, then later started going to the evening sessions. Unfortunately, I never got to see the Beatles, but my sister did go to one of their shows. The BBC wanted to make a programme about the Liverpool groups in Hamburg, and so took a group of us Cavern regulars over to the Star Club in Hamburg for a programme called *Wacker Mach Schau*: the title was based on the Hamburg club owner's exhortation to the various bands: 'Make a show!'

During this time I read about karate, which, as far as I could gather, seemed to be a kind of 'advanced judo'. I guess I had heard about it the same way most people did, just from books and movies, and bits that were on television at the time. You would see these either serious or comical demonstrations of breaking wood. I had read R. W. Smith's *Complete Guide to Judo*, which mentioned karate, E. J. Harrison's *The Manual of Karate*, and anything else on the subject I could get my hands on. But the biggest problem was finding out where karate was taught in Liverpool.

I walked the length and breadth of the city, looking. I kept hearing of karate clubs in different parts of Liverpool, but they usually turned out to be ju-jutsu clubs. For example, I went along to the Alpha Ju-Jutsu Club in Sheil Road, and spoke to the legendary Jack Britten, who had been teaching self-defence since 1936. He had first been taught in 1910 by the touring ju-jutsu exponent Yukio Tani, a diminutive Oriental who took on all comers in no-holds-barred challenges. Knowing what I know now, I would have liked to have chatted to him longer, but since he didn't teach what I was seeking – karate – I left.

After leaving school, I worked in the BICC Prescot, the huge home of British Insulated Callender's Cables, which at one time had 14,000 employees producing paper-insulated cables and ran its own football teams, fire brigade and even an on-site hospital. It had a judo section as part of its Sports Club, and while I was training there one evening, a chap turned up and asked to put a poster advertising a karate demonstration on the notice board. This was Frank Vernon, who I would later work with on the door of the Top Rank. I went over to him like a shot and found details of the demo and the karate group. The demonstration was to be by four Japanese masters. I also found out where Frank trained, which was the Red Triangle gym in the Everton area of Liverpool.

On Friday, 23 April 1965, I went to St George's Hall in

Liverpool city centre, where a capacity crowd was treated to an awesome display of sheer athletic ferocity. At that time Japanese Karate comprised four main systems, or styles. Shotokan was based on long-range engagements, big, powerful moves and low stances. Goju-ryu was a close-range system, attacking groin, throat and eyes. Wado-ryu was an offshoot from Shotokan, with Ju-jutsu mixed in. Shito-ryu can best be described as a mixture of Shotokan and Goju. The four Japan Karate Association (JKA) instructors, Masters Kase, Kanazawa, Enoeda and Shirai, were on a mission to spread Shotokan karate around the world, so they really pulled out all the stops in putting on a show. They moved like cats, yet their techniques resembled powerful machinery. Their punches and kicks shot out like pistons. The force was immense. They performed for a couple of hours, going through the entire repertoire of techniques, *kata* (forms) and sparring routines. That was my first live sight of karate and what impressed me most was the dynamism of it, and just what it was – something totally different. This amazing power output from these guys who were able to move and react in this completely unusual way. Kanazawa, Shirai and Enoeda were all former JKA champions, and Kase had started in karate during World War Two, when martial arts training was especially severe. And each one of them, any one of them, would have been a tremendous sight, but to see them all together – in fact, we were a bit spoiled because now those top Japanese never do demonstrations anyway, and we had them all in one go. You probably won't see something like that again. It was fantastic, and I was entranced.

And so, the following Sunday, I turned up at the Red Triangle karate club at the YMCA in Everton Road. It was a training day, but apparently there was a waiting list, as they restricted membership at the time. I was told my name would be put on the list and I would be contacted when there was a vacancy. After a couple of weeks I was invited to join, so I went down again and paid my £5, filled in a sheaf of forms, including references, medical clearance, several oaths, in short everything short of registering my hands with the police. That was the British Karate Federation in those days; it was almost like joining the Masons. In fact I'm still sworn to secrecy, so I can't say much about it. It had been founded by Essex man Vernon Bell, who was said to be the first British man ever to hold a karate black belt.

Then when I actually managed to set foot on the dojo (training hall) floor, I was instantly bawled at by Terry Astley, a pugnacious blue belt, for not bowing. In judo such etiquette wasn't strictly enforced, and I found the karate guys rather more serious than their judo counterparts. Training was hard, with numerous repetitions of the basics, as well as lots of callisthenics, including push-ups on knuckles and sit-ups done over the edge of a stage.

At the St George's Hall demo, the local guys had put on a short display and I had noticed that one of them was a young doorman I had seen working at the Cavern Club. A couple of weeks later, I went along to the Cavern, saw him again and mentioned I had seen him doing karate. This was Terry O'Neill, and that first conversation became a lifelong friendship.

The senior guys at the Red Triangle were Andy Sherry, Joe Chialton and Alan Smith. Andy, who had previously studied ju-jutsu with Jack Britten, was the most dedicated enthusiast there. He pushed himself relentlessly. They were the first lads to be graded black belts by the JKA in the UK. Strangely, Joe stopped training shortly afterwards, while Andy went on to numerous championship titles and to his current position as the leading British Shotokan instructor. Alan Smith gained his black belt shortly after my arrival. He was a toughie, a real Scouse lad with lots of street experience and bags of guts. He worked a couple of doors in his time.

We were very fortunate to have Keinosuke Enoeda become

resident instructor in Liverpool. Born in 1935, he was a fear-some fighter who had won the JKA All-Japan Championship in 1963. Following this he was sent to Indonesia to train their military, including the presidential bodyguard. Renowned for his hard training, he was a hit in Liverpool. He suited us and we suited him. Although I was a white belt I was allowed to train with the seniors as well, so started training twelve sessions per week (five evenings plus Sunday, two sessions back to back per time).

Training as directed by Master Enoeda was severe. Probably the most intense drill was *jiyu-ippon kumite*, a semi-free sparring routine where, because the attack was pre-set, it was delivered full force: the defender had the task of blocking, then countering with controlled force. This drill was done two at a time, monitored by Master Enoeda, with the rest of the class seated in a circle. It was restricted to the more senior colour belts. We were encouraged to develop our 'fighting spirit' with deep shouts, firm stances and darting attacks. There was a guy who had trained for several years, who I'll call Mike. He was something of a bully, always dominating the lower grades. Terry O'Neill knew him well and told me that he worked in the morgue, where he practised wristlocks on the corpses! Like many bullies he was a coward, and during semi-free sparring I saw him chased right out of the door of the gym.

Later we were introduced to full freestyle sparring and again this was done with two lads taking the centre of the floor in highly atmospheric conditions. Today, you see whole classes all engaged in light sparring. What we did at the Red Triangle was far from light; it was serious, intense and martial. Master Enoeda considered Liverpool his flagship dojo and wanted to turn out a strong cadre. He was harder on the Red Triangle lads than on those who attended his courses in other areas.

Terry O'Neill took a year off from karate; and during this period got a regular day job, got married and started the weights seriously. He did go down to London at least once to train with Master Kanazawa but basically he stopped training. When he came back we were the same grade. Then we sparred. I can still remember that first time facing Terry in freestyle sparring. The only way I can describe it is like being in the sea and being taken by a huge wave. It just goes to show that belt ranks are not always a real reflection of skill.

A lad from York turned up at the Red Triangle one day. Steve Cattle had already trained in karate in his hometown. He had chosen Liverpool for college in order to be able to train with Master Enoeda. Steve and I became good friends, and when he started a class at a teacher training college in Huyton, I often trained there. Steve was a keen judo man who competed in the World Student Judo Championships in Tokyo. He stayed on to do some training and later told me that the judo training at a Japanese university was the hardest he'd ever done. Steve became British Open Karate Champion and a noted instructor. The last time I spoke to him was when we were both travelling back from London on a long Sunday train journey. I had been to a shotgun shooting course, Steve had been teaching karate. We caught up on old times. Not long after, Steve died after suffering an epileptic attack alone on a train.

Eventually I reached the brown belt grade in Shotokan, then started training with various other karate groups. One was based in the Conservative Club in Green Lane, where they had two floors for their exclusive use. The main attraction was frequent hard, virtually full-contact, sparring. Quite often, when getting changed afterwards, we would have vivid footprints on our chests. Harry Benfield, who I later worked with on the Top Rank, ran this group.

Harry had a brother, Tommy, who trained in some weird style of martial arts. One time he was involved in a road rage incident, resulting in dire threats being exchanged, so Tommy got out of his car and stood, ready to fight. The other driver started to get out, took one look at Tommy in his knock-kneed fighting stance, and got back in saying, 'I'm sorry mate, I didn't realise you were a cripple.'

Later I trained in a dank dungeon on Everton Brow. The floor was black stone, we were barefoot, and we finished with cold showers, and this was winter – and we loved it!

* * *

At about this time I became interested in Goju-ryu karate, the 'hard/soft' system, originating in Okinawa. I had read a couple of articles about Goju, and while I was intrigued by all Okinawan karate, more so than just by one style of it, the most available style turned out to be Goju. It combines hard striking attacks such as kicks and close-hand punches with softer, open-hand, circular techniques for attacking, blocking, and controlling the opponent. A book that influenced me a lot was *The Karate Dojo* by Peter Urban. Although its historical accuracy was dubious, it was a very good motivational book, and it pushed me in the direction of Okinawa.

After seeing the two leading Goju instructors, Steve Morris and Brian Waites, perform a terrific demonstration at the Crystal Palace, I contacted Brian and he started coming up to Liverpool, where we started a small group of interested guys. Brian was a great lad, a real London character, with superb classical techniques. His flexibility was impressive and, like Terry O'Neill, he was into bodybuilding.

It was also during this time that a young lad from Scotland Road joined the group. Paddy Phillips eventually became my top student and would work on the Miss World competition and a couple of other bodyguarding jobs with us. For several years he was a member of the Fire/Rescue Service, before going on to a great career as an osteopath. Paddy treats all the top bodybuilders and martial artists for sport injuries. Both

Terry and Gary relied on Paddy to keep them functioning. I suffered a shoulder injury which Paddy completely cured in about three visits. Recently I injured my wrist while overseas and Paddy fixed it in a few treatments.

Goju suited me. It wasn't that it was better than Shotokan, more that it was what I was looking for. I wanted a good arsenal of short-range techniques, like elbow strikes. However, the conditioning was very, very hard. We used to do an exercise – and this was at basic, white-belt level – where you would stand facing your partner in a cat stance, and you would kick to the inner thigh and try to make the other guy flinch, or try to take it without flinching. Looking back, you couldn't pay me to do that; I don't think it's very good for you and I'm sure a lot of people still carry injuries because of it. It was a good physical and mental conditioning drill, but it was very hard. I also learned how effective it could be. I had been working on the door for a while by then and the Goju elbow strikes definitely worked. They became one of my main techniques.

Unbeknown to me, my path was about to cross again with Terry O'Neill, a chance meeting that would change the course of my life.

Terry O'Neill, aged sixteen.

CHAPTER 2

THE KARATE KID

THE CAVERN CLUB became one of the most famous music venues in the world, almost entirely because of its connection to The Beatles and the Merseybeat sound of the early Sixties. It was also, I am sure, the location for many a life-changing encounter. As mentioned in the previous chapter, it was here that I first saw Terry O'Neill. I was a customer, and Terry and Tommy McNally were doormen there. When I started training at the Red Triangle, I recognised him, so the next time I went to the Cavern, we got talking. Terry went into red alert straightaway when I mentioned karate, which was clearly his passion.

Terry was then a blue belt, which was between green and brown in the old grading system. I got talking to him on a regular basis. He almost immediately pointed out that what we were doing was karate-do, which was a sport version of a combat system, and he made that distinction very clear to me. So right from my introduction to karate I was aware of the difference between sport, art and real fighting. I must admit that I was always more influenced by Terry than by anyone else because he was the guy who was actually doing it, night after night, in the city centre. That impressed me more than the more traditional aspects, even though that's the system I was training in. He told me things then which have influenced me ever since, that very first time we talked: about the difference between 'do' and 'jutsu'; about the way things are different in the street from the dojo; about how techniques that we used in training might not work in the street.

Terry was born in 1948 and so was close to my age but already had a wealth of experience. This is his own story of how he embarked on a lifelong martial arts journey:

I first became interested in physical culture through Tarzan, the Edgar Rice Burroughs character. My father enrolled me in the Tarzan Club and there were two weekly magazines, Tarzan's Adventures, *which he used to get for me. I actually learned to read through the Tarzan books, even though they were adult books, not written for children, with tearing people's throats out, killing all the natives, and so on. So Tarzan was a great interest.*

I always wanted to be fit and strong. I was an only child, with no interest in team sports, but I got an interest in judo. When we passed down Catherine Street, my father pointed out Skyner's Ju-jutsu club, where he had trained. I don't know how much training he'd done, he was a policeman. Anyway, I would show him armlocks I had tried to learn out of Pat Butler's books. [Butler, the founder of the UK Amateur Judo Association, wrote books like Popular Judo *(1958),* Advanced Judo and Self Defence *(1961) and* Judo For Juniors *(1966).] Pat Butler came into my life in a big way.*

We were living in Benson Street, off Mount Pleasant, in the city centre, in the original police flat they had given to my father. Just before my father had died – aged seventy, when I was only thirteen – I had started taking judo lessons, only twenty yards up the road in the Mount Pleasant YMCA. I promptly broke my collarbone; someone threw me with a tomoe-nage (stomach throw), which bothered my mother. My dad then had a stroke and died, so I was sort of in charge of the household.

Neither of my parents were particularly athletic; my mother had bronchitis. At an early age I'd had operations on my knees, for lumps, like TB of the kneecap. The surgeon, Mr Dwyer, had operated on my knees and I was excused games; I was on a stick for about a year. The surgeon told me I would never play sports. Many years later, I broke my ribs competing in the European Championships, and went to hospital when I got back to Liverpool. This Mr Dwyer came round to examine me and I remembered him and told him, 'You told me I'd never play sport.' He said, 'Yes?' I told him, 'Well I'm on the British karate team.' He said, 'These things happen,' and moved on. If I'd listened to him it would have been the kiss of doom.

I've never been any good at football, always last to be picked. I failed the eleven-plus, I was more interested in Tarzan. I'd gone to St James', the most cosmopolitan school in Liverpool; if they asked who needed to be excused during religious education, half the class went out. I'd never seen black people, Chinese, and the school was full of them. The playground was on the roof and somebody had been thrown off; my mother was terrified what would happen to me. Fortunately I befriended a lad called Lloyd Henry, a black guy, who had a great interest in Tarzan, and he used to look after me. Anyway, I passed the thirteen-plus and went to Toxteth Tech. Later when I was doing karate one of the teachers, Charlie Penrose, the English teacher, found out about it. I was always good at English and Mr Penrose found out there was a karate class in St Helens on a Wednesday night, which was always hard for me to get to, but he had a car and would take me up there. He joined, he's listed as a member of the British Karate Federation. Anyway, suddenly I became one they wanted on the football team. I still couldn't play football to save my life, but I wouldn't be kicking the ball I'd be kicking them on the head, so they all wanted me on their team.

I had heard of this thing called karate but the only book about it that was out was E.J. Harrison's The Manual of Karate, so I wrote to Pat Butler asking him about it. I had read somewhere that you could damage your hands badly, that was a prerequisite to karate mastery, so I asked him if you had to damage your hands, and also where could you go to train. I've still got his letter in response, which I opened in the presence of my mother, unfortunately. He said, yes, you did have to damage you hands in karate, which was an art for just killing people, whereas judo was far better, and he gave me the address of the Amateur Judo Association. My mother read it and *responded: 'Oh Christ, you're not doing karate.'*

About eighteen months later, I discovered there was a karate club just a bit further up the road, at the top of Mount Pleasant, in Harold House, a Jewish community centre. The class was on Sundays. I went in, was allowed to watch a little bit, and they said you had to be sixteen years old to train; I was fourteen at the time. Anyway I lied about my age. You needed a letter from a doctor, a reference from a police officer or similar. It was like joining a secret society. This was the British Karate Federation. I lied about my age and got a police officer, who had known my father, to write a reference. I started training just after my fifteenth birthday. To jump many years ahead, thirty-five or forty years later I happened to be with Vernon Bell, he was like the Funakoshi of Europe, he brought karate from Paris, he introduced it to Britain, and was interviewing him for my magazine Fighting Arts. *When I told him the story – I still to this day don't know if he was joking – he said, 'This is a very serious matter Mr O'Neill, I'll have to amend the records.' And he went to some files. I still don't know if he was bullshitting or not.*

Anyway, I started karate and gave up the judo. I had been in for two gradings and got, I think, a 'temporary yellow belt'; that's as far as I got. It was under the British Judo Council, and at the same time I had been for a few courses at the Bromborough Judo Association on the Wirral. Brian Moles was a sandan (black belt, third rank), and they had Kenshiro Abe Sensei, a leading judo master who had his own association. He would come round strangling everyone. I was watching them go down, and he came to me from behind, and I always remember how fast it was, and then I woke up with a tremendous headache, and afterwards didn't sleep for hours. In that class he had an assistant coming round doing katsu [resuscitation methods]. Also under the BJC there was aikido going on, run by a man called Ken Williams, very impressive, from the Aikikai of Uyeshiba Sensei, the founder of Aikido. They also had Noro Sensei and Nakazono Sensei, both senior instructors resident in France. I went to one course with Noro Sensei, at Kelvinator's in Bromborough, when I was fifteen, and he snapped my wrist, with the nikkyo lock. All I remember was he put this wristlock on and I'm going, 'Ow, ow, ow,' and he's telling me, 'The pain is not in your wrist, it's all in the brain.' Anyway, he broke my bleeding wrist!

I thought the aikido was incredible. I've jumped ahead of my time space here, but at the time I'd seen top karate sensei like Murakami, and Kanazawa, and couldn't understand how anyone could fail to be hit by someone of that skill; yet watching Noro and Nakazono, who were senior sixth and seventh dans of the Aikikai, I couldn't understand how anyone could hit them. Of course I now realise that the aiki instructors were being attacked by aikido students and all that.

At Harold House, Andy Sherry was the senior. Having filled in my application forms, I was allowed to watch a course with Tetsuji Murakami Sensei and Vernon Bell. I couldn't understand a word Murakami was saying, he kept slapping people around the head, but something appealed to me, it was different. Prior to that at school we'd done yoga, and I was the only one able to sit in the lotus posture. I was still only fourteen, and I was sitting there eating sweets; Vernon Bell was walking round looking at things and started chatting to me, telling me he was sure I'd be soon able to join in. Murakami was teaching a group at the end of the room, and I couldn't see. Bell turned, and put his hand out behind him. I thought he wanted to take my hand and lead me up to watch the class, so gripped his hand; which he shook free. It was a sweet he wanted! Most embarrassing.

Bell was a very good ju-jutsu man and he introduced karate into the country, it was down to him, so whatever anybody says, we all have a debt of gratitude to him. But the stories about him! When Kanazawa Sensei was first here, Bell bought fish and chips and said, 'You'll have to eat yours here because the wife doesn't like Japs or Chinks,' and left him outside on the doorstep. Many years later we were at a meeting of the British Karate Control Commission, they were all there, in collars and ties. I was there, never interested in politics, but we'd been to a World Championship. Anyway, it came up about the Japanese, and Vernon was anti-Japanese, took a Union Jack out of his bag, wrapped it around his body, climbed on the conference table and marched up and down singing 'Rule Britannia'! Chairman Alan Francis, a chief superintendent with the police who had been given the BKCC job to keep control of the nutters, which he did, tried in vain to talk him down. It was just one of those incredible things which I wouldn't have believed if I hadn't been there.

Once I started karate, I used to go up and practise basics and kata in the same YMCA where I'd done judo. One day I saw these two big guys in there wrestling. Turned out it was Tommy McNally, who became a great friend of mine, and Tony Buck, an Olympian and champion wrestler. The smaller of the two, Tommy came over, asked me what I was doing, and I told him about karate. He invited me down to the Cavern Club, where the Beatles played. I had never been to a night club, ever. I went down one day with John Kerruish, a school pal of mine, and Tommy showed us around, VIP'd us. It wasn't really my scene. He met me again at the YMCA and had me showing him some of the karate blows, which he integrated into his stuff. Tommy was an amateur wrestler but he was doing some pro wrestling, and he integrated some karate-type moves under his mat name The Great Kwango or something, while he wore a mask.

Anyway, he asked me if I'd like some work. I was just sixteen and he got me work at the Tower Ballroom, over the water in New Brighton. He had me bulk up by wearing all kinds of sweaters under my shirt, had my hair cropped short, I'd never done anything like that. The first time I worked there was, I think, a concert by the Walker Brothers. The Rolling Stones was another. Tommy then said he would get me working on the Cavern. Paddy Delaney, who was in charge of the Cavern Club door, said I was too young. But playing on Paddy's origins Tommy said, 'He's a good Irish lad, looking after his mother.' Paddy, however, was adamant; under no circumstances would he wear me working. The wages were then £1.50 per night, and Tommy finally said, 'He'll give you ten bob from his wages every night.'

Paddy instantly replied, 'He's on Monday, Tuesday, Wednesday in the daytime, then Friday and Saturday nights.'

So that's how Tommy first got me on. He then suggested I start bodybuilding. I had never done weights before, just push-ups.

Anyway, I had started work at Robinson Buckley, a shipping office. I'd been knocked back from the police cadets, the only job I'd ever considered. I failed the eyesight test, which devastated me. My whole ambition was to join the police. My two schoolmates, John Jeffries and the lad I mentioned before, John Kerruish, they joined the police. Jeffries is possibly still in. John Kerruish had great success; he retired as a Detective Chief Superintendent, in charge of many murder cases. He was the lad I first started judo with. By the time I was nineteen, I could have got in with contact lenses, but I realised they would stop me doing karate. My dad never wanted me to join the police. With my mother being a police widow there were often police calling round. I'd go up to Mather Avenue regularly, put all the pads on, and run round for the dogs to tackle me. I'd be fourteen or fifteen at the time.

Anyway, I joined the Universal Health Studio, in Lord Street, and I was twelve stone plus when I paid my membership. It was a terrific gym. One of the instructors was a guy called John Pinnington, who later turned out to be a doorman, who put me on a course. I'd never done weights before but I got the Universal award for the most progress in nine months because I'd always trained hard in karate, but if you train hard on the weights, and then start to eat a lot, you can really progress. I think I gained almost a stone in just over six months. So much so, that I was able to start taking those sweaters off on the door; instead it was just me.

Tommy said that bodybuilding is good self-defence, he was always a pragmatist. He reckoned you're less likely to be attacked the bigger and stronger you look – and he was right. I mean, nowadays there are people who would attack a buzzsaw, but back then the bigger and stronger you looked, the better. Nobody wanted to fight Tony Buck, for example, he was huge. Yet he might actually have been the softest, *slowest to react. Tommy was always the one to react first. Plus, when it did come to the crunch, if you didn't spark them, didn't kayo them immediately, then it would usually come to grappling, and the bigger and stronger you are, the better it is. So that's how I got onto the Cavern, it was down to Tommy, who looked after me, was like a guru to me for many, many years.*

My first confrontation at the Cavern was at an all-night session; the most memorable fights there were when we had all-nighters. Everyone would be turfed out from the early session, and they'd queue again to come in. I was watching the queue, told not to let anyone queue-jump, when I saw these two fellers jump in. I wandered down to them and told them to get to the back. I always hated being called 'son' or 'kid' and this guy said, 'Something, something, son.' Tommy had always told me what to do, you know, steal it on them, never give them a chance. To use a pre-emptive technique, or in other words, a sucker punch.

This feller has fronted me, won't get out of the queue, so I said, 'Just wait till this policeman's gone past.' As he turned his head, which is what I wanted, I kneed him in the groin. At the time, I thought someone had punched me from the back. What had actually happened was that when I kneed him in the balls, which was a successful strike, his head shot forward and butted me in the face. Now I'd done this knee in heian yondan, the number four karate kata, but you've got to either turn them around or put your arm across as a barrier, because their head will automatically shoot forward.

As it was, the feller recovered faster than me, but fortunately Kevin Connelly, another pro-wrestler, who unfortunately is dead now [Kevin died in the 2004 Indian Ocean tsunami: D.M.] ran down and helped me out, stiffened the guy. I still thought that someone else had hit me, but Kevin put me straight and took me down stairs. My nose was pouring with blood. That was one of those things. Karate works in the dojo, but you're pulling it so you don't get the reaction. It's like doing mae-geri chudan/oi-tsuki jodan [front kick to body followed by punch to face]. If the mae-geri is successful, the punch may be too high. You do have to train to hit things.

Another time, I went down to the Grapes pub, where Paddy Delaney used to slide off for a drink and come back stinking of onions so Ray MacFall, the Cavern owner, wouldn't know he'd been drinking. This night I went to fetch Paddy to tell him there was a problem on the door, and as he was finishing his pint I walked back and saw a guy running away from the door, with Bob Wooler, the Cavern DJ, running after him shouting, 'Stop him!' I grabbed the guy, he grabbed me, and I spun in for a really good hip throw. I threw him, landed on top of him, and he was unconscious. Which prompted Bob Wooler to write that 'Terry is the toughest and best looking bouncer'. The landlord from the Grapes saw the action too, and years later in a radio interview with Pete Price told of the fastest technique he'd ever seen. It was mainly that the feller was running, and his own momentum worked for me.

I was just a kid there at the Cavern. I had never seen headbutts. I remember we were doing a thing with Sandy Shaw and Petula Clark, it was being filmed for French TV. I was put in charge of Petula Clark, walking round with her. I got hit on the back, and when I turned round it was a girl holding a chair. I grabbed the chair and she started kicking me. I didn't know what to do. Kevin jumped in and butted her in the face, and asked what I was doing. I had bruises all over my shins. I really didn't know what to do, and would probably still be standing there now! Afterwards Tommy told me, 'If they're hitting you, hit them back.' He always looked after me.

I never did that much fighting at the Cavern because I was sort of a junior to Tony Buck, Tommy McNally and Kevin Connelly. I remember the first time I saw Tony Buck. There was this huge back standing by the squat rack, bar bending across his shoulders. I thought he was squatting, but he pressed it, dropped the weight back onto his shoulders, then after a minute pressed it again. This with a weight that strong men were squatting with! The biggest, strongest man I'd seen. Tony was immensely strong, but never the first in, whereas Tommy and Kevin, who were smaller men, would fight anyone.

I was still only seventeen when the Cavern closed. Then there was a period of about a year when I was doing odd nights here and there, at places like the Grave. Then I went to a club called the Downbeat, which later became the Victoriana. Stan Roberts was the owner. I was about nineteen when I started there and that was the first club that I was ever in charge of, head doorman sort of thing. At first there was only me and Jimmy Parry, who still remains a friend. This was a time of, shall we say, racial tension, so we employed Frank Gibson, who was black, to avoid accusations of discrimination.

The Cavern was the first place I used the roundhouse kick. I used to be able to do it without showing anything in the left shoulder, kicking with the right, and I would flick coins up, and if I flicked five coins I'd hit four of them. I used to put lights out with my feet, just by flicking the switch with my foot. I started keeping a diary of techniques, and at one time I had over eighty listed. Eighty separate techniques I'd used. Usually roundhouse kicks. I often say when teaching, 'You get good at hitting people by hitting people.' I always remember the first person that I mawashi'd [roundhouse kicked] to the head, and at that time, it would be 1968, because from '69 onwards, after I'd been to South Africa with Ticky Donovan, he'd shown me how to get extra distance with less damage by kicking with haisoku, the instep. Anyway I kicked this guy in the jaw, and there was a delay. I went to do something else, then he went right down, unconscious. It was at the Victoriana, though it was called the Downbeat then. It was the Downbeat for four or five years until they had a big makeover. By that time I'd gained a decent reputation, you know.

A funny story. It was early, we had just opened. I knew this guy Terry, who was a boxing trainer, and he came down with this older guy, collar and tie, skinny feller; who asked, 'Who's the doorman who's kicking people in the head.' I told him, 'It's me.' With that, he starts taking his coat off, then his tie, and asked if I'd kicked someone in the head the previous week. I told him I did. Anyway it turned out that the older guy was Jimmy Molloy, and he'd been a middleweight or welterweight professional boxer and was still working on doors, a *right hard case. And he'd heard of a doorman who was kicking people in the head, not knowing I was doing it while they were standing. Jimmy thought I was doing it after they were on the ground, which he thought was out of order, and had come down to knock me out. Which he probably would have done, I wouldn't even have looked at him as an opponent. Anyway this trainer, Terry, put him straight and told me to show him, so I kicked with control to Terry's head, and Jimmy, who was rolling up his sleeves ready for action, said, 'What the hell was that?' We later became friends. It turned out he'd known my father. Jimmy was working the door of the Odd Spot in Bold Street. Once, after being kicked in the groin, he came to the Red Triangle to learn how to defend kicks, and Enoeda Sensei, who if you remember had no time for people other than karate, I introduced him to Jimmy Molloy and he told me to take the warm-ups while he chatted to Jimmy. Later Enoeda Sensei said, 'He is warrior.'*

Richie Molyneaux was a pal of mine. When I was on the Downbeat, Richie was on the Rumblin' Tum at the top of Hardman Street. We started training together, going to Arnold Dyson's gym in Princes Avenue. I was still training with Tommy, wrestling at Crosby Barbell Club. One Sunday I went up and there was a competition on, Liverpool against Bolton. I threw my first opponent, then in the next round, a guy called Wally Booth started shouting advice to my opponent, 'He knows nothing,' meaning me; which I thought a bit off as we were working together at the time, but he was wrestling for Bolton. I got behind my opponent but didn't have a clue.

Dennis Martin (left) at a Liverpool Goju-ryu dojo in the early Seventies.

CHAPTER 3

THE VICTORIANA

IT WAS CHRISTMAS, I was eighteen and I was skint. So when I was offered work on the door of an open-all-night Indian restaurant in Bold Street, I took it. Basically the job was to stop people leaving without paying. I learned pretty fast how to handle drunks and groups of guys. I was then given the odd night on the Blue Angel, a famous club owned by Alan Williams, former manager of the Beatles

Then, in about 1969, I bumped into Terry O'Neill in Liverpool city centre one Saturday afternoon. I had lost contact with him, as I had been training with a different group of karate guys and had spent the summer in London training with a group down there. It was good to catch up on news, and I asked him if he had the latest issue of *Black Belt* magazine. Back then you couldn't buy it in many shops but I had picked up a copy in London. Terry said he hadn't seen it, so I said I'd bring it down to the Victoriana Club that night.

The Vic was in Victoria Street, one of two clubs owned by Jimmy Roberts, who had won his money on the football pools. His other club was the Mardi Gras in Mount Pleasant. I shot down that night and got talking to him. While chatting to Terry, I saw him knock a guy out with *mawashi geri*, a roundhouse kick, to the head. Two other doormen were trying to drag this guy out from the main room but he was resisting. Terry just turned, kicked him unconscious and carried on the conversation. I had never seen anything like it.

I had never seen him fight at the Cavern, although I'm

assured there was a lot of trouble there, but he performed this *mawashi geri* and the guy was out. I later learned that Terry would be surprised if they didn't go unconscious from one of his kicks. Over the years I think I only saw it happen once, where he had to hit a guy again, and I think he had just been a little sort of relaxed, brought his foot up and not quite put as much power in as usual, and was turning away to see to something else. And the guy was staggering, he wasn't quite unconscious. So: 'Oh, need another?' Bang! That was it.

Terry was a black belt by this time, actually the youngest guy to achieve this rank at the time. I started popping down to the Vic quite often and met the other lads, who included Richie Molyneux, a big, strong guy who, when in training, could bench-press 400 lbs. Another doorman was Frank Gibson, a black lad who was often the target for Terry's humour. Terry would hide behind the front door as a group of townies sauntered past, and call out, 'Keep moving, honky.' The group would stop, look in the club, see Frank seated at the desk, and start giving him grief. Frank became resigned to this.

Jimmy Parry was another victim of Terry's pranks. Terry would innocently ask, 'Are you hungry?' and when you said you were, would hit you on the head with a bar of chocolate; then offer you one of the broken chunks. Jimmy started to retaliate with his own choc bar, and this escalated into a war. Jimmy pulled out the big guns with a large bar of Cadbury's Whole Nut, which had Terry staggering. Terry planned his revenge. The karate team went to Switzerland for a competition, so Terry bought the biggest bar of Toblerone they made, brought it back, put it in the fridge until it was rock hard, then hid it down the back of his belt. Catching Jimmy off guard with 'I'm starving, are you?' he whacked him with the massive triangular confection, scoring a clean kayo.

There were big kick-offs in the Vic virtually every night. I pitched in and helped the lads and eventually was given a start, covering when one of the regulars was off. The music policy was soul, and they booked live acts. However, instead of Ben. E. King they'd have 'Benny' King, a lookalike (but unfortunately not a soundalike). Frank Gibbo often did a spot as an 'American soul artist'. This usually resulted in complaints, arguments and fights.

I'd already had my first confrontation at the Blue Angel. It wasn't really a fight, but a big guy, much bigger than me, came in to grab me, and I stepped back and hit with an *ura-tsuki*, a close, low, snapping punch in what I call the corner of the ribs. It put him on his back, and I was quite impressed with myself. He was impressed as well because he didn't want any more trouble. It was a punch which I never had success with again, at all, but it did wonders for my confidence, which is always a good thing, so when I had a few failures, it didn't discourage me too much. I sometimes hit people and nothing happened, or not as much as I expected to happen. I was rather disappointed that people didn't explode when I hit them!

One night we lashed out a drunken Scottish guy. We heard him shouting and saw him up the street by a shop. 'I'm coming back,' he yelled, 'and when I do, this is what you're getting.' He then kicked the shop window. His stuck in the shattered glass and blood flowed down the gutter towards us. We laughed at the time. The postscript came about eighteen months later; a policeman was passing the Top Rank Suite, where I then worked, recognised me from the Vic and told us that the Scot had had his leg amputated.

After starting to work with Terry on the Vic, I was privileged to train with him every Saturday morning at the Liverpool University Sports Hall. We used the fencing studio, which had a beautiful wooden floor, a full mirrored wall, and stretching bars, ideal for karate. When Terry competed in Tokyo as part of the British team at the first World Karate Championships in 1970, he regularly sent me postcards telling me that he'd been to visit the dojo of a superb Okinawa Goju-ryu teacher called Master Higaonna – and when Terry said somebody was good, the guy was good – and that he'd met a really interesting 'Aussie' bloke called Gary. Terry stayed on after the team went home, and this Gary put him up and took him to various dojos. Little did I know that these two men would become major influences in my life.

* * *

I first met Gary Spiers on the day he arrived in England in 1971. He had turned up at Terry's in the middle of the night, having travelled from Japan overland via Russia, which he had crossed on the Trans-Siberian railway. Terry and I were scheduled to take the train to London the next day and Terry arrived up with this guy who I took to be a Yank. He had a crewcut, a big camelhair overcoat and a Hawaiian shirt on. We got on real well.

Gary was in fact a New Zealander, not an Aussie, though he had spent some time in Oz and hard trained there under the karate organization of the redoubtable Bob Jones. Jones also supplied doormen to licensed premises, and Gary had already cut his teeth working as a bouncer. In fact, though only a young man, he was already a figure of myth, this mysterious half-Maori who had trained in the brutal dojos of Japan and worked some of the roughest doors in Australasia.

Nick Hughes was another formidable student of Bob Jones's who heard the legends of Gary's exploits and how he had gained his reputation. Nick later recounted some of them to me:

I was living in Melbourne at Bob's house and we would sit around at night talking about various personalities and characters. I had heard tales of Gary 'The Animal' Spiers and so I asked Bob about him. Bob's first story involved the night he and his wife Christine were enjoying a night out on the town. Bob had nearly lost the tip of his finger in a fight the week before hence the night out. He decided after dinner to go visit some of his guys working on various club doors when he ran into three guys he'd thrown out, and banned from clubs, on previous occasions. During those fights they'd always been one-on-one affairs. Now there were three of them and Bob had a dodgy hand so he shoved it in the air, settled down into a cat stance and began fighting them. Christine ran inside to get help and ran into Gary, who was at this point a high-ranking green belt. Gary came outside and found Bob in the thick of it and waded in.

After they were done and the three guys were out on the ground Gary dragged his guy over to the gutter, placed his head up against the drain and proceeded to boot his head until it went inside the opening. The drains in the gutters in Oz have a grate and a gap. The gap is approximately an inch or two narrower than the average person's head but Gary managed to get this guy's head through it. Bob told me the fire trucks had to come down with their specialized cutting tools to get the guy out. It might sound brutal in retrospect but those were the rules of the game in those days. Had the tables been reversed, in all likelihood those three guys would have kicked Bob to death on the ground. That was the night though that Gary earned his stripes and his nickname 'The Animal'.

On another occasion, Gary had gone to a party. Someone there took offence to his presence and a group of Italian kids ambushed him with broken bottles and weapons. During the melee Gary got sliced from the top of his forehead all the way to his chin, deep enough that his skin flapped off his face like a piece of steak. Undaunted, Gary left to get some reinforcements and come back and even the score. They pulled up in a car outside and were planning their foray when a cop walked up to the car and tapped on the window wanting to know what was going on. Gary apparently turned to look at the guy with half his face hanging off, causing the cop to flinch and visibly blanch.

The third story I was told was the one that involved Gary having to *leave Australia. There are several late night restaurants in Australia that cater to the staff of the various night clubs. Affectionately known as 'chew and spews', they're in every major city and Gary was in his favourite eating dinner after work when two Army guys came in causing trouble. They were drunk, rowdy and out to pick fights. They roamed from table to table grabbing girls, stealing food off plates and pushing people around. Unfortunately for them they made the mistake of slapping Gary across the back of the head and tipping his drink over.*

The fight was on and by all accounts it was a purler. At one point, Gary was heard to say, 'My granddaddy used to eat white boys like you for dinner,' as he bit three sizeable chunks out of one of their faces. The other one either jumped or was thrown out of the second-storey window, where he either landed on or was run over by a cab in the street below. Bob heard the story from the detectives assigned to finding Gary, so the dialogue and what went down is fairly accurate.

Gary was not to be found, however. Friends managed to get him on a boat out of the country and he was gone. Rumour was that he'd gone to Japan, another said back to New Zealand and yet another that he was in England.

In fact, as Gary himself tells in Chapter 4, he had gone to Japan, then England. I set up a group in a community centre in Broadway for him to teach, and learned a lot from him, at the club and in one-on-one lessons. His karate was less classical than either Terry's or Brian Waites's. However, he had a good, practical, street-oriented approach.

Gary didn't teach Okinawan Goju. I used to call it Gary-ryu. It was a mixture, better oriented to the street than a strict style. Gary also really taught – apart from kata, which you've got to teach – he'd tend to practicalise it, if that's a word. He had you fighting from guard positions rather than with your fist in a chambered position.

We went up to Glasgow to referee and demonstrate at

an England versus Scotland match. Gary decided to demonstrate a kata using an Okinawan forked weapon called *sai*. I
introduced Gary and really bigged up this demo, saying this
was the first time this kata had been seen in the UK. Gary
started well, and then caught the points of the *sai* in his
sleeves every time he flipped them; finally throwing them on
the floor and walking off in disgust. Backstage I persuaded
Gary to continue with the second part of his routine, which
consisted of performing *seipai*, one of the advanced formal
exercises of Goju-ryu; then demonstrating the application
on me. He did a perfect *seipai* and then, to make up for
his earlier embarrassment, really slammed me during the
bunkai (applications). One move involved throwing me and
I literally bounced a couple of feet off the hardwood floor.
Good demo.

Eventually Gary decided that he needed a more regular
income and stopped teaching karate, to do other things, such a
driving a taxi. It was also about this time that Terry, Steve Cattle
and myself decided to form a martial arts magazine. Terry
had previously edited *Karate News* and I had written several
articles for that publication. We envisioned a really serious,
professional publication, with in-depth reports and technical
articles. This was launched as *Fighting Arts International* and,
due to Terry's perfectionism, was eventually acclaimed as the
leading publication in the martial arts world.

* * *

I worked at the Vic for about a year, before moving up the road
to another club, the Top Rank Suite. Terry, meanwhile, stayed
at the Vic, and it was there that he had a brush with the law.
He had kicked a guy quite severely, putting him in a coma. A
couple of CID came down to arrest him. One was skinny, the
other a bulky rugby player: they said one was to catch him,

the other to stop him (some chance). Terry was charged with GBH and told, 'It could be murder yet, son.' The case dragged on, and meanwhile I started working at the Top Rank. One Friday a group of guys crowded the Vic door and asked, 'Are you Terry O'Neill?' Terry said he was, and the group parted to allow the guy at the back to hurl a huge iron spike at him. It was a piece of road-building equipment and weighed 40 lbs. Terry managed to swerve it and kicked the nearest couple of guys. The rest legged it. The door crew screamed all over the town looking for the rest and caught a couple near Scotty Road.

The next day we were due to go to London for karate squad training. Gary Spiers and I heard the story on the train down. We offered our help, and on the Saturday night nipped off the Rank door to stand off outside the Vic in case of another gang retaliation. We really thought it could have kicked off big time. Gary armed himself with a big carving knife from the Top Rank kitchen, and really psyched himself up: 'I'm gonna stab a heap of people!' Nothing transpired and Terry was acquitted of the GBH.

Looking back on those days, it seems strange that door crews could chase guys all over the city. Now, stepping off the door is strictly forbidden and the ubiquitous CCTV enforces the rule. Back then, we once chased some guys right into the Mersey Tunnel. We were also always messing around, throwing kicks, putting headlocks on each other. Terry was the main instigator, but one night Frank Gibson and I were play-sparring and I threw him, using a foot-sweep technique to his ankle. He went down screaming that his ankle was broken. Terry told him it was just a sprain and started twisting his foot to ease the pain. Frank went to hospital where he was told, 'Your ankle is broken, and someone has been messing with it.'

The Vic had a Chinese cook and that made it attractive to hungry doormen, even when we were working up the road at the Rank. We would pop down and have a plate of fried rice, and, more often than not, join in a fight. We were a bit conspicuous in our tuxedos, as the Vic crew all wore sports jackets and slacks. Once, Harry Benfield and I were having a scoff when it kicked off good-style. We got well stuck in and some damage was done. Then we went back to our own door. Meanwhile, the injured punters called the police, who gathered the Vic door crew together. The punters insisted that the lads responsible were wearing tuxedos and the police chased them for wasting time. Reminiscing with Terry about it, he mentioned that a guy was trying to hit Frank Gibson and Harry ran up, drilled him with a karate reverse-punch in the middle of his back, and stiffened him. Terry said he'd never seen a punch like it.

Tommy Mac no longer worked at the Vic but popped in sometimes. He gave me a lot of invaluable advice, such as what to say when arrested and interviewed ('nothing'). I later worked with Tommy at the Banyan Tree and he is now one of my best friends.

* * *

In 1972, I went to Paris to watch the Second World Championships. A highlight was when the British team, captained by Terry, knocked the Japanese team out of the event (a couple of years later the Brits, again captained by Terry, won the world title). In Paris, I met Master Higaonna for the first time. He was due to spend an extended period in South Africa teaching for Hugh St John Thompson's karate group, and together with Hugh, they stopped in Liverpool for a few days en route. Hugh was one of the pioneers of karate in South Africa and had co-founded the first training school in Cape Town in 1962. Terry had met him while touring RSA with the British Team in 1968. Master Higaonna taught at our club, and demonstrated the sai kata, as well as the advanced suparumpai form to a spellbound class.

Terry, Gary Spiers and myself were involved in a group training commitment, which involved working on the door on the Friday, then nipping off early – the other lads covered for us – and catching the midnight train to London, which in those days took over six hours for the overnight trip. We didn't book sleepers and usually talked for the entire journey. From Euston we'd go by tube to whichever venue was being used, then train until about 4 p.m. We would then catch the train back to Liverpool, eating the famed British Rail dinner en route. Upon arrival we would go to the club and work another part-shift, then catch the train and go down to London to train on the Sunday. We would usually go to the West End after Sunday training and watch a new movie, have a meal, then catch the midnight train back, getting in to Liverpool about 7 a.m. on the Monday. We didn't really think that this was a hardship. We enjoyed each other's company, we were training, it was fun.

After hearing all the tales of training in Japan from Gary, Hugh and Brian, I decided that I must make the trip, and started saving my money. Meanwhile, after keeping in contact with Hugh, I arranged for him to teach in Liverpool, following an invitation for him to be chief referee at an international match in London. During the visit, Hugh announced that I should take the black belt grading. He arranged for Terry to be my partner for the sparring, and told the lad to 'make it hard'. It was. I managed to pass the test, however.

I started a training class at the Vernon Sangster Sports Centre, in Stanley Park, between the Liverpool and Everton football grounds. For my door work, I adapted what worked for me from the traditional training and also picked up tricks of the trade from the other guys on the doors: not just fighting tips, but also body language, assessing people, intervention, defusing aggression. It was a mix-and-match process: if it worked, use it. Working with several wrestlers helped me pick up the grappling aspect that was lacking in karate. Though I was practising and teaching a traditional martial art, for my personal use in doorwork it was stripped down, a very applied version of what we were doing in the dojo. Later on I came to develop this into a much less traditionally based system applicable to such things as bodyguarding and more adaptable to personal self-protection. All of the leading self-protection instructors currently on the scene have a background in the martial arts. Some trained in very traditional systems. However, each has adapted his original training, sometimes radically. This is essentially what I did back then too.

A young Gary Spiers in Japan.

CHAPTER 4

GARY SPIERS

Part I

'Yes, I do make my living out of fighting; and it's true that a large percentage of my opponents end up in the hospital, because I'm good at what I do. I've spent the past twenty-five years learning to do just that. And no, I don't see anything wrong in using karate for that purpose, to me that's what the martial arts are for, for heavens sake.'

THIS QUOTE OPENED an interview with Gary Spiers by Terry O'Neill published over four issues of *Fighting Arts International*. It became the most popular, and controversial, interview in *FAI*. Gary here tells his own story better than I ever could. I have edited it slightly by removing much of the Japanese terminology, leaving just the English translation.

TERRY: *The opening quote is indicative of the hard-line approach expressed by interviewee, Gary Spiers during our four and a half hours of taped conversation. I met this big New Zealander in 1970 in Tokyo, where he was living at the time. Discovering that we had a lot in common – a mutual love of karate and we both had been employed in the physical security field – we became friends. When he was ready to leave Japan, I encouraged him to come to England. This he did, settled in Liverpool and he has been here ever since (we can't get rid of him – only joking). We began training together and he started teaching his style of karate, Goju-Kai.*

During the first year of his stay, Gary tried to obtain work in his

*trade as a slaughterman butcher, but due to the high unemployment
situation in the area, he was unsuccessful and soon found himself back
at his old job of what is commonly termed 'bouncing', or 'minding'
on night club doors. That's what I was doing at the time, which left
my days free for karate, and I had no difficulty at all in finding Gary
security work in Liverpool, which has probably the largest percentage
of night clubs and discotheques of anywhere in Great Britain. He was
tailor-made for the job actually... With his size: around 6 foot and
240 lbs. (at that time, nowadays he is 280 lbs. plus – that's 20 stone!)
His ability: along with lots of wrestling and judo 'know how', he'd left
Japan with a 3rd degree black belt from Master Gogen Yamaguchi
('The Cat') and his experience: he'd worked for years on nightspots
and working men's clubs in Australia.*

GARY: One of my earliest memories, it was my first-ever pinup,
was a centre-page from *The Ring* magazine. It was a close-up
of Rocky Marciano's fist splitting Jersey Joe Walcot's nose in
half with a punch. I wanted to box at seven years old but my
mother would not allow me to do this, so I started wrestling
instead, and I really loved it. I loved it that much that since
that time, I have always spent a large proportion of my waking
hours in gymnasiums and dojos all over the world, learning and
practising combat. I remember my mother constantly giving
me earache and criticizing the fact that I spent so much of my
time learning to fight, but then she didn't have my arguments
at school and she didn't have to defend herself to and from
school or on the rugby field, where, because of my large size, I
found myself up against older, wiser people.

My parents were warned several times to put me into
something to take the aggression out of me before I got into
serious trouble. Apparently I was always in fights as a youngster,
but you see at that time, in the early fifties, New Zealand was
inundated with immigrants of every European culture who
brought over all their ethnic, religious and political bullshit
with them. Their kids obviously reflected their attitudes and in

a school of say, a thousand pupils, a good forty per cent were immigrants. Now, through no fault of my own, I have Maori blood in me – of which I am in fact extremely proud. However, in that school at that time, there were only about seven of us with Maori heritage. As a consequence, because we were the smallest group, we got the most stick.

The main fellow who taught me wrestling was a fairground fighter who used to nightly take on all-comers. He'd also fill in for the boxer if he wasn't available; sometimes they would take a hammering from an unknown challenger and be unable to put in an appearance. Now he was so good, I did not realise just how good until later on when I was exposed to other forms of training and trainers. I realised just how lucky I had been to have him as my first teacher when I compared what he taught to the stuff that was being handed out under the heading of self-defence around the country and the wrestling that was being taught at schools and colleges. The collegiate wrestling that I watched being taught was nice and by that I mean they had locker rooms and showers, a nice environment, and on the mat, they did classical, dead-correct wrestling moves – and they wouldn't have handled him, my teacher, for one minute, because of his fighting know-how and super experience at taking on anybody and everybody who cared to climb through the ropes to face him.

Once I started combative training, I never stopped. Wherever I would travel to find work, all over New Zealand and Australia, I would find a gym to work out in. The first thing I'd look for in a strange place was accommodation and the next thing I'd find would be a gym, 'cause I loved it! My friends would go to the pub after work and I used to go to a gym.

During my teens I became interested in karate. I had heard about all these special blows and kicks that they did and I eventually read E. J. Harrison's *Manual of Karate*. But at first I started practising judo. I was working at a big meat works in New Zealand – that's what I am by trade, a butcher or slaughterman – and I met a chap from Auckland called Charlie Sterling. He was only a brown belt but that was a high grade at that time and I began training with him, not only because I admired his judo but I also liked the way in which he conducted his life. He was a thorough gentleman. It has been my experience that the more physically competent people are, the more confidence they have in their own personal lives and the more gentlemanly this makes them. Because they don't have things to prove, the minimum of aggression is normally displayed by these type of people in their everyday lives.

So I was learning to throw, trip, hold down, apply locks, strangles and chokes. I found it very interesting and easy to do because of my wrestling training. I also found it very effective, because it taught you the ability to get hold of clothes, which everybody wears, and it's very practical to, say, choke people with their own jacket. This and other judo techniques I learnt have a great usefulness outside the environment of the gym and I particularly liked that aspect of it.

Why the preoccupation with street effectiveness?

Well, I was working in a job where you had knives in your hands all day. I was living on a work camp where there was all kinds of gambling, drinking, bringing women back to the camp on a day-to-day basis. I was a young fellow at the time and that was what is regarded by contemporary society as a very hard lifestyle. The fact that in the canteen, you were quite liable to lose your issue of food to some older, bigger and harder fellow, or if you had a nice motorbike parked outside or a nice sports coat and he wanted to borrow it, if you refused you would be promptly bashed.

A regular thing that used to happen to the younger fellows, the boy butchers, was that when they got paid, the older, harder ones would ask them for a loan and it would never be repaid, no matter how many times you asked, unless you were willing to fight over it, and then if you took second place you still wouldn't get your money back. So this creates a pressure; it's commonly called bullying. There was someone teaching karate in New Zealand at that time but no one could tell me where it was at, it was all conducted in semi-secrecy and all that nonsense.

I travelled to Australia for work and it was in Brisbane that I first began formal karate training. I would be around nineteen years old at that time. There was a chap running a dojo. It was called Okinawan *shorei* style. His name was John Ryan and I liked what I saw there. They didn't have the hand dexterity or the bobbing and weaving of boxers, nor the rough and tumble of wrestling, but I liked the kicks. I realized that if I could learn the kicking, it would augment the ability I already had at grappling. I also liked the aspect that they trained you to fight several people at once. So I trained there for a while until my work took me away from Brisbane. I trained at various other dojos including one called the Silvertop Karate Club.

Silvertop was the name of a big taxi firm and they had specifically brought over two really good Korean tae kwon do instructors; they called their style Moo Duk Kwan, as I recall. Mr Kim was the name of one of them and I'm not sure of the other one but he was also a 6th dan at judo, or yudo as the Koreans call it. Anyway, Silvertop had engaged them because two taxi drivers working for the company had been murdered – had their throats cut in robberies. So these Koreans were brought out for the specific purpose of training the company's employees to defend their bloody selves! One of the founder members of the club was Jack Rozinsky, who is a well-known figure on the martial arts scene today in Australia. Another teacher I trained under was Mr Kato, who was one of Masu-tatsu Oyama's good *kyokushinkai* people, a very fast, hard karate man. I liked that training: the *kyokushinkai* in Australia got real good by fighting each other all the time and they kicked the groin immediately. Other systems didn't concentrate on that kind of thing.

Now, karate was becoming more and more popular and lots of schools were opening up but I wasn't too impressed by a lot of what I saw. I used to go all over the place to train. Sometimes I'd pay a whole year's affiliations just for a handful of lessons before my work would force me to move on. And I would find that, in many instances, I'd go to train or watch a karate class and I would not reckon much to the teacher's chances against me in a real fight.

Surely that wouldn't stop you training under him?

Yes, of course it did. I only wanted to be taught by people who looked more proficient in combat than I was. See, I'm a big person, I come from a large race of people and I've always thought a good combat teacher should have the capacity to put someone of my size out of the game. I never thought I could have 'copped for' [beaten in a fight] either of the Koreans, nor the Japanese, Kato, and that's why I stayed with them for as long as I could. In some of the karate clubs that I attended, we were given thousands of push-ups to do. That was not what I wanted. I joined one karate club, the first goju training I ever did, and although the instructor, Tino Ceberano, was excellent himself and taught me real good ways of using groin kicks and joint-kicks etc., he constantly stressed all the time that we must not touch at all in the sparring. And that I could not understand nor agree with.

Another policy that many of these people had was to take you for a run. Well, if I had wanted to run I'd have continued playing rugby. Running has a lot to do with stamina if you intend fighting a number of three-minute rounds. But my object has always been – because the situations I find myself in have always demanded it – to finish off my opponents as quick as possible, before they can get support from other people. So it used to actually annoy me to pay a training fee to learn karate, go along to a dojo and be taught how to run. I thought it was wrong.

Well, I can't agree with your sentiment that any karate instructor that you felt you could best in the street, had nothing to teach you.

Well, okay, I didn't mean what I previously said as a blanket ruling. It is just that I was that interested in learning good techniques that I went to every conceivable place that I could go. In a lot of karate schools that I went, they only kicked and punched the air. You had no way of knowing how strong your blows were. They deliberately barred any form of contact whatsoever. And if I thought that they didn't have some proficiency at hurting me, I used to get frustrated and leave. It used to really frustrate me, marching up in line, just hitting the air. I liked to hit things and people. And I never minded being hit back if I had dropped my guard or made a mistake, because to me that's what it is all about, the avoidance of pain and the retaliatory dishing out of pain.

I liked the Okinawan system of training when I got to Okinawa, because they utilize a lot of striking pads and other equipment in their training. I liked the Tae Kwon Do because they used to put you in half-armour and you immediately learnt how to hit each other. You would start out slowly, just touching, and then build the speed up as you got more used to it. A lot of the ju-jitsu type systems being taught at that time were strong contact systems: you had to work to get the lock on your opponent, you had to work to get any strangles or chokes on him. I have been to lots and lots of different schools in my time and sparred with them whenever possible. I've even tried some French *savate*, where the guys were incredibly supple, as in the ballet, but really, all I had to do was to charge in and I'd have them all on the floor.

What you have to understand is that I was living a totally different lifestyle to the average citizen, who simply does not put his physical well being on the line for the sake of a job. I was travelling around the country on my own, with one bag full of my working tools, another bag full of clothes and my sole finance in my back pocket. Everywhere I went with an alien accent was dangerous. When I turned up at an ironworks that I had travelled hundreds of miles to, and twelve Maltese guys blocked me at the gate, told me there was no work there, and I wanted to see the manager or foreman and have him tell me there was no work there, I needed to be able to fight – and fight well, I'll tell you! Another thing was that by then, I had started to do some security work in pubs or clubs. Whenever I went to a town and got a day job, I'd see if there was any work to do looking after places at night and I'd take that as well, so that I could bank one set of wages. In that way, I had a higher standard of life and could afford more things than people who just had one job.

Exactly when did you first start using your martial arts to 'flatten' people in clubs?

What? That's a bit strong isn't it, Digger?

Perhaps … Let me rephrase the question. When did you first start moderating people's behaviour in clubs?

That would have been about 1963/64. I started with Bob Jones, who today has a large security firm and a big karate organisation in Australia. Also a chap called Bill Bowling. I was in a dojo there with these two and I was asked to help out in a situation that had occurred. A group of dance halls in Melbourne had had an outbreak of severe trouble and we were able to put an end to that problem.

Before we get too deeply into the incidents you have been involved with over here, could we back track a little and talk about some of the 'battles' you had in Australia? I know some of them were quite severe

Correct... I suppose we could start with this (Mr. Spiers traced with his finger, a faded but still noticeable eight inch scar that runs through the centre of his face), which I got at a party when I was around 21-22 years old. An Italian put a knife in my face. It was a big party and whilst everyone was drinking, up until this point there had been no trouble whatsoever. I was there with a group of my friends and there was a large group of Italians there as well. It started with one word, or rather the misinterpretation of a word, and by the end of the fight, twelve of us had been stabbed. One of my friends was in fact stabbed twenty-two times in the back and wound up on a kidney machine. The word in the Maori language for 'mate' apparently translates in [Italian dialect] as 'homosexual' and that's what it was over. We were told later by witnesses and police that we were very successful in not being killed by these Italians, who were armed right at the onset with blades. They waited for us in the car park and ambushed us, Christ knows how many of them there were; but there was heaps more than us. I was the first to get it. Because I was the largest in our group, I was instantly stabbed to get me out of the way. One minute I was walking along, both of my arms occupied in carrying a large case of beer and the next thing was I got slashed from under my right eye, right down through my nose – it sliced one nostril in half – through my lips to my jaw. It was only a small stiletto but you can see how much damage it did.

Did you go down?

No, I didn't. My face was literally cut in half and as I was breathing out, there was so much blood spraying out in a mist through the hole in my nose that I couldn't see anything in front of me. I still got right into him. I cannot truthfully say what the sequence of events was – I must have been in a state of shock – but I'm told that I locked his arm up, which prevented him from sticking me with the knife again, turned him over (threw him down) and then smashed his spine. He managed to crawl under a parked car outside the premises, otherwise I might well have killed him on the spot. I apparently damaged thirteen of his vertebrae and nine months later, when the case came up in court, he turned up there still in a wheelchair, which I thought was marvellous. I count myself very fortunate that I was training four or five days a week in karate and wrestling. I believe that this saved my life at that time and many times since then.

Another time I was stabbed in the groin with a broken bottle. That was back in New Zealand at a Maori community centre that I used to like going to. There were always a lot of Samoans and Fijians there. I'd helped a doorman put a fellow out. He had been having great difficulty with this large fellow after an argument about sport. It's like here in England, where if you go to a football match wearing a different coloured scarf to somebody else, you are quite likely to find yourself in some physical difficulty. Anyway this fellow's girlfriend ran out into the street, found a milk bottle on a doorstep, 'prepared' it by smashing the neck end off it and, after hiding it until an opportune moment, she stuck it between my legs. Actually it was right under the balls, so I guess I was lucky, if you can call that being lucky. I did the appropriate thing: I passed out and woke up in hospital.

I had another very serious fight when I worked on a nightclub in Australia. It was a really nice place and I refused admission to these two fellows who were, in my opinion, too drunk to come in. I was the head doorman at this place and I was very courteous to them. They claimed to be military this and military that but after some awkwardness – they were not touched at all – they went away. That was that – I thought.

At around 2.30 a.m., I finished work and went to have a meal in a restaurant, a Greek place, before I went home. In walk these two characters, changed from their civvies into their full military kit, including, of course, their boots. They came straight to my table where I was halfway through my steak and started the verbals about my attitude to soldiers. I hadn't been hard to track because a lot of nightclub people ended up eating at this place after work.

So we got into a fight because one of them put it straight on me at the table. He hit me a good right-hander in the face whilst I was still sitting down. So I 'shot' the table at his friend and immediately grabbed the leg of the one who had punched me and took him down to the floor, with me on top of him. As soon as we touched the floor, I had him pinned by my body-weight and was just getting into seeing how he liked having his face punched in, when he reached up, grabbed me by the lapels and pulled me right down, close to his face. His friend by this time had got out from under the table and proceeded to use my head, which his partner was holding nicely in place, like a bloody football.

So they weren't beginners at this sort of thing – they could fight?

Well I certainly could and they were doing quite well with me up until then. Now I don't know if I actually lost consciousness but the thought did occur to me that these bastards were going to kill me. After the first few kicks from those big army boots, I was bleeding from the nose, the mouth, the ears, I was being given a real good working over. I didn't think of doing it, it just came natural I suppose, but the one who was on the bottom, holding my head in place, lost his left ear. Well, I bit it off ...

What, right off?

That's right, but it couldn't be found when they looked for it later.

Surely you didn't swallow it?

I don't know. What I do know is that I was in a lot of pain and facing more where that came from. There was heaps of blood, all mine up until that point in the proceedings. His friend, the 'footballer', had kicked me at least once full in the eye, so that was closed up and I could see only half of what happened next. I was then hit over the head with a stool, which split my head open. Again it did not have the desired effect of polishing me off and I got up off the floor. 'One ear' had let go of me at this point and the other one decided it was time for him to leave. I chased him across the restaurant and he missed the banister at the top of the stairs – we were on the second floor – and he sailed right out of the window. I was later accused of throwing him through the window but I did not recall that at all. The incident was savage. It was instantaneous. There were possibly thirty people in the place screaming their heads off but nobody was inclined to help me, as nobody is inclined to help anybody in these type of incidents, unless they are friends or family. Even then, in such circumstances, sometimes even your friends hesitate sufficiently long enough to get you killed.

What happened to the guy who had lost his ear?

I haven't the faintest idea, nor am I at all inclined to care. I suppose if he wore glasses, he'd have to use Sellotape on one side of his head to keep them on!

When and why did you go to Japan?

April 1968 from Sydney by ship, I was twenty-five years old then, and 'why' was to continue my martial arts study. I knew that there was an awful lot for me in karate but I wanted to learn it from the best people, because karate done poorly isn't worth a pinch of shit.

I'd had a few fights with up-and-coming karate fellows in clubs. Now they could kick fast, I'll give them that, and with me being big, that was the first thing they'd try to get me with. But I'd get inside their legs by charging them, take them down and once they were off their feet they were mine. Now the goju system of karate attracted me because it preached super-mobility, lots of footwork and lots of twisting the torso to get away from the blows, while staying in close proximity to the attacker, so you could sweep him or whatever.

So I enrolled in Mr Yamaguchi's dojo and I was immediately impressed by a Mr Yamamoto, who was one of the top boys there. He could really put the kicks in properly. I've always thought that a good kicker was more dangerous than a good puncher. A Mr Takahashi was another great fighter there who could really do the business. There was no shortage of really good, hard, fast fighters around in the various dojos, definitely. I did get some good 'treatment' [punishment] there – more than I ever would have believed I could take. You see, most people teaching in a Western society were teaching for money, which meant that they took it really easy on students, because they didn't want to bang them around and lose their custom. But in Japan it was different, particularly in the universities, where I would often go to train. The first thing they would do there was try to 'work it' to the big *gaijin* [foreigner]. I did take a lot of stick at those places but it was good, because the more you learn to cope with that, the more competent you get. When you turned up at a strange dojo, senior students would usually go out of their way to try to do you in.

Brian Waites and myself, plus other people who I used to get around with in Japan, were injured consistently. I've had black eyes on top of black eyes. I have been served up a severe black eye on the Monday night and then I've got the same dose in the same eye on the Thursday night – which meant that I wasn't looking after my eye too well! I did eventually get sick of the constant hammering and continual injuries that I got at the colleges and universities there. Because of my size,

I would more often than not be put up against opponents of three times my karate ability and I was just looked upon as a big dumb foreigner to kick the Christ out of.

And of course, the higher I got up in the grades, the more savage the fighting tended to become. So I really got too much of what I had gone there to look for. I got sick of the militant students' attitude where they had been nowhere, seen nothing, done nothing, had their education subsidised by the government – lots of them had never had to work in their lives – and they thought nothing of trying to cripple you permanently in the dojo. And they worked on the basis that they, your *sempai* (seniors) in the ranking system, could hit you as hard as possible, as often as possible, and yet if you were to use your size and strength to grab them, throw them down and then to drop your knee into them as a follow-up, to maybe rupture their bowels or spleen, they would have a shit-fit. Eventually a lot of us got fed up with this attitude and we began to stop it in the only way that you possibly could: to knock them right off their silly feet and put them out of commission.

Didn't you try to hide the fact that you were already injured when you next went into the dojo?

Yes, of course, but you soon had that many injuries, they were impossible to conceal. I mean, I have always been a believer in that. I have had bad injuries from the night clubs and kept quiet about it, never let anyone know about it, because in my work I cannot afford to let the opposition know that I am vulnerable in any way. I had some smashed vertebrae in my back once and I was wearing a corset for support whilst guarding a door on my own. This was in England several years ago. I had a very hard time to just move and turn around. I just had to hope that I would not get into any serious difficulty. I never told anybody about this, I travelled twenty miles away to get my corset strapped up each night so that it would not become known in the area I was working that I was injured. Because I knew that if it did become common knowledge, or even rumoured that I could hardly move, there would be no shortage of would-be contenders.

I was in Japan for just over two and a half years and I did everything from teach English to waiting-on in restaurants. It was hard but then I wasn't there to live in luxury. A group of us formed what we called the Ikebukuro Jujitsu club – that was the name of the area – and we used to have special training 'meets' on the roof of one of the universities. We were all learning different things in different dojos: some of us were doing *goju* karate, *shorinji kempo*, judo, *shotokan*, *kyokushinkai*, *aikido*, and we would all exchange and pool our knowledge. Then we'd practice it all against each other. People sometimes question the relatively short time, just a couple of years, sometimes even only one year, that foreigners train in Japan. But in my case and even more so with some of the other people I mentioned, you have to bear in mind that you trained almost every day. Some days you would go into the dojo at one o'clock in the afternoon and not leave until 10.30 p.m. Sometimes you'd even sleep there and get right back into it, first thing in the morning. Apart from your little jobs of teaching English and whatever, there's virtually nothing else to do but train. After you have paid your monthly dojo fees, and bought food, you usually haven't got much money to go anywhere else except the dojo.

I had some good friends amongst the foreigners who were there at that time, people like Brian Fitkin, Steve Peck, John Robertson – he's still there actually, got his 4th Dan in judo – Brian Waites, Ray Edler, Steve Morris.

You were always in trouble with Morris, weren't you?

Correct. Whilst I was in Mr Yamaguchi's dojo, Steve Morris was the senior and he was put in charge of the foreigners at the

Goju-Kai. Now I liked him a lot and all that, but I would go off to the pub sometimes at the slightest provocation to drown my sorrows . . . and I also slept too long for his liking, he did not like that sort of behaviour at all. Now Morris was a fanatical person at training. He was physically very strong and also very strict in his attitude because of the way in which he had been brought up. This, plus the fact that he was living on a minus budget, would result in him going nearly berserk at us, and me in particular, if we did not do as he told us. He trained daily, day in, day out, I mean he never missed, ever, and I'm afraid I did develop a habit of doing a disappearing act sometimes. Now, to him, not showing up for training was like going AWOL in the bloody army. My rather flippant attitude at times used to drive dear Steve to bloodshed – mine. But we were different, you see. He was a really gung ho, rigid trainer and very respectful of the traditions. Now I didn't really believe anybody was better than me, of whatever nationality, until they could knock me on my behind and show their superiority. Remember, I'd been doing this stuff for real for four years before I ever set foot in Japan.

I [also] visited Okinawa and trained at various dojo there. The Okinawans did impress me, not only with their karate and their ability with weapons but with their helpful, friendly attitude to students, foreign students included. The *shorinji kempo* people are very good. It's a fast, flowing style, lots of joint twisting, throws, lots of two-man drills. I was also impressed by the linear systems of the Japan Karate Association (JKA) and the Wado-ryu: dynamic, driving, hard. One of the most spectacular people that I related to in Japan was the JKA's Yano, whom everybody nicknamed 'The Animal'. He was built on the same lines as me, you see, and Jesus could he perform!

Then there was the kickboxing. My friend Ray Edler was a really good, strong, able fighter from the USA. He took up kickboxing and became the middleweight champion of Japan.

I also trained a little at one of the kickboxing gyms in Tokyo – not much, because I couldn't afford it, but I'd do the next best thing, I'd watch the training and then practise it on my own, until I could add it to my repertoire. Something that really, really impressed me during my time in Japan: Ray Edler was good, but I saw this Thai kickboxer just annihilate him in a big challenge match. It was a Japan vs. Thailand match and Ray, of course, represented Japan in his division. Well, he was doing okay until this fellow – he was tall for a Thai, close to 6ft and very lean – polished off Ray with no trouble at all. He hit him with a perfect shot, a Thai-style roundhouse kick in the head. He took the full shin in his temple and it effectively retired him from kickboxing. At the time, it looked like it had killed him. I thought to myself, 'Yes, you'll do for me, mate, that gent with that kick would see you right off, dear Gareth.' I thought he was bloody marvellous.

You also did a lot of training under Master Higaonna, the famous Okinawan goju ryu karate teacher, didn't you?

Yes…. actually at the time I met him, I had had so much karate over that twenty-month period in Japan, I was ready to pack my bags and leave. I stayed on there just so that I could train with him. He had a really nice, genuine nature and so did all the people in his dojo. Mr Higaonna is an Okinawan and they have a different mental outlook to the Japanese. He was, and is, a perfect gentleman, a bloody marvellous karate person, and it was a pleasure to be taught by him. His classes were hard with lots of exercises to strengthen the body, lots of *makiwara* (striking board) to strengthen the mind and good effective karate, but he did not allow his students to use you as target practice.

He is a very practical teacher, isn't he?

Oh yes. He's that practical he fractured my skull and caved in one of my nasal passages!

Deliberately?

Well his technique was deliberate, yes, but knowing him, I'm sure the amount of damage he did me was not intentional. What happened was that ... well, I deserved it, actually. I had taken a liberty. I touched him during a *kumite* (sparring) practice, with an open-hand technique to the groin, twice. I got away with it the first time and I should have left it at that, but I was that pleased with myself that I did it again and he did a really excellent jumping front knee-kick into my head. And I never again bothered trying to tap 'The Boss' in the groin. It cured me completely

Did that finally stop you? You were always looking for people who could do that.

Well, it didn't knock me out. The whole dojo stopped at the sound of the air coming out of my sinuses: one of them just collapsed. I just stood there, astounded I guess, with blood coming out of my ears and nose like a beauty. They took me and sat me down in the changing room.

So you finally met someone who stiffened you?

He didn't actually 'stiffen' me.

What I'm getting at is – did you fancy a return match with him?

No. I did not! No thank you. I mean, really it was wonderful... look at the size of him, he's only up to here on me (Mr. Spiers indicated his own navel – a slight exaggeration but anyway, Higaonna Sensei is quite short) and he did 'fix me up'. He actually did remark later about the fact that I had not fallen over and 'died', that I still had the ability to stand there.

I considered my stay in Japan to be the most important part of my life. My experiences in Japan really woke my ideas up about life – having to go to the dojo continually every night, where I knew that I was going to get bashed good and proper, taught me a great deal about the martial arts. I would say that that period was invaluable in the building of my spirit. For whilst the consistent hammering can't help but sicken you, it is good for your mind, because it exposes you to a far higher level of physical and mental stress than you would ever get in a Western dojo. I think you will learn more actual technique in a Western dojo but not more spirit. It's just that, well, I have never in my life done what seems to be a Japanese habit of knocking bits off the junior grades. I consider that a liberty. I would not, as a 4th dan, kick a first-degree black belt all over the place. The Japanese mentality makes no allowances whatsoever. If you can't do it, they just force you anyway.

I personally believe it creates a weakness, in the society of today, in that it develops an attitude that is really not conducive to civilized behaviour. If I decided to adopt that attitude to my life, I would not work, I'd just take anything I wanted off anybody that couldn't stop me. There are people like that of course – and I do know what they need, in huge quantities, and it's something that I can dispense really well. It's called pain.

I'll give you another example of the karate attitude that was prevalent in Japan when I was there – it may very well have changed now. I used to go to one dojo which belonged to a well-known 6th degree in the Goju system. He was rumoured to have lost a testicle in the collegiate karate fights when he was a young buck. Now he would actually encourage his 4th and 5th degrees, in Japanese of course – but after a while you learn to speak the language quite fluently – to really take a brutal, merciless shot at you. Now I had the physical size, the capacity and the attitude to cope with this to a large extent. I was brought up on very hard manual work and used to getting into it with all sorts of assorted idiots back home in the clubs I worked in. This was towards the end of my stay there and during the time when I was bashing them back. But the other foreigners had a lot less ability to handle this type of punishment and this instructor, through his senior students, used to put them through the meat grinder. And I thought it was an appalling liberty. But I understand that from the dawn of karate, this has been the Japanese way, whereas the Okinawan attitude is that you are there to be taught lots of things before they expose you to any real physical danger in the *kumite*.

I was with Mr Higaonna one day and he introduced me to the then captain of the Takushoku University Karate Club. We bowed and then shook hands politely and as soon as he had hold of my hand, he kicked me straight in the groin. 'How do you do?' Whack! 'Hold that one Spiers, you're a man of property now – there are two "achers".' Mr Higaonna had told the captain I was practising karate and he wanted to see if I was what they termed a 'weak Westerner'. He wanted to see what my reaction was. I don't consciously remember doing it but I had my foot in his balls before he could return his kicking foot to the ground. Both our kicks were pulled of course but they both landed on target and after that, we got on real well. But that's the Japanese.

I'm not anti-Japanese. They are just like that, they are different to us. It's the same mentality that made Japan such a tough and universally feared military power, until Hiroshima and Nagasaki cured them. That was a terrible thing, I know, but they would never have stopped otherwise. They are only a small nation of physically small people, most of them anyway, but they are super-tough and that's a historical fact. I believe the Japanese spirit, their code of *bushido*, to be the strongest of its kind in the world.

Would you then recommend a karate instructor going to Japan to improve his karate?

Yes, or else find some other realistic, true-to-life way of experiencing combat before you put up a sign advertising that you teach karate as a fighting art.

Well, I don't think it's very practical to say that before becoming an instructor, you have to either go to Japan, or else work on a nightclub door to get the sort of experience that you have.

Let's put it this way. Would you go to a dentist and pay money to have your teeth taken out by a fellow who had never done it before – he'd only half or even quarter practised it? You have to understand that I do not, have never and probably never will, regard karate as a sport. My personal idea of sport is having two women to splash around with in a big bath – do you know what I mean? I have always participated in karate as a method of physical combat.

But shortly after you first arrived here in Great Britain, you competed as a member of the national squad and team?

Yes, and I enjoyed it, but I enjoyed the travel and the meeting of people more so than the actual competition. Now I'm not against sports karate per se, I fought in several tournaments and matches in Japan. It tests your judgement, timing, speed – it's fine for them, but not for me, that's all I'm saying. I'll soften up a bit: for the vast majority of people, sport karate is an excellent aspect. It encourages them to participate, it takes up a good period of their life, becomes a hobby or interest, it improves them physically, they learn discipline, control of their bodies. But it does not equip them psychologically to fight for their lives and I have to be ready to do this every bloody night of the week. And that's it.

Former doorman Tommy McNally revisits the world famous Cavern Club.

CHAPTER 5

TOMMY MAC

TOMMY McNALLY WAS something of a mentor to both me and Terry O'Neill on the doors. Some years back, Terry came on a knife course I was holding at the YMCA in Liverpool and we sat in the upper gym during a break. On the left was a storeroom where they now keep chairs and Terry mentioned that it used to be the weights room. One day he was training in there, and a guy came in to complain about the noise he was making. That guy was Tommy Mac.

Tommy kindly consented to an interview for this book to fill in some of the detail of how he met Terry and of those early days when we worked together as martial artists on the doors. The questions are mine.

DENNIS: *Tom, tell us about that first meeting in the YMCA.*

TOMMY: I was in there training with Tony Buck and we could hear this banging going on. I went into the weights room and there was this young lad hurling a barbell into a stack of mats. It was to develop explosive power, for punching. Anyway, he came out to watch us wrestling and asked if he could have a go, so we showed him a few moves on the mat. He mentioned that he was doing karate. I had heard of this and asked him to show us some and he did this side-kick, to the head, which was very impressive, because even at that age he was the height he is now, which is 6ft 1in.

He was fifteen, still at school. He was training heavily on the weights, doing judo and was learning karate as well. And he had developed a very powerful side thrust-kick, which was impressive not just for the height he reached with it but for the power he obviously generated with it. Terry had done a bit of judo and when we got on the mat he could obviously move around, though he was limited by the fact that we weren't wearing jackets. Anyway, he started training regularly with us.

Karate was largely unknown then, apart from a few Charlie Chan movie scenes?

Yes, and that was usually limited to a chop, in fact it was called a 'judo chop', to the villain's neck.

So Terry started grappling with you and Tony in your daytime work-outs. Tony Buck was a champion amateur wrestler wasn't he?

I got into wrestling when I went to a [pro] wrestling show, and asked the promoter where I could learn. He sent me to Crosby Wrestling Club, which was run by a guy called Johnny Mack, who been a professional boxer and wrestler for years. The training concentrated on very basic stuff, it wasn't a technically skilled class, we were there as punchbags for Tony Buck really, who was the champion. He'd come in every night from a ten-mile run and wrestle everyone in the gym two or three times, or until they were too injured to continue, then he'd go and do what I can only call a professional weightlifting session after that.

He was long-reigning British Heavyweight Champion, unbeaten for about fifteen years. He represented Britain in the Empire Games. He was a total inspiration. One day I said to him, 'You're doing reps there with British record poundages, why don't you enter the powerlifting tournament?' But he wouldn't go, he had no interest in winning medals. At a later date I was in his house and he showed me two walls completely covered from ceiling to floor with trophies, for wrestling and for boxing – he had boxed in the Army – so he had no interest in more medals to collect dust. He is still working on the doors now at over seventy years of age.

There was an incident where Terry wasn't really bullied so much as taken advantage of. He was training with the instructor, a black belt second dan, who locked his arms and threw him so he couldn't breakfall. Terry landed and broke his collarbone. He came in the gym, and it was very much a clique up there, and when he told us what happened, with him being a novice at judo and only being fifteen, I thought it was a liberty, so I went down to the judo dojo to confront the instructor. He wasn't there, but when I told the fellow who was in charge at the time, who was a brown belt, what I had come down for, he said, 'That's easily sorted, I'll fight you.' So we had a bit of a set-to. Rather foolishly, I put a judo jacket on. Anyway, I managed to get him into a side headlock, cranking the back of his neck, and submitted him.

So you started wrestling professionally? Wrestling back then was very popular, it was on the TV every Saturday, and the stars were household names, rather like the WWF became in later years. There was one guy who was legendary, Bert Assirati?

Bert was a heavyweight from London who was just a natural wrestler, nobody could do anything with him, he just loved hard wrestling. He was highly skilled and tremendously strong. He was the original Guv'nor, he lorded it over the London nightclub scene as a doorman.

Yes, I spoke to a guy who managed a club and had Bert on the door. He said he was absolutely fearless. One night the receptionist buzzed him to come down as there was a problem on the door. Bert had refused entrance to a group of guys because they weren't members. When the manager got there he almost fainted because it was the Kray twins with a few of their boys. Anyway he told Bert that it was okay, they could come in. Apparently, there were no comebacks because the Krays respected Bert's fortitude.

He was a legend. He found it very hard to get bouts because he wrestled at full power and full speed. He was so strong and skilled his opponents would be injured and have to miss forthcoming fights, which caused a bit of dissent. Eventually promoters stopped booking, so he'd turn up at a venue and wouldn't let anyone else into the ring unless he got a match.

What about Les Kellet?

Another phenomenal hard man who unfortunately went on television after his best days were over. His tag partner was his son. He was very tricky with a great sense of humour in any situation. Often, if he didn't like the outcome of a bout he'd continue it in the changing room, and at the end of the night he'd be doglocked in a corner while his lad was waiting to drive him home.

Another Liverpool wrestler, Kevin Connelly, who I met a few times with you, also worked on the door with you and Terry?

He was from the Crosby Wresting Club. I got him onto the Cavern door, and he got me into pro wrestling. Kevin sometimes used to partner Les Kellet in a tag team.

I remember a story I heard when there was a fight at the Cavern and some guy grabbing Kevin in a headlock, not the best thing to do to a wrestler. Anyway Kevin twisted his head to look at the lad, said 'Is it on?' then picked him up and slammed him into the floor. When you were growing up, as a young man, the way men would fight was very different to today. Often men would arrange a fight, to sort out their differences on a bombsite, or bit of wasteland. Can you tell us about that?

It would be what they call a straightener today. Somebody might have taken a liberty, beaten someone up who was older, or battered somebody when they were drunk. The local champion, who may not have been a particular friend of the injured party, would sort it out. In the fight, what was different from now, since karate and this full-blooded street fighting, was that the moment a bloke went down his opponent would let him get back up. I've seen many a fight where one party would go down on one knee and that was the fight over. They had both fronted up to each other, won a bit of respect and one guy might have a black eye, and that would be it, instead of like now, where a bloke ends up in hospital on a life-support machine.

When I was about fourteen, myself and a few mates, like Denny Regan, would sit outside the Grafton, a famous local dancehall, and watch the fun. There'd be two or three fights, blokes would be getting thrown out by the doormen, that was our entertainment in those days.

One night a fight kicked off at the Grafton door between two local hard cases and a group of hard lads from the city centre, and it went right down to Lime Street, a distance of well over a mile. The two locals took on pairs from the city centre in succession, the occasional kick was slipped in but a roar would go up from the crowd, 'Fight fair, you dirty bastards,' and the punching would resume. As I say, right down into the city centre.

Somebody came down to the wrestling club and offered Tony the job on the door of the Cavern. But Tony, the gentleman, wasn't interested in being a bouncer; so I told them I'd take it. I got Kevin Connelly down there, Johnny Mack, the trainer, down there, then eventually talked Tony into coming down and working there – and, of course, Terry.

Terry always credited you with teaching him the ropes on the door. Being a doorman is a lot more than fighting, isn't it?

Yes, obviously there's some doormen who enjoy that side of the business, but in the long term it's counter-productive. My attitude, which I relayed to Terry, was that it's easier to stop them on the front door, before they go into the club, than it is to deal with them inside the club and have to drag them out, particularly in places like the Cavern, which had a very steep, narrow staircase. Plus the amount of witnesses in the club, their friends, who were likely to join in and kick off a brawl; whereas at the door you could isolate them and with a few harsh words deal with it.

Yes, as a lad who went to the Cavern I can remember very few fights inside, I never saw what happened up on the door, but you certainly kept the club itself free from trouble.

Which is what the job's all about; you very quickly learn to spot the likely lads, front them, and quite often their attitude would indicate whether they were the sort of people who'd kick off inside.

What else of this sort of knowledge did you pass on – how guys would use distraction and deception to get close and steal it on you, that sort of thing?

Right, how to stand in an on-guard position, a covert on-guard position, and be watching them all the time, don't get distracted or complacent.

We can't leave the Cavern without mentioning The Beatles. It was the most famous club in the world and the reason is that the most famous group in the world played there. So you must have worked all the time they were playing there, but neither you or Terry really mentioned them.

As far as the doormen were concerned most musicians were just a pain in the arse. They were young, they tried to take advantage by getting their mates in for free, many were druggies, whereas myself and Terry were both into heavy training and weren't interested in drink or drugs, so there was very little rapport between ourselves and the groups.

So you never bothered collecting The Beatles' autographs or getting photos with them?

Another fortune I missed out on, would have been a good eBay investment.

I remember Terry telling me he had to wear a couple of pullovers under his shirt to bulk himself up a bit.

An old bodybuilding trick! Terry was quite young, very tall, slim build, wasn't carrying an ounce of surplus anywhere; and his boyish face didn't help. So to make himself more impressive I insisted he wore so many sweaters he couldn't get his jacket on! Then, when he did get his jacket on, with the help of everybody, he couldn't move his arms.

I believe in those days Terry was very uncoordinated, and was always falling over?

Yes, it was amazing. One minute he'd be doing these Olympic-level acrobatic moves and karate, next minute he'd drop his bag out of his hand, or trip over his own feet.

Then he suddenly changed?

Oh yes. What brought this to light, we were walking down from his house to do our shift at the Cavern. They'd put these waist-high barriers along the road near Lewis's in the city centre. I walked up and kind of slid over it; then Terry jumped, I don't know what you'd call it, he was facing square on and just leapt up, both his knees coming up by his chin, and cleared the barrier. Not a vault, he leapt right over it. I'd never seen anything like it in my life. That's when it all started locking in place and he became the superb athlete that he was. It was a pivotal point, going from being a big, clumsy feller, particularly when he locked on to somebody or when it had become like a street wrestling match, but then it quickly reached the stage where nobody could get close enough to put their hands on him without falling to the floor unconscious.

Another aspect, you were probably the first guy to work on shop security, in Liverpool anyway. So you really started what is now a booming business.

What happened was large gangs of shoplifters were going around, and one of the shops, a men's style outfitters called Brass & Jackson asked for a couple of doormen to work there on Saturdays.

Did they come down to the Cavern looking for doormen?

That's right, they asked for a couple of lads, because the Cavern had a reputation for being well run. So Terry and I went there on Saturdays and had lots of fun and games. By this time Terry was so quick at picking anything up, it was very easy to spot people coming in the shop and decide whether they were going to be a problem or not. The tactic was, we'd let them in, because they would still buy stuff, but stand obviously looking at them so they wouldn't steal stuff. But some of them would still try to have gear away, and fun would commence. The most memorable row happened one Christmas Eve when a couple of fellers were in the shop, acting the goat, half bevvied, and I caught one stealing a pair of socks. I led him out but he started arguing the toss, so I put a hold on him and in the struggle we fell through a 5' by 5' mirror on the stairs. Anyway we got them down the stairs and threw them out. The smaller of the two ran at me, right onto a front kick which put him through the plate glass window. The street was crowded shoulder to shoulder with Christmas shoppers and a big crowd gathered to watch. This bloke was a right warrior, really wanted to fight, even though I'd already got the better of him a couple of times. After the window incident the crowd backed him up and blokes were rushing at us, as Terry and I held them off with kicks, punches and lots of good verbal discouragement. Then a couple of rugby players who were in town decided we were the good guys and ran in the doorway and stood on with us. This went on for quite a time, and word obviously spread because a couple of karate fellers from Terry's gym ran through and very visibly braced themselves in stances next to us, and we thought the incident was over. However the little feller was still looking for a fight, and about twenty minutes later came into the shop and told me he wanted to fight me on my own, but I persuaded him he was on a loser and told him to shake hands and have a happy Christmas, and that was it.

You also worked on the Victoriana Club with Terry?

Yes, we went from the Cavern to the Victoriana. That's where we started working with Richie Molyneaux. Richie was a very strong man, particularly in the bench press.

The Vic was where I first worked with Terry, in 1970. By then he was a highly experienced doorman with hundreds of fights. My memory of him from that time was that he was so adept at knocking people out without any hesitation, he was like a machine the way he produced it. Actually, I was under the impression that this was normal, and that most doormen could kayo people so efficiently. Of course that's far from the case.

That's right, and just around that time, say from the Cavern, where he first started and was struggling a bit, by the time he reached the Victoriana he'd reached the level that it wouldn't matter how many people were involved in the scuffle; with a display of perfect technical strikes he would knock the lot of them out, sometimes more or less in one movement. I've seen him kayo three fellers in one movement without putting his foot back on the floor.

Did you go into karate training?

A little bit, but I missed the physical hands-on stuff of the wrestling at that time. I have to say that Terry crossed the boundaries between classical karate and practical fighting, more so than any other karate man I've ever seen, and I've seen a lot of champions.

Not a lot of people know that Terry did Tai Chi Chuan, you did it together didn't you?

Yes, up in Manchester, with Rose Li, who was one of the greatest in the world, a fierce competitive fighter back home. We were impressed with the stuff. She was a highly accomplished martial artist and would insist that Terry attack her at full blast, but he just couldn't do it, you know, attack this little Chinese woman.

I guess it kind of shows his open mind; a guy who was famed for classical Shotokan trying something as different as Tai Chi.

That's Terry for you, he's interested in everything that applies for martial arts.

Then you came back on the doors, and worked on the Banyan Tree, a nightclub within the famous Adelphi Hotel. I worked with you there as well as Terry, and of course, Gary Spiers. That was a bit of a crew wasn't it?

Yes. Gary came to work there because Terry was always taking weekends off to go away for karate tournaments or courses, which left me as the front man on the door, which was a bit more than I could handle. So I told Terry I was leaving unless he brought Gary in. So the Maori came down and started working there regularly.

Do you remember the first time you met Gary?

Yes, it was in the Khardoma coffee bar, just around the corner from the Cavern. By arrangement Terry told me that this feller Gary was coming down, a phenomenal fighter from Australia. Anyway, Gary came in and was just my type of feller, he was laughing and joking, a perpetual grin on his face. He said,

'Terry's told me a lot about you,' and I said the same and we got on like a house on fire. We both came from a wrestling background, and as the wheels turned he eventually, many years later, ended up doing wrestling sessions with Tony Buck at Kirkby Stadium.

As you say, Gary was literally larger than life, very easy to get on with, big laugh, big grin, lots of stories. What was it like for you working with him?

It was a doddle. Gary and Terry were chalk and cheese. A big point was, say four or five fellers come to the door looking for trouble, I'd be busy wrestling with one, while Terry would knock the other four out, then finish off the one I had hold of. With Gary, it was different. Gary had this amazing verbal skill, were he would start off in this avuncular way, putting his arm round them, talking to them in a very friendly fashion. Suddenly these fellers would realise that this monster of a guy, about nineteen stone at the time and over six foot, had about three stone of arm around his shoulders, lifting him up and rocking him around like a baby. Many times I've stood there watching in anticipation of some aggression, then after about thirty seconds of Gary talking to him and slowly increasing pressure on his shoulders, I'd see his face turn white and his knees buckle. I've seen it many times, and used to watch for it happening, and they'd go off about their way.

He really was adept at the verbals, wasn't he? He had that easy, fluent voice and the Aussie slang, I mean if you ever read his articles or interviews that's exactly how he talked. In NLP (Neuro-Linguistic Programming) terms he was almost hypnotising those guys.

That's right, I've never seen anyone handle aggression the way Gary did. In NLP we talk about disarming aggression but I've never seen anyone do it like Gary. They'd be there, full of fight, the next thing, the blood would drain from their face, their knees would start to shake, and Gary, with his arm round the shoulder, would be more holding them up as he led them out the door!

By the same token, if he needed to be, he was fearsome.

Ferocious, and for a big man he was like lightning, tremendous speed; and talking about power, I've seen him punch a feller in the middle of the back, he went down and couldn't get up.

And he could take it too.

Nobody could give him enough, he loved fighting. However, as I say, he was so good at the verbals that it seldom came to fisticuffs.

I heard a story about when you were facing a problematic customer and had to send for Terry, with quite an outcome?

Terry had gone to have a meal elsewhere in the Adelphi, I was on the front door of the Banyan, and this bloke came in, about six foor four, went inside and caused some problems. The barmaid came out and told me that the guy was out of order. I decided to wait until Terry had finished his meal, hoping that the feller would behave until then, but she came back and said he was taking people's drinks and needed to be thrown out now. The manager phoned to the restaurant and told Terry that there was going to be trouble, whereupon Terry replied that Tommy's a doorman, tell him to handle it. So I went in, just slipped past the bloke and asked him his name. When he told me it was Tony, I told him 'Your kid wants to see you outside...' an old doorman ploy. The idea was to get him out into the street then close the door in his face without any physical stuff.

Anyway, we were a few feet from the door when he asked me what my game was, and started obscenities. So I thought, okay, he's just right for a groin punch, his groin being about level with my chin, but just as I was about to launch there was a thump and he slid down the wall. What had happened Terry had come down, saw me crouching and setting myself, and leapt the full length of the hall to side thrust-kick the feller in the face, right over my head, which was quite impressive. There was a huge dent in the wall, as if someone had pressed a football into the plaster when it was still wet. The feller slid down the wall, unconscious and we dragged him out and left him outside. Anyway we're looking through the spy-hole and the bloke is still lying there. I look at my watch and it's been twenty minutes. We decided to go out and move him a bit further away, but as we approached, he stirred and slowly got up. We went back in thinking that was that, but about three minutes later the hall porter called down to say that a feller was causing murder at the hotel reception. Terry shot up. It was the same feller and Terry knocked him out again.

So he had a good night out in Liverpool's fascinating clubland. There was another story which is quite famous in our circles, about Father Christmas?

Again, I was pretty well involved in this because I knew the bloke, he owned a shop and did a bit of business with him. He came down to the club, dressed as Father Christmas, which he used to do that time of the year, working with kids, probably on every paedophile register in the country. He was a real rough character, a townie, been in and out of jail a load of times. I let him in, and based on the fact that he knew the doormen, he started taking liberties inside. Anyone who has worked the door will know this, it's the friends you let in for free who cause the most problems. He was taking people's drinks, twisting their noses and going, 'Ho, ho, ho!' I told Terry I didn't want to fall out with the feller and asked him to deal with the problem. So Terry went in and told the feller he had to leave. Santa refused to budge so Terry put a wristlock on him. Anyway, the feller started calling for me and when I went in found Terry trying in vain to get him out of the chair with this wristlock. Meanwhile the bloke's roaring at the top of his voice, 'What a trick, hitting Father Christmas. You've got no heart. Happy Christmas mate.' Terry got a bit upset with me for not playing an active part but I was laughing so much at Terry struggling with a roaring Santa Claus. Anyway Terry solved the problem in his usual way and Father Christmas was out.

The next night Terry was still having a go at me, that the feller was coming back with a team, a regular happening on the doors, and I told him that we were in for trouble, because Santa had recruited a gang of dwarves to take us on.

You mentioned the wristlock. I know Terry had trained in aikido and was very impressed with it. I've never found aikido that useful, but then I've never really trained in it. You both did aikido for a while, under Ken Williams, wasn't it?

Ken Williams was a warrior, been in a few street fights and built up a reputation for himself.

Didn't he have a special punching method?

Yes, he did demonstrations were he'd punch somebody, with full power, in the stomach. He picked a bloke who'd done a lot of karate, punched him hard in the guts and the feller withstood it. Then Ken said he'd use his intrinsic energy, his *ki*, and delivered what was a relatively light blow and the bloke ended up on the floor in agony.

Let's talk about the actual techniques Terry used. His number one knockout was the head-high mawashi-geri. He also used side-kicks, back kicks and spinning kicks, all with great effect. But he used to try out new and different techniques, and log the results in a diary. That would be an interesting read! What can you remember about some of the techniques he used?

As you quite rightly said, he'd regularly change techniques and use the whole syllabus. I've never seen him headbutt anyone. He asked me to show him how but he never had to use it really – if they were close enough to butt they were already unconscious! Regarding hand techniques; I've seen him use the straight punch, obviously, as well as ridgehand, axehand, leopard's paw, hammerfist, front and rear elbow...

He used the elbow strike in competition, didn't he? He was the first guy we ever saw score points with the elbow.

Absolutely, he was just as impressive with his elbow as with his feet. It's just that his kicks were more pretty to watch.

What about knee strikes?

Knees, then every aspect of the foot; ball of the foot, heel, side of foot. He used to cycle through the lot of them. He'd use palm-heel, open-hand slaps ... I've seen him knock people down, stun them. He didn't knock them out with slaps, just stun them.

He'd use something like a slap if he didn't want to knock them out, wouldn't he? If he wanted them unconscious, he'd kick them.

Yes, that would serve as a telling off in Terry's terms!

What about footsweeps? I remember him using sweeps a lot.

Oh yes, another one. He started off sweeping down at ankle level, then he would work up so he could get them down with a sweep at knee height. He kept working, getting up near the midline, until he could make contact at the seat of the pants with success. He did this one night at the Banyan. A Scottish football team were down there, causing a lot of trouble. I was struggling with one feller, I front-kicked him and he caught hold of my ankle. I was holding on to the wall for balance, trying to shake him off, when Terry ran up and swept him with a straight leg across the seat of his pants and spun the feller like a top.

He must have had a thing about sweeping footballers because I remember at Rupert's, some guys from Tranmere Rovers were kicking off downstairs and he swept this guy continually. He'd let him get up and he'd sweep him again with the other leg.

Yes, I'd think that would be based on the fact that most athletic people go into clubs and cause trouble. It's just one of the general rules of the game.

What about other types of techniques, such as grappling? I know he wouldn't have grappled a lot, because as you so succinctly put it, 'if they were close enough they'd already be unconscious', but he liked grappling didn't he? I recall once where he voluntarily grappled with a guy just to have a pull. Can you remember any such instances?

Oh Terry loved the wrestling. When he first started he entered a competition and didn't even know how he was supposed to win. From the Banyan Tree we used to get free train passes and we'd go down to London. Every time we'd get on the train, Terry would get us an empty compartment and I'd have to wrestle him all the way to London. By then he was just too strong and canny; I could never do anything with him. Anyway, one day we were strolling through London's Chinatown and I thought here's my chance, I'll get him here, and I caught him low, took him to the ground and slipped him into a side head-lock, which is just a containing hold really. He was on the floor saying, 'Get up, everybody's watching,' but I was determined to embarrass him as much as he'd done to me for the last three hours on the train.

Do you ever remember Terry using chokeholds in the street at all?

He'd catch people round the neck, but I've never seen him choke, or even half choke, anyone. Just a restraint. He knew the chokes, but really, as I've said, if he was close enough to choke they'd be unconscious.

Yes, I think the use of the chokeholds came in a bit later with the spread of CCTV, when we didn't want to be seen to be striking people. You talked about going to London with him, Chinatown with him, just being in Terry's world was always an interesting place, there was always a buzz about him, never boring, just sitting having a cup of tea would be interesting.

Yes, the lad was an absolute human dynamo in everything he did: karate, weight training, social, conversation. He was just on his toes and up for anything that was going on at the time. And he could turn his hand to anything at all.

Yes, people who only know him from seeing him in movies and on TV might get the impression that he's a rather serious character. He's typecast as villains, soldiers, police in serious dramatic roles, but we knew him as a joker.

He couldn't talk for more than a minute without putting a humorous twist on it, from outright clowning to very subtle observational skills.

He was the same in training. We trained together under some prestigious instructors in very strict and serious karate classes. Terry would always be standing on your foot or pulling your jacket over your head or something else to embarrass you. But always great company. I've gone to London with him in his car just to spend a day chatting with him.

I've done the same, spent a weekend with him while he's teaching, again just to spend time in his company.

I had the privilege of working with Terry and Gary, but you worked with Terry, Gary and Tony Buck, three of the most exceptional fighting athletes ever.

Terry and Gary were always ready for violence. Tony Buck considered himself a sportsman, he was a gentleman, and his favourite tactic was just to grip a troublemaker on the arm, just above the elbow, with his massive hand, and they'd squeal like a pig. I've never seen him physically struggle with anybody, just a pinch grip to the elbow and lead them out.

I worked with a guy who had been a barman in a place Tony worked when he was in his sixties, and he told me in amazement that Tony picked two guys up and carried both of them out, one under each arm.

Yes, you couldn't describe to anybody Terry's skills as a fighter, you couldn't do him justice if they hadn't seen for themselves. Tony Buck was the same, one of the strongest men in England, could apply his strength and his wrestling skills.

Gary, in a gym, was surprisingly not very strong, he was shy of heavy weights, but put him in a situation of manhandling, he was phenomenally strong.

He was one of those anomalies, just born to fight.

You mentioned earlier that Terry and Gary were two guys who could really put their training into practice on the street. I've always said that Terry's karate was absolutely textbook perfect in the gym: his form was faultless, upright, back straight, stances immaculate. He was also like that in competitions. There's a lot of photographic evidence of Terry winning a tournament with textbook techniques. However, he was like that in the street as well. Unfortunately we don't have any photos of him in action on the doors, and there was no CCTV in those days, but we both know that his street techniques were absolutely classical.

Yes, as I said, I saw him knock three blokes out without putting his foot back down on the ground. As he kicked each of them the heel of his supporting leg stayed flat on the floor, I just happened to notice that. Perfect posture. And he wasn't doing it on fresh air, where you can easily throw multiple kicks without losing your balance; he actually hit these blokes, knocked them out without losing an ounce of balance, or, faulting his technique at all.

Your son, young Tommy, trained with Terry and became a black belt. He also worked in the clubs, firstly as a glass collector. Tell us about the incident where he and Terry came out of a club at the end of the night and were ambushed.

This is more or less word-for-word what my son told me: They came out of the club and five fellers were waiting there, with clubs, to attack Terry. The fellers were rushing in, and next thing Tommy was down on the ground. He later realised that Terry had put both hands in his back and flung him right out of the arena. By the time he gathered his wits and looked up, four of them were unconscious and Terry was running up the street after the other one! Now, I don't know whether his heel stayed on the floor during that, but I'm quite sure it did do.

What an amazing story, but it's typical of Terry, in both looking after a mate and in his total fighting mastery.

Terry's unbelievable. I could quite well imagine you could walk up the street with Terry, bump into four fellers who wanted to fight, and Terry would say to whoever he was with, 'Walk on ahead, I'll take care of these myself.' He was the best friend anyone could ever have.

The Trio: a rare picture of Dennis, Gary and Terry together on a club door.

CHAPTER 6

THE TOP RANK

THE TOP RANK Suite was a massive place built over the shopping centre in St John's Precinct. The main ballroom held 2,000 and the function room held a few hundred more. At the time it was considered a very modern set-up, a bit like a nuclear shelter with music. The Rank Organization opened several of these venues throughout the country. Their expertise was in the movie business and unfortunately, they tried to operate ballrooms using the model of their cinema business. They didn't employ doormen, they used 'attendants', paid by the hour, with no aptitude or training for the type of violent confrontations common in the nightclub trade. Entrance to the Liverpool suite was via an escalator up to the fourth level. The first three levels were car parking, which was still being built for the first year or so. The fifth floor was the function room. While punters were being admitted, the way out was an elevator. This process was reversed when the front doors closed, and the direction of the elevators was reversed too.

The music was mainly live. There was a full dance band in residence, led by Clive Carnazza. The stage would revolve and a guitar duo would take over. Records were only played during intervals, as this was before club owners discovered that employing a DJ was a cheap alternative to live music.

When the Rank opened I was working at the Victoriana with Terry. We used to see police Jeeps scream up the hill to the Rank every Friday and Saturday. What happened in every new city centre venue was that there was a lot of jockeying for dominance by gangs from the various suburbs, who used the town as the arena to settle disputes and sort out who was the hardest bunch. In the Rank this was done on mainly racial lines, with the black lads from Toxteth claiming the club as 'their' territory. This came to a head when the crew of a Royal Navy ship, I believe it was HMS *Eagle*, were ashore and a major race riot ensued. We heard that the police dragged the Toxteth lads down the fire escapes by their feet, heads bumping on every concrete stair. That was the last straw and the police closed the place.

One of the Victoriana lads, Richie Molyneaux, was approached to run the door, and he took me with him. Richie was an unusual guy. He was tall and well built, with a shaven head. That was unusual in those days and, together with his goatee, gave him a very distinctive, severe appearance. He was, however, a hippie, into love and peace. He had spent a year hitching around America, with a couple of months in the communes of San Francisco. When he returned home to his flat in Liverpool Chinatown, he decided to turn his bedroom into a cave, much to the consternation of his elderly mother. He used chicken wire and plaster to build the walls of the cave, then painted it to look like rocks, threw in some fur rugs and crawled in to sleep. Unfortunately the paint fumes nearly killed him and his mum had to drag him out unconscious. Richie would much rather talk people out of fighting and his imposing presence, together with his hippie attitude, did indeed prevent much trouble. This being Liverpool, though, we still got loads.

We had two other guys, Harry Benfield and Frank Vernon, who were both karate men. Frank was the guy who had come into my judo club and first told me where the karate club was. He had a day job as a welder at Cammell Laird shipbuilders and was involved in the trade union. Naturally he became our negotiator. Harry and I had trained together quite a bit. By trade he was a plasterer. Neither Frank nor Harry had worked the door before, Richie had several years experience, and I had about a year. We all got on well and watched each other's backs. They still employed a team of 'attendants', who earned an extra hour's pay by stacking the chairs at the end of the night. Most of these were a waste of rations, but one or two were staunch and got stuck in when trouble erupted – as it did, regularly.

At first, when they reopened, they targeted the over-twenty-five age group. Then, after seeing us keep out the scallies successfully, they asked us if we were okay with them going back to an over-18 policy, which is where the real money is. We had no problem with it, so the place really took off again, and was soon operating at capacity. The problem they'd had earlier was that the attendants never controlled the door. Guys who had caused trouble previously were readmitted because the attendants were easily intimidated. Having a proper door crew meant we KB'd (knocked back) known troublemakers, which lessened the trouble inside. However, with 2,000 people there were bound to be kick-offs, and we had our share. A code would be broadcast over the PA system. Each bar was numbered and the dance floor was coded as 'six'. So 'staff to bar six' meant a fight on the main dance floor. We could hear this at the front door, so two of us would sprint up the escalators, leaving the other two on the door, and steam in to sort it out.

The Rank was really where I learned the job. We had some major events there: concerts by David Bowie in September 1972, during his Ziggy Stardust era, Emerson, Lake and Palmer, Wilson Pickett, and so on. Terry used to join us for the odd night, when we needed extra lads, and although there were just four of us fronting the door, we did bring in other guys for special events. Terry ended up working there a lot. He would sometimes double up, putting in appearances at the Rank and the Vic alternately through the night and claiming two pay packets. Those were the days!

The cash desk in the reception area was circular, with panes of toughened glass. We were told it was bullet-proof. One night I was perched on the ledge of the cash desk talking with Terry when he playfully gave me a mighty shove. I went straight through the glass – so much for it being bullet-proof – and lay with the remaining half pane above me, waiting to fall like a guillotine. I scrambled like a cartoon dog trying to get clear, while Terry was rolling up laughing.

We brought Steve Cattle in for a night and he had a great time. There was only one kick-off, but it was a big one and Steve got in very enthusiastically. Steve was a member of the British karate team alongside Terry and was a British champion. He and Terry fought a famous battle for the title one year, which went to several overtimes. Terry eventually won but gave a lot of credit to Steve for a gutsy performance. One time Steve was on crutches, having been injured in a competition. Walking down Rodney Street three scallies tried to mug him. He battered them unmercifully, including throwing one over his shoulder with a classic judo throw into the pavement and unconsciousness. The police actually considered charging Steve!

As mentioned, when we first started they were still building the car park, so the front door was at the end of a temporary tunnel, quite a distance from the actual reception area. There was no heating, and since we started in winter, we froze. We all wore heavy sheepskin overcoats over our tuxedos. Frank introduced a novel idea, which I've never seen on a door before or since. He had been a shop steward at Cammell Lairds, and the form in the shipyards was that if two men were assigned to a job, only one actually worked at a time while the other took a break. This probably accounts for the fact that we don't build ships there anymore. Anyway Frank persuaded Richie to use that system at the Rank, and so a pair would be on the door and the other pair in the staff room. Harry and I didn't really like sitting in the smoke-filled staff room so we would only take a short break, and consequently we spent most of our time actually fronting the door. Some commentators criticise doormen as working in a gang. Well, for much of the time there were only two lads on that remote door, facing all comers. The punters who had caused all the trouble previously really wanted back in, and we had to convince them otherwise. It was a hectic time.

We did have a good social life at the Rank (which has since been demolished). There were often stay-behinds after work, or parties in someone's flat. We had a teen disco on Tuesdays, which closed a 10pm, so a group of doormen and barmaids would go over to the Shakespeare Theatre Club to catch whatever act was topping the bill. We saw such stars as Tommy Cooper, Roy Orbison and Dave Allen. If the show was good I'd come back on Thursdays, my night off, with my girlfriend for a night out.

* * *

Every year, a karate tournament was held in St George's Hall, and one year the after-party was held in the Function Room at the Rank. I had been handling the commentary at the tournament, so attended the party, along with Terry, who had been a referee and demonstrator. Numerous top champions and instructors were present, including Terry's teacher, Master Enoeda.

During the evening, Richie came in and asked Terry and I to give him a hand, as a situation was brewing. We went into the main ballroom to eject some rowdies, and the whole place kicked off. Terry, Richie and I all went down under sheer weight of numbers. When you see those two go down, you think, we're in trouble now. But we all fought our way back to our feet and the game was on. Someone told the rest of the karate blokes that we were fighting, and they all steamed in to help. Steve Cattle and Glen Haslem in particular were dropping guys enthusiastically. The brawl went on for quite a while, then we dragged the unconscious bodies to the fire exits and lashed them. One memory was a guy who was dragging me by the waist while his mates were trying to punch me. One of the karate guys pulled him off, slammed him through an inner door, and I saw him a bit later lying unconscious in the elevator foyer, with the lift doors closing and opening on his head.

* * *

Most doormen learn the specifics of pre-violence control. An aspect of this is assuming an unobtrusive 'ready' position, with your hands ready for defence or attack, but not obviously so. Old school doormen often tucked their thumbs into their tuxedo lapels, so that their elbows were up as a shield in a tense situation. The author and martial artist Geoff Thompson has widely described the 'Fence' methods which he learned while working with a number of door crews. My favourite was to hold my right hand in my left, at chest height, and start cracking my fingers. This led to a funny incident.

I had been down to the Vic for a bowl of fried rice and a chat with Terry. On my way back up the hill, I saw that Harry was fronting three blokes who, from their body language, were a problem. I stood behind the guys, listened to what they were saying, and unconsciously started cracking my knuckles. They saw this and quickly legged it, to the amusement of Harry. Apparently he had KB'd them and they started getting aggressive, asking if he was going to stop them by himself. Seeing me approach, Harry said, 'It's up to you lads, but I'll tell you what's going to happen. See this lad coming up the hill? He's going to listen to you, he's going to start cracking his knuckles, then he's going to knock you all out.'

Another time, Terry had been inside the Rank and when he came out he saw that we were confronting a group of abusive guys. Every time we went out to them they backed off; every time we went back in they came back giving us verbals. Terry sussed it out and strode passed us as if he didn't know us. The guys outside didn't realise he was a doorman because he wore a sports jacket. Once close, he launched four kicks and there were four sleeping beauties.

* * *

Gary Spiers didn't really want to work on the doors, due to the circumstances of his leaving Australia, but since he couldn't find any work as a slaughterman, he joined us at the Rank. On his first night, a couple of Italian seamen approached the door and Gary KB'd them for some reason. When they argued, Gary pointed to his scar and told them, 'A wop did this to me.'

The first confrontation I saw Gary handle was after we had ejected a guy via the rear exit, and he was trying to get back in past Gary, who had his back to him while trying to handle the crowd. Gary told the ejected punter to desist a couple of times, then ended the discussion with a rear headbutt. This was the first time I'd seen a headbutt done backwards, and I was impressed, especially since the punter was horizontal, unconscious, with several of his teeth lying in a bloody pool beside him.

When we had courses in Liverpool, the guys would often come down to the club and hang out with us. Brian Waites, a Goju-kai [Japanese Goju-ryu] instructor, came down quite a few times. They were great times. But the Top Rank changed hands several times, becoming Baileys and Cinderella Rockerfella. The rates on the site were enormous and it was impossible for a business to make money there. Eventually the place closed and the structure has been demolished.

I left in 1973. I'd probably had an ambition to go to Japan

ever since I started in karate, but it was a vague, unspecified ambition. Then one day I woke up and said, 'I'm going to Japan.' I made a serious commitment to go, took several months to get the money together, and in April set off on the journey of a lifetime. I would be there for six months.

Terry and Den on the ship to Okinawa, Japan.

CHAPTER 7

JAPAN

ON FRIDAY, APRIL 13, 1973, a couple of days after my twenty-sixth birthday, I took a Pakistan International Airlines (PIA) Boeing 707 to Japan. The flight stopped at Rome, Cairo, and Karachi before landing at Tokyo's Haneda Airport. Unfortunately, my luggage went to Peking. Terry had arranged for me to stay for a couple of days with photographer Arthur Tansley, who supplied some brilliant photos for *Fighting Arts*. Arthur was a judo black belt who had been in Japan for eight years. He earned a living by teaching conversational English and by appearing in movies and TV as a foreigner. He also appeared in numerous adverts, and once, when we were on the bus, together a gaggle of giggling schoolgirls pointed to him as 'Mr Ebi Fry', as he was the chef on a popular brand of stir-fry prawns; it was rather like sitting next to Colonel Sanders. Back in England, Arthur had been part of a group of judo-trained doormen before emigrating to Australia, then Japan.

I arrived in Tokyo late Saturday night, and then early Sunday went to Yoyogi to scope out the famed *shurenkai* ('severe training place') and meet Master Higaonna. He took me to the local McDonald's, a chain unknown in England at that time. Later I wandered around various parts of Tokyo, marvelling at the neon and just absorbing the fact that here I was, realising my ambition to train in Japan. After a while I was hungry, and noticed a machine featuring a steaming pot of noodles. I inserted some coins, expecting a delicious hot snack, and was dismayed when a solid block of noodles emerged. This was my introduction to pot noodles, and the realization that you needed to add your own hot water. I ate a lot of this cheap meal while in Japan and have never eaten them since.

On Monday morning I did my first class at Yoyogi, taken by Kokubo-san, who was the *deshi*, or apprentice instructor. I needed to wait until the next class to speak to Master Higaonna, so ended up training at two classes back to back. It was hard, but didn't kill me, so at least two classes per day was my schedule for the entire stay. Before training, I had nipped over to find the Tokaido shop, which sold karate suits, equipment and books. I picked up a book, in Japanese, which detailed all the weapons *kata* (training drills). I took the subway train to Yoyogi and decided to have a snack before training. I chose a coffee house near the station. Only one seat was available, at a table occupied by a young Japanese couple. Seeing me leafing through the book, the man asked, in English, if I trained in martial arts. As the conversation continued, I was amazed to find that he had taught aikido in the Vernon Sangster Centre in Liverpool, where I taught karate. Small world indeed!

Training at the Shurenkai was high repetition work. We drilled basics endlessly. Also the kata had be perfected, again by repletion. Goju emphasises hard conditioning, and we pounded our arms against each other, lifted the *chi'ishi* (stone weights) and slammed thousands and thousands of punches into the *makiwara* (punching board). The floor of Yoyogi was the worst I'd trained on, worse even than cold black stone. The planks were all uneven and often nails popped up to rip your bare feet. After a week I had no skin on the soles of my feet and no skin on my knuckles from hitting the hard rubber pad on the *makiwara*. I asked the seniors what treatment to use and they wrote a note for me to take to the chemist. It turned out to be Mercurochrome, which gave a dramatic blood-like hue to my knuckles. This solution contains mercury and I had heard on the news that the local fish was also polluted with this heavy metal, so I was ingesting large quantities of a toxic substance. I took so much mercury that I grew six inches in hot weather!

After I had been there a few weeks, Terry came over in advance of the British contingent for the forthcoming JKA World Championships. Up till then I had done little except train at the dojo and visit the zoo on the Sundays when the dojo was closed. Terry, who was staying in my apartment, immediately arranged for us to visit several notable martial arts experts. He was determined to meet and interview as many top masters as possible for his magazine.

The first of these was Donn Draeger, an American who had settled in Japan after serving as a major in the US Marines. Originally Donn studied judo and then expanded into numerous other martial arts, to the point that he held over seventy black belts or equivalent rankings – all earned, not honorary. He had also written ground-breaking books about Asian fighting systems and was the role model for all martial arts writers. We met Donn at the Shimizu Jodo Dojo, which specialised in the use of the three-foot stick. Everyone and his dog wanted to meet Donn, so his friends tended to shield him: but we were able to arrange a meet through a Canadian, Howard Alexander, who would take us to the dojo. Well, this won't come as a shock to those who know Terry, we were late and Howard had left. Terry denounced him; after all, we were only about two hours late! Anyway, we eventually found the dojo, after a hilarious conversation with a policeman, who kept insisting we meant 'judo' whenever we asked where the 'Jodo' HQ was. We linked up with Donn, got on well with him and met quite frequently after that.

Donn was physically impressive. He was over fifty but had the body of a twenty-five-year-old athlete. His arms, especially, were amazing, with layers of muscle from all the different weapons training. Donn came to meet us at Yoyogi once and waited at the door watching the session. The instructor, Kokubo-san, came over and asked me if that was Draeger-Sensei, and when I confirmed this, Kokubo said, 'I thought so, I saw his arms.' They were like the gnarled branches of an oak tree.

Donn was probably the most highly qualified instructor in the world, yet with all this knowledge, he was the nicest guy you'd ever meet. You just wanted to ask him questions, but he was equally interested in your views, your opinions. Good sense of humour too. We were having a cup of tea one day and Donn was moaning about his publisher. He said, 'I'd like to punch him on the nose.' Terry and I just looked at each other and burst out laughing. Donn was perplexed; what were we laughing at? We told him, with all your grades, all your skills, you just want to punch the guy on the hooter? Surely you'd use a Siamese Death Lock or something. He saw the point and laughed too.

After several meetings, Donn invited us to his home in Chiba, where he arranged a demonstration of various weapons systems that was simply astounding. Then another time Donn arranged something special for us. He was no longer living at the famous Ichigaya house, having moved to Chiba area. Terry and I took the train out there where Donn had arranged to show us his movies of South East Asian martial arts. I especially remember a twelve-year-old *sai* expert and a guy who was lightning with the *kerambit* knife. Donn told us this guy had won numerous knife fights, and I think that was the point I really started realising the lethal threat of the knife. Donn also arranged for us to meet a senior instructor of the Katori-ryu, and after talking to us for a while, he told Donn to get changed into training kimono and they gave us a demonstration, a real privilege as Katori-ryu usually only show their stuff at the New Year festival. After demonstrating Iai-jutsu, the sensei paired up with Donn for Bokken versus Bo. It was absolutely terrifying ... I was holding my breath.

The speed and power was awesome and it didn't look like a kata, which it was, but a fight to the death. It was a highlight which I still look back on. Donn's death was a real shock, which upset Terry and I greatly.

Karate originated in Okinawa, one of a group of islands between Japan and China, and it was the place I most wanted to visit. Terry and I took the train to Kobe, then the ship to Okinawa. Master Higaonna had arranged for us to stay at his home dojo, the Jun-do-kan, run by Master Miyazato. As we disembarked at Naha, the capital, a young Okinawan greeted us. He had been sent by Master Miyazato. In the car we asked him how he recognized us, as there were lots of *gaijin*, or foreigners, on the ship. He explained that he had just looked at everyone's hands, on the assumption that any karate guy would have big, conditioned knuckles.

We saw quite a bit of Okinawa. Mark Bishop, an Englishman training at Jun-do-kan showed us around quite a bit. Although the island is not really attractive I liked the people a lot. Unfortunately Terry, who suffered from asthma, had a severe attack, requiring a visit to the hospital. I arranged for him to fly back to Tokyo while I finished the trip then came back by ship alone.

Back in Tokyo, another *gaijin* joined the group. Bakkies Laubscher, from South Africa, was a student of Hugh Thompson and a noted international competitor. Built like a bull, he was very strong. One day Bakkies was reading a newspaper from home with the results of the Miss South Africa competition. Little did I know that I would meet the winner within a few months.

The British team arrived and Terry moved in to the Imperial Hotel with them. I spent a lot of time with them, mainly to get some free meals on their expense account. It turned out that, because of some mix-up, they were a guy short, and being on hand, I was invited to join the team. The JKA

World Championships was held in the huge Nippon Budokan, the national hall dedicated to the martial arts, and taking the tournament stage there was a daunting experience. We were knocked out of the match by the very strong South African team. I must record my thanks to Master Enoeda for his hospitality to me during this event. He ensured I was included in many banquets and dinners. Master Enoeda died tragically and suddenly in 2003. It has been said of him that 'he had the fearless attitude of a hero and the loving heart of a child'. His contribution to British karate was immense.

As spring became summer, training became arduous. The heat and humidity were fearsome. Many clubs ceased training during August; we trained as hard as ever. There was no break during the class and you weren't allowed to drink. There was a single tap outside the front door to be used when the class was finished and I would gulp gallons of tepid water after every session. Sometimes, before I'd get a chance for a drink, Master Higaonna would grab me for some extra, after-class training, usually hitting the board or kata. The phrase every guy who trained at Yoyogi will remember best is *mo ichi do*: one more time. You would perform the drill, and the teacher would say, 'Mo ichi do,' again and again. You might have to repeat the kata twenty times, at full speed and power, before he was satisfied. However, this training was exactly why I had come to Japan.

In between training, I managed to fit in some interesting visits. Master Higaonna was invited to the opening of the new Karate College by Gogen Yamaguchi and kindly took us *gaijin* along. Mr Yamaguchi, known as 'The Cat', was a famous teacher, famed for ascetic shinto routines, such as performing the sanchin breathing kata under a freezing waterfall in winter. Gary Spiers and Brian Waites had trained in the Yamaguchi form of Goju and I was delighted to attend this formal demonstration.

Some mornings, before training, I would go the Nippon

Budokan. There was always something new, something fascinating, to see there, such as a women's *naginata* (halberd) class, or soldiers studying *juken-jutsu* (bayonet fighting). Some Saturday nights I would blag my way into the Korakuen Stadium, where the full-contact kickboxing fights were held. Often fighters from Thailand competed and the power of their *muay thai* was impressive. I saw some great fights.

In October, the dojo took an official party to Okinawa to participate in the festivities celebrating the twenty-fifth anniversary of the death of Goju-ryu founder Chojun Miyagi. A group of us *gaijin* from Yoyogi performed *shisochin* kata, which was a great honour for us. Every top instructor of Goju-ryu was at the festival, from all over Okinawa and Japan. After seeing all the famous teachers, I can say that in my opinion Master Higaonna was the technically most proficient exponent of Goju in the world. While in Okinawa, Master Higaonna also put me through the test for black belt, second dan. I passed and became his first British black belt. Higaonna was the epitome of the martial arts master. He was very modest, very polite, very easy to get on with, and yet he was an awesome martial artist. It was the two things together. He was what many people believe martial arts instructors are like, but most of them are not.

There was so much to take in in Japan. We went to an aikido dojo one night, where they did a kind of *randori*, or sparring, with a glove on the striking hand. Englishman Arthur Tansley took us to the Kodokan several times to watch the judo training. Those guys trained hard. I also went to the All-Japan Judo Championships to do a magazine report. The guys all looked real toughies, broken noses, cauliflower ears, all the corners knocked off – and that was just the spectators. I also enjoyed visiting the Budokan. I used to turn up there and blag my way into whatever event was on. I saw several martial arts contests and once a rock concert this way.

Terry and I went to a few other dojos, to Master Nagamine's

shop and his dojo, and to see Uechi-ryu, which was the style I most wanted to see over there. But unfortunately we went there on a Saturday night and there were only two white belts training, with Master Kanei Uechi himself teaching. So we never saw the full style, and I never got to see Uechi-ryu at all when I was there. And that was the style that interested me the most.

Nagamine was a very approachable man for such a high rank. He had a record, music for karate, which I bought. It was called 'Springs of Okinawan Karate-do'. His style was Shorin-ryu, the foundation style of Shotokan. His guys were very good. They had a lot of focus, a lot of power. They used the circular, split *makiwara*, and they practised fearsome blocks on it. It's considered a hard style, and I thought it was. I wouldn't have liked one of them to block my shin. It was quite basic, but very effective.

However, Nagamine didn't particularly like free sparring. He sort of asked us about it in a rhetorical way: 'How can you do it? How can you compete in karate, karate is for fighting, so how can you make a sport of it?' He was very much of the old school, but very approachable. I enjoyed going there. We didn't get round to all the places we wanted. We had introductions to instructors from Master Hirokazu Kanazawa, he gave us his card and wrote on messages for people for when we went to see them, but time just ran out, we didn't get to see them. It's a pity because a lot of them are dead now.

Several years later, martial arts writer Graham Noble interviewed me about my training and work. I've included large sections of this interview throughout this book, primarily in the chapter At Close Quarters, but the following excerpt is most appropriate here:

GRAHAM: *In the Jundokan, wasn't it the case you'd turn up and more or less train as you wanted?*

DENNIS: It's nice. It's an Okinawan cultural thing where you go on the floor and one of your seniors will grab hold of you and put you through something, might be *makiwara*, might be kata, might be conditioning, using training equipment. And then one of his seniors will come over and grab hold of him and do the same, and then you'd be left to continue on your own and it's great for the handful of people who can train that way, but for most of us, myself included, the drilling is better, and particularly on a short stay like I was.

A little after going to Japan, you wrote an article on conditioning methods – chishi, makiwara and so on. How important was that as a part of Goju?

It was important. But I've got deep reservations about a lot of the conditioning now. The hard, body-to-body conditioning, I disagree with now. I did it, and enjoyed it while I was doing it, but looking back, I wouldn't do it, I wouldn't teach it, I wouldn't let anybody do it to me. I think it's bad for you, the *ude-kitae*, that kind of thing.

Why's that? Is it breaking down the body, something like that?

Yeah, and it doesn't relate to anything I'm doing now, which is close-quarters combatives. You can train hard and you can go through pain barriers without the concomitant injury factor. The *makiwara* – okay, great, I enjoyed *makiwara* training. But looking back now, is the *makiwara* the best device for developing punching power? Does it resemble any kind of human target? Does it give you the same kind of resistance a human body does? I just automatically assumed the *makiwara* was great.

But I don't punch any more and I don't use the *makiwara*. The other stuff, the *chishi* and the *sashi*, are very specific for karate and I think they're excellent because of the leverage: you get a lot of advantage from quite a light weight. But to be frank, we didn't do a great deal of that at Yoyogi. We had them there and I used them sometimes, but I was more or less left to my own devices. I saw them being used more in Okinawa, but it was only afterwards that we really got into it, when Goju developed in the UK.

My six months in Japan was over and I flew back with PIA, learning why this airline was popularly known as 'Perhaps I'll Arrive'. The aircraft developed technical problems so we were stuck in Manila for a night, no hardship apart from martial law being in effect. We were then stuck in Karachi for three days. I was very short of money, having budgeted just enough for a few drinks en route, then my train fare back to Liverpool. Stuck in the airport hotel, a group of female passengers wanted to visit the Bora Bazaar downtown and asked me to accompany them as a bodyguard. This turned out to be a fascinating experience. The taxi drive was quite long, and when we tried to pay the driver, he told us he would wait and take us back, despite our telling him we'd be a few hours. After wandering around the stalls, and seeing the fakirs with spikes in their arms, we found the taxi and returned to the hotel. We paid the driver twice what he asked, and the whole deal still cost about fifty pence. Amazing.

Departing Karachi, I found myself seated next to a stunning Pakistani lady who was en route to New York, where her husband was an international banker. She was scared of flying and tightly grasped my hand during take off. I tried to relax her by asking about her culture, and the flight became a very nice experience. Back in London I had several hours to wait at Euston for my train, and no left luggage lockers were in operation, due to the IRA bombs. So I was stuck lugging six months' worth of luggage around.

* * *

Paddy had done a great job in keeping the dojo running while I was away. The Bruce Lee movies had started to catch on and martial arts were the new fashion. We built up a solid training group at the Sangster. A young lad called Billy Jones joined. He was dead keen and quickly established himself as a serious trainer. Billy eventually became a senior black belt, helped on the Miss World team and also worked the doors [I later worked with him on the Chelsea Reach and also the Quad]. He trained to become a professional diver and progressed to being a top saturation diver. During a transit of the Straits of Hormuz, his ship was hit by an Exocet missile and his eardrums burst, ending his diving career. As he was a keen bodybuilder, I introduced him to Vic Imundi, who ran the gym I did weights at. It was a fortuitous match, and with Vic's coaching Billy won the Mr Universe title. Today he runs Gym 21 in the Kensington district of Liverpool. We had several good students who reached black belt level. Paddy and Billy both gained third dan. Other black belts included Bobby Hayes, Sue Kingswell, Bob and Maureen Newitt and Paul Hennigan.

One day a young lad asked to join. He was actually too young, but as his granddad had taken the trouble to bring him along, I let him sign up. His name was Tony Rimmer. He really applied himself and had great natural ability. At age thirteen he was hitting like a man, a strong man. He never missed a class and had terrific self-discipline. Tony later worked the doors, starting on the Quadrant Park nightclub when he was just eighteen. Terry O'Neill is the best doorman and best fighter I have ever met but I rate Tony Rimmer as the best of the next generation. He is now one of the partners in Premier Security in Liverpool.

Gradually, the demands of running bodyguard courses, bodyguard jobs and other projects gave me less time to devote to karate. In about 1991, I wound up the class and moved on to other things. Looking back, I am amazed at some of the things we did in karate. Few people today would do that kind of training – including me. A lot of traditional karate training is non-functional for street application. It may have self-discipline, sporting or artistic merits, but for self-protection much of it is excess. The only guys I know who can pull off classic karate techniques in the street are Terry O'Neill and Nick Hughes.

Den keeping watch on Miss Israel, Dana Feller, as she goes jogging in 1979.

CHAPTER 8

PROTECTING MISS WORLD

I HAD BEEN home only a couple of weeks when I was called and offered the job as a bodyguard for that year's forthcoming Miss World contest. The contest had been started by Eric D. Morley at the Festival of Britain and had grown into a massive international event, with a TV audience of about twenty million in the UK alone. Morley, known always as 'EDM', had risen to be chairman of Mecca, the biggest entertainment company in Europe, with dance halls, restaurants, bingo halls and hotels. His wife Julia, known as 'JEM', headed a subdivision called Mecca Promotions, which ran the Miss World contest, then organized the subsequent itinerary of the winner, which was mainly charity appearances.

For many years, the Miss World entrants had needed little in the way of security. A number of chaperones were employed, mainly ex-flight attendants, and each had about half a dozen contestants to look after, grouped mainly by languages. A group of Mecca managers, mainly from the bingo side, were used as security, with three of Mecca's actual security staff, former police officers, to oversee the operation. That changed with three events in the early 1970s. The Women's Liberation movement famously flour-bombed host Bob Hope during a live transmission at the Royal Albert Hall. A domestic terrorist group, the Angry Brigade, planted a bomb and blew up a BBC transmitter outside the Albert Hall. Finally, the murderous 1972 attack by Arab terrorists at the Munich Olympics demonstrated that anyone representing the State of Israel was a target. Since the Miss World contest always included Miss Israel, her government insisted on enhanced security.

The Morleys turned to Alan Francis, a friend of the family, who was a chief superintendent with the City of London Police and also chairman of the British Karate Control Commission, the government-sponsored regulating body for karate. Alan recommended Brian Hammond and myself to boost the Miss World security effort. His brief to me was 'to be around in the hotel corridors when the breakfasts are being served'. Brian was a big, suave guy who did both bodybuilding and Kyokushinkai karate. He fitted in well in a five-star hotel and had excellent people skills. I turned up at the Britannia Hotel in Grosvenor Square and met JEM and the team. I was given the primary role of protecting Miss Israel, and this became a task I fulfilled for the next dozen years.

The contestants arrived at Heathrow or Gatwick, on pre-arranged flights, and a team of security guys were based at those airports to meet and transport the girls to the hotel. With Miss Israel things were different. She was delivered by a team from the embassy, without prior warning. Later, as they began to trust me, they included me in the team, and we would go to Heathrow in a diplomatic vehicle to meet the El Al flight. Eventually, they handed the whole thing over to me, so I guess they had faith in my abilities. Each contestant had a sponsor from the host country, and for many years Rachel, the sponsor for Miss Israel, and I worked closely together to ensure good protection.

During the first week of the event, the contestants would attend numerous press calls and also go on various sightseeing events around London, taking in theatres, restaurants, the ballet, and famous landmarks such as the Tower of London or Windsor Castle. The second week would be mainly rehearsals for the show, which was held on a Thursday night. Security was tight. The girls were accommodated on a dedicated floor of the hotel. The lifts were programmed not to stop there and all exits were guarded. Access was via the staircase, through a checkpoint. All visitors and deliveries were screened. Whenever the girls left the floor, they were escorted by security and chaperones. The press were fascinated by the security measures and called the hotel 'Colditz'.

The Provisional IRA was also very active and we had to be aware of the risk of bomb attack. We were given threat assessments by the police and had procedures in place for evacuation of the hotel. By 1975, it was crazy. There was a concentrated campaign by a particular IRA active service unit, with hotels and restaurants being hit with bombs and drive-by shootings. Places we had visited the night before were hit the next night. Places we were scheduled to visit were hit before we arrived. It seemed only a matter of time, but fortunately we avoided attack.

On one of the first days working, I was involved in what I considered a minor incident. We were escorting a group of three or four girls across into Grosvenor Square for a photo shoot. Traffic in front of the hotel was heavy, and as we were halfway across I realised one expensive car was in danger of hitting the girls, so I stood in front of it until the girls were safe. Having to stop incensed the driver, and he tried to get out. I simply leaned on his door, preventing him opening it, until Brian had the girls well into the square, and then stood back. He was now even more enraged and launched himself at me. A footsweep put him in a heap. He tried again and again went down. Eventually he gave up and drove off. Apparently the admin staff had watched this from their office window and my willingness to act was noticed. While this was happening a reporter from a Turkish press agency was snapping photos, and wrote it up as an attack on Miss Turkey, foiled by British bodyguard 'Jeremy Port'. Many years later, the same reporter published a photo of another one of the lads escorting Miss

Turkey, and he too was identified as 'Jeremy Port'. I never found out where the name came from.

We had to establish a working relationship with the media, as the Miss World received unprecedented press attention; no other event, other than the major sport tournaments, had two weeks of constant international media coverage. Personally I found that most of the photographers were OK, they just wanted their picture. Since the whole object of the exercise was publicity, we co-operated, but of course prevented them from getting any shots we deemed negative to the wholesome Miss World image. The reporters were a different matter. They were always earwigging for titbits and I found most of them slimy. Two exceptions were Ann Leslie and Philippa Kennedy, who we still didn't trust but who played it pretty straight. Philippa's husband was a major in the Paras.

The three Mecca security staff were Jim C and Morris F, both former Met bobbies who now investigated any fiddles within the bingo halls, and Alec M. Alec was a real star. A former DCI on the Manchester force, he was a quiet professional, and I learned a lot from him. He had been a wartime Commando but didn't boast about it. I had to drag it out of him. Alec suggested that I go in advance to locations we were scheduled to visit and scope them out. Using my common sense, I would gather what information I thought useful, such as arrival points, timings, exits, fire precautions and contact numbers for venue management. I eventually compiled a checklist and this became the basic template for subsequent 'Advance Recce' tasks.

Brian and I took the job seriously. The security guys would usually eat with the contestants while out on visits, but we would position ourselves at vulnerable points and stay on watch. After that first 1973 event, won by the gorgeous Miss USA, Marjorie Wallace, we were both asked back, and were also asked to provide other guys to boost the team. I supplied a couple of lads from karate and shooting. I decided that VIP protection was something I could pursue – I found I liked it and had a certain aptitude for it – but realised that I needed a specific array of skills and knowledge, so I set about acquiring them.

At that time there were no commercial bodyguard training courses, so I acquired the material piecemeal. There is more on this in the chapter on Close Protection.

* * *

Back at the Miss World contest things got very busy in about 1980. Firstly there was a 'palace revolt' in Mecca, when the bean counters ousted Eric Morley from the company. Since he owned the rights to the Miss World title, he took it with him and set up his own company. I was given the job of running security each year, with a team of over twenty guys. Since the Mecca men had left, I recruited the new team. One was John Clark, who was one of the guys who showed me the ropes when I first started pistol shooting. John also worked the doors and for many years was one of Gary's main men. John had been on the Miss World team for several years and now became a team leader. He was what the Americans call a 'senator' – a fixer, and great to have on any job. He was brilliant at getting hotel staff onside, and I sent him to liaise with various agencies. Once we needed to get some stuff that Customs had impounded off an incoming contestant. Despite them quoting laws, rules and regulations John persisted, and in the end the Customs guys gave in and told him, 'Take it and piss off.' Karate guys like Paddy Phillips and Billy Jones also joined the crew, and learned on the job fast. Others were guys I had worked with on the bodyguarding circuit.

Julia Morley was very security minded and we started putting guys on the smaller events, such as the Miss UK and Miss England competitions. I was also able to organize the

Miss World security in a much more efficient manner. We split the lads into five teams of four BGs in each, plus myself as OC. On a rotating basis we had an advance team, a static team (covering the hotel and running the ops room), two mobile teams (one for each coachload of contestants) and a night team. John Clark liked working at night so he was made Black Team leader, in sole charge during the silent hours.

Right from the first contest I worked, I had been given the task of escorting the celebrity judges into the building as they arrived at the Albert Hall. The first of these was Gregory Peck, who, with his imposing stature and tan, looked every bit the film star he was. Another was Christopher Lee, who was best known at the time for playing Count Dracula in the Hammer horror films. When he arrived at the stage door, he was told, 'This is Dennis, he'll be your bodyguard.' In his deep voice he asked, 'Do you think I need a bodyguard?' I replied, 'Well, there's a guy downstairs with a wooden stake, so I wouldn't take any chances.' That went down like a lead balloon.

* * *

It was at a Miss UK final, in Hammersmith, that we had a major incident. Alistair, one of the press photographers, told me he had been tipped off that the Animal Liberation Front were planning a demonstration. At the time I'd never heard of the ALF, but I passed the information to the Cunard Hotel security manager, who was our link with the police. In the event, he failed to pass on the tip and we were hit by a full-on attack to disrupt the show. As the crowd stormed up the hotel escalators they made quite a noise, and this alerted the TV crew, who are programmed to protect a live show. They rushed to keep the demonstrators out. This was fortunate because there were only two bodyguards, Dave Hague and myself, on what was expected to be a low threat event. I wore a Velcro belt with my tuxedo, and quickly tied the main doors shut with it, but a few got in through another entrance. One mounted the stage and I had to grab her and drag her off. As I turned, I saw a gauntlet of cameras aimed, so did the only thing possible in the circumstances and smiled. That photo of me with a headlock on this tiny female, hand across her mouth to keep her quiet, was on the front page of most of the papers the next day. I flew to Manchester with the winner for an appearance at Old Trafford and it was a weird experience to see my face on all the papers being read on the aircraft.

Although it was quite funny to see that photo, the actual attack was violent. As they stormed into the hotel the ALF broke the arm of an elderly commissionaire, and when the police eventually arrived several were injured while trying to eject the demonstrators. The reason the ALF attacked the Miss UK was that the sponsor was a fur coat company. Subsequently I got quite a bit of work guarding fashion events against ALF disruption. And even when the Miss World had no further sponsorship with the fur trade, the ALF still targeted the contest. Their reasoning was that several contestants represented countries which killed tigers, fought bulls, hunted leopards and so on. Obviously, none of this was the fault of the event, but the ALF were more interested in gaining publicity than any common sense. They were, in effect, a terrorist group and resorted to incendiary devices and car bombs.

At a subsequent Miss World, I was looking after Astrid, the winner, at an appearance in Top Shop, Oxford Street, the day after the final, when I was discreetly approached by two officers from Special Branch. The ALF had become such a problem that the Branch had set up a dedicated unit. They informed me that ALF were planning further attacks, and since we were due to tour Top Shops all over the UK I should liaise with them and they would arrange for local police to provide appropriate resources. We immediately beefed up the team, and that tour with Astrid, who was from Venezuela, became very active.

When we visited Birmingham the threat was especially high and a large-scale demonstration was brewing. I called up two ex-Regiment lads, Jimmy and Ginge, over from Hereford to augment the team. That Special Branch contact became very useful as I did more and more jobs in the fur/fashion trade. They also put me in touch with the SB Terrorism desk, and they were a great aid in our threat analysis on future VIP protection contracts.

After the Black Team had taken over for the night the day lads would often gather for a hot chocolate to chat about the day and to decompress. We'd often discuss the strokes the press had tried to pull. Once, they set up a photo shoot for one of the girls who was celebrating her eighteenth birthday. Rather than buy a cake, the photographers made one out of crazy foam, then all claimed for the cost of a proper cake. Another time, Miss Hong Kong was an inspector with the Royal Hong Kong Police and had brought her uniform with her. The press wanted a shot of her with a British bobby, so we trooped around to the local nick to set it up. It went something like this.

Bobby on desk: 'Can I help you, sir?'

Photographer: 'Daily Mirror, mate. We have Miss Hong Kong here, who, as you can see is an officer in their police, and we want a nice pic with one of your lads.'

Bobby: 'Just a sec, I'll get the sergeant.'

Sergeant: 'Can I help you, sir?'

Photographer repeats his spiel.

Sergeant: 'I'll get the Inspector.'

This went up through the Inspector, until finally the station commander was called down.

Superintendent: 'Can I help you, sir?'

The exasperated snapper again trots out his request, as myself, Miss Hong Kong and the chaperone roll up laughing.

Super: 'I'll phone the Yard.'

Photographer: 'Forget it mate, life's too short.'

We went outside, spotted a passing bobby and the photographer asked him if he wanted to be in the *Daily Mirror*. He agreed like a shot.

Knowing the press so well was something of a two-edged sword. On one bodyguarding job we were looking after a senior royal who was booked into the Cromwell Hospital for some serious treatment. Also in there was the comedian Benny Hill, and there was a press contingent doorstepping the hospital for news of the comic. Most of the press guys would have recognized me from Miss World and, being professionally nosy, would have started asking who was being protected in the hospital. I had to use a side door to dodge them.

Every year the contestants would organize a talent show, with songs, sketches and dances. One year, a group of the girls put on a sketch about the security escorting a party of tired contestants. It was very funny. Several girls had dressed up in suits and borrowed spare radios to act as the security lads. Mariasela, Miss Dominican Republic, made herself up to impersonate me, complete with heavy moustache. She went on to win the Miss World title that year. Another girl who did well in the talent show was the 1975 Miss Venezuela, Maria Conchita Alonso. She sang and played the guitar with real talent. Afterwards she gave us all copies of a record she had made. A few years later, Maria-Conchita became a Hollywood movie star, playing opposite Arnold Schwarzenegger in *The Running Man*. Another contestant who went on to movie fame was Miss USA 1986. I can still remember the impression she made with her bikini during the swimwear section. Halle Berry went on to win an Oscar.

Den and Mac, a former Royal Marine and expert
bodyguard, on close protection duties.

CHAPTER 9

CLOSE PROTECTION

AFTER MY FIRST Miss World contest, in 1973, I decided to try to gain as much relevant training as I could. One of the first things I did was to take up firearms training. Although British civilian bodyguards (BGs) are unarmed unless working within diplomatic premises or vehicles, knowledge of shooting, ballistics and weapons seemed an obvious requirement. Plus, while working overseas there was the requirement of being armed. The firearms world opened many doors. I met guys with a range of backgrounds. For example, a senior NCO from the Explosive Ordnance Disposal Unit shot with us, and he gave me much valuable information on the Provisional IRA bomb threat. It was actually through shooting that I met a number of lads from Special Forces who got me onto some good BG jobs. First aid was another topic of prime relevance and I started training, something I have kept up to this day. First aid skills have proved useful on numerous occasions.

Many of the tactical procedures we developed were based on common sense: how we positioned ourselves with the VIP, how to escort through various types of environment, how to work car drills. Having access to a group of guys in karate and shooting, we could work out and practise these elements. Later, as I worked with more guys on different jobs, I would always try to learn from them and shamelessly picked their brains. I have continued this process to this day. I love learning new skills and acquiring relevant knowledge, and it is a delight to attend a presentation by a top instructor.

In 1975, I made my first trip to Southern Africa, which has continued ever since. Over there I was able to do advanced firearms training, including in automatic weapons, and work on attack drills, using vehicles on the shooting range. A good mate at this time was Dave Hague, who had served with the Royal Marine Commandos. Dave was a keen shooter and had been Corps pistol champion. He came to Rhodesia with us in 1977 and stayed to join their Boat Squadron, until the terrorists took over the country in 1980. We then worked together on several BG contracts. Dave is still in the industry, being a permanent team member for one of the prime companies in London.

We worked together on a few firearms/tactics courses in Southern Africa, and he endeared himself to a group of women when, teaching the use of shotgun for home defence, one lady asked what would happen if the intruder picked up her baby to use as a shield? 'No problem, a shotgun will go right through a baby,' was Dave's reply. He also did door work and was actually on duty with Gary when he had his famous fight with Eddie Palmer (see Chapter 16).

I continued to do as much professional training as possible. For example, I attended the American Pistol Institute Program, under the legendary Colonel Jeff Cooper, and graduated as 'expert'. With contacts you can do amazing things, and I had great contacts. One mate was on the staff at the secret Special Forces Training Area near Hereford. He invited me to assist in training a group of police firearms instructors in room combat and vehicle drills. At a security conference I met Peter B, who was setting up Burns International Special Operations Division. Burns was a large, US-based security company with a massive presence in the uniformed guarding sector. They had a Special Services Division, which was, basically, the guards put into blazer and slacks to add more prestige to a company foyer. Burns decided to break into VIP protection, and so the Special Operations Division was established with an office off Piccadilly. Peter invited me to join their team, who were mainly ex-Special Boat Squadron with one guy from 'The Regiment' (22 SAS).

Two main jobs came in. One was the training of a protection team for the head of a province of Nigeria. We used a stately home, Balcombe Place, near Gatwick, which reminded me of how the Special Operations Executive used to train their agents in such grandiose venues during World War Two. The other job was to set up the security for a very prestigious hotel in Miami. I wasn't on that, as I had to go to Africa for something of my own, but several of the guys stayed in Florida for a couple of years. That was it as far as Burns went. Security companies are constantly starting and finishing.

Also in the early 1980s, I was phoned by one of the ex-SBS guys I had met at Burns, who offered me a job on a team in London. Since there were two places available I roped Dave Hague in, and the next day we took the train down to Euston and made our way to the Dorchester. The team leader was Mac, a former Royal Marine, who then went into 'the Det', the undercover Special Forces unit working on hostile surveillance in Northern Ireland. Meeting Mac was one of those fortuitous encounters and we worked together a lot over the next six years.

Mac was a total pro. He had passed out top recruit in the Marines and was actually used on their recruiting poster. His suit was always immaculate and his shoes were like dark mirrors. There was a whole group of VIPs from a particular Gulf state, and after a chat he put Dave and I on the 'Gold Team' as personal protection for the main VIP – who, I was surprised to learn, was their queen. She went about in a Rolls-Royce Phantom 6, with diplomatic plates; we followed in a back-up car. Following this first contract, I later worked with the royal families of half a dozen countries, including a couple of heads of state. We were always working in the Dorchester, Hilton, Intercontinental and Savoy hotels, as well as numerous royal residences. I once estimated that I had spent over three months of my life in the Grosvenor House hotel alone.

One such job I was looking after a group of sheikas, or princesses, a mother and three daughters, who were seriously into shopping. We would go to a major department store and spend all morning buying clothes and bedding. We would go for lunch, then back to another store for a full afternoon of more retail therapy. At night we would stop at an all-night supermarket in Marylebone and the girls would spend about £25 on chocolate. The youngest was four, but was the size of a ten-year-old. She had to visit the dentist because her teeth had rotted from sweets. After the treatment, the dentist told the mother to give her nothing but water for the rest of the day, then some light food and soups for the rest of the week. In the car she ate a Mars Bar.

Another job I did with Mac was to provide security for a character known as Doctor Sheik. We were contracted by a company called Counterforce, run by Major Ram Seeger, former commanding officer of the SBS (Ram is now secretary of the Special Forces Club in Knightsbridge). Doctor Sheik was under severe threat. An assassin armed with an assault rifle had been intercepted at Heathrow on his way to kill him. Apparently he had insulted a member of a rival royal family and their government sponsored the hit. Initially, we did a security survey and boosted the existing security. Then, after we submitted our report, Ram pulled us off the job, saying, 'They've had a look at us, if they want good security we'll provide it.' It worked and we got the full job, and I was called back down on Boxing Day, 1983. We needed thirteen lads to man three four-man teams, plus an OCBG (officer commanding bodyguard). Each team worked a week of days, a week of nights and a week of leave. Mac acted as overall co-ordinator, running several other jobs for Ram. It was difficult to man the teams, due to it being New Year, and the fact that Doctor Sheik had a bad name on the bodyguard circuit; if I tell you his nickname amongst us was 'The Madman', you'll get some idea. He drank a bottle of brandy a night and smoked the shisha, inhaling the smoke of rotting vegetation, which combined to turn him into a mindless puddle. Despite this, he was a religious leader with over a million followers. He was connected to the Saudi Royal Family by marriage, and much disliked by many of them.

Our point of contact was Alvin, a Miami lawyer who looked after the numerous interests of Doctor Sheik. There was also a young guy, Sheik Shariff, who used to breeze in every so often and would greet us in perfect American English. I thought his language skills pretty good until I found out that he was actually American, the son of Alvin. I thought it weird that a Jewish American was part of the Saudi royal family.

We eventually got the teams up to strength and I managed to get a day off after working continuous sixteen-hour shifts for three weeks. I was part of a team under Pete S, who had recently left 22 SAS after about twenty years active service. Another member was Pete V, who had been on the Burns set-up. As OC we had Steve F, another guy from the Regiment. Dave Hague was on another team, along with Jimmy L (Regiment), Dave O (Rhodesian Light Infantry) and John H (ex Det).

The Madman had houses everywhere. His son-in-law, Prince Turki bin Abdul Azziz, had a massive estate outside Slough and Doctor Sheik had a mansion there. The BGs had our basha [house] in Langley Corner House, near to Pinewood Studios. Other properties included a penthouse overlooking Hyde Park and houses in various London suburbs. Despite this, for the four months I was with him Doctor Sheik stayed in hotels, firstly the Royal Lancaster and then the Savoy. So we had to slog in from Slough every day, which added an hour at the beginning and end of the twelve-hour stag.

One Sunday morning we were driving from along Oxford Street at about 7am when our VIP told the driver to pull over, as he wanted to drive himself. There was no arguing with The Madman. For some reason I was acting as personal BG and was up front in the Rolls-Royce. I called the BG back-up car to overtake, lead the way and keep the speed down. Fortunately the street was deserted and he slowly zigzagged across two lanes. Inevitably we were pulled by a passing police patrol, who were decent about it (the diplomatic plates helped) and the driver resumed control for the rest of the drive to the Savoy.

For obvious reasons, guys kept leaving and we were short-staffed again. The final straw for me was after Pete S left, and I had to take over the team. I had just got back to the basha when the duty driver turned up to give me a warning order for a quick move to Morocco the next morning. Dave Hague came to pack the kit for his team and take me to the Savoy prior to deployment. I had bad vibes and told him to drop me at Euston; I was binning the job. At first I regretted it, as the money was good, but then the news filtered back. The team had been aboard a Royal Maroc Airforce C-130 loaned to Doctor Sheik by the king, and the crew had stacked a mountain of baggage, including aluminium containers in the cargo bay without any securing straps. The lads, most of whom were trained in air despatch and heavy-drop, refused to fly, knowing that the slightest turbulence could cause the load to topple, and were thrown in prison for insulting the king. After intervention by the Foreign Office they were released, and Dave Hague had to use his Amex card to buy flight tickets for the team. They reimbursed him later.

Mac and I later worked for Prince Turki in the south of France.

* * *

Bodyguarding is completely different from door work. You have to be able to do things like recognition and search for terrorist devices, firearm threats, ambush drills. The medical side is also completely different: you have to be ready to deal with gunshot wounds and blast injuries, rather than the cuts and scrapes you get in clubs. It's a different role. You are very much into avoiding trouble; the last thing you want to do is drag the VIP through a firefight. Your planning has got to be there. You're working in liaison with people to sort things out. It can be a totally interesting and absorbing job.

I had some dangerous moments. We worked for four months looking after a guy who had a government assassin after him. That was in the UK. They picked up a man at Heathrow with an Armalite rifle. He had a contract from a foreign government. So that was quite interesting. We worked in London all the way through the IRA terrorist campaigns of the Seventies. They used to just miss us. We'd go to a place, the next night it would be blown up. Or we'd be due to go to a place and it would blow up before we got there. We weren't being specifically targeted, it was just the West End of London. If you were going to prestigious places, that's where they were blowing up.

I think a lot of people go into it for glamorous reasons. Certainly the first job I did was by most definitions a glamorous one, but I never took it as being glamorous; I was always more interested in doing the job properly. And some of the stuff you do as a bodyguard has little relation to protection. You become a facilitator for the Principal. One of the biggest jobs I did was to be in charge of the team for eighty members of an Emirates royal family at the Mayfair Hotel. We picked them up at the Heathrow special south side terminal, which we used for many of the jobs, and got them settled in. As the baggage was being delivered, a huge consignment of fruit was off-loaded on the pavement in front of the hotel. It turned out that this was a special fruit from the royal gardens. The hotel manager was having none of it. He told me that the last time this fruit was delivered, it rotted in the rooms and the smell took weeks to dissipate. He was adamant and said he was prepared to see the party leave, he could easily fill eighty rooms in the summer. However the leading sheika said, 'Mister Dennis, please, you must bring our fruit to us.' A bit of a dilemma. I compromised by having the lads smuggle some crates in through the service entrance, while others very obviously loaded the rest of the spiky, minging produce into a van for disposal.

On another job, the Principal despatched Mac and myself to organize the purchase of heavy artillery pieces. We walked round to a discreet arms dealing office behind the Dorchester and entered the fascinating world of the legal arms trade. I was surprised to find that the UK placed very few restrictions on who they would sell weapons to, apart from the Soviet Bloc. The South Africans, whose G-5 cannon was state of the art, were very discerning as to who they would allow to purchase them.

Despite long hours and constant vigilance, we still managed to have a laugh on BG teams. While on a job in the Far East, one of the guys got one of our police counterparts to write, 'The occupants of this room are homosexuals', in Chinese, then stuck the label on the door to the hotel room occupied by two of the lads, telling them it was a good luck sign. The local staff giggled every time they passed the door. On a job in London, one of the guys stuck in the hotel on static duties arranged for a gay outcall masseur to visit one of the lads later that evening. Sure enough, the well-toned date swished up to the security checkpoint and announced he had an appointment with Ian. Needless to say Ian, an ex-Para, vehemently denied all knowledge, but the slagging was relentless.

Den and Terry at Ruperts, a lively nightclub in Birkenhead, Merseyside..

CHAPTER 10

OVER THE WATER

AFTER RETURNING FROM Japan, I crossed the River Mersey to work on doors on the Wirral, while at the same time pursuing my growing VIP protection contracts. The Wirral had only recently become joined with Liverpool as the county of Merseyside. Previously it had been a part of Cheshire, and many residents resented being lumped in with Scousers. Some parts of the area were very upmarket, such as Heswall, Caldy and West Kirby. But then there were sink estates that were among the worst in Europe.

When I went over there in late 1973, there were only three nightclubs in Birkenhead. The oldest, the Golden Guinea, catered for the general crowd. The Hamilton was a huge theatre club, featuring top acts (I saw Ken Dodd there). Ruperts, where I first worked, catered for the upmarket crowd, so the main job was maintaining a strict door policy to keep the scallies out. At first I worked with a local called Paul, then later Don Woods, another Birkenhead guy, who had been a seaman, took the job when Paul moved to the Hamilton.

Ruperts was fairly small, a far cry from my previous door over on the Top Rank. Although we didn't have the mass brawls of the Rank, we nevertheless had numerous kick-offs. These were mainly on the front door, but, being Merseyside, sometimes inside too. The actual front door had a spring-loaded stop at floor-level which only allowed the door to be opened a foot or so, until we released the catch by foot, allowing the door to be fully opened. This stopped a crowd rushing the door and was a handy device, one I have never seen before or since. At first the door was reinforced with a sheet-steel backing, but the owner decided it was too aggressive-looking and removed it one day. Inevitably, that night we had trouble with a crowd of local lads who resented being refused admission. The first tried to force his way in. I let him, then pushed the door shut behind him and put him to sleep. However, his mates kicked the now-flimsy door panels in, then started throwing rocks through until we opened up, and Don and I steamed out and got amongst them. The police arrived and were a bit concerned by the unconscious bodies, but a new inspector, recently transferred over from Liverpool city centre, just told his guys to 'lock that shit up' and the gang was arrested.

The Bruce Lee movies were all the rage, and people started getting into the martial arts in a big way. A lad was found unconscious in an alley near to the club, with a pair of Nunchaku [rice flails] next to the body. The police suspected a martial arts attack, until the chap awoke and, somewhat sheep-ishly, admitted that he'd been trying to learn the flail, and was whizzing away with gusto, when they bounced off the alley wall and knocked him out.

Don had a nephew who was more like his brother, being about the same age, named Laurie. He was a police officer, initially in uniform in Birkenhead, then on the Task Force in Liverpool. Laurie needed to pass his firearms course to join the Task Force, so I took him to the shooting club and gave him some extra tuition. He later came back to Birkenhead in the CID Drugs Squad, where his sergeant was Ellie Davies, a larger-than-life figure who later became the main character in the documentary series *Mersey Blues*, before being convicted of corruption. Ellie was a great guy, regarded by the officers he worked with as 'a copper's copper'. Birkenhead was rife with drugs, and the drugs squad used Ruperts as their unofficial HQ for planning their jobs.

In those days it was normal for off-duty police to flash their warrant cards and gain free entry to most night-clubs. The local uniform officers would also pop in and have a swift beer while on duty patrolling the streets. They would stand near the door, and whenever the bell rang they would cover their pint with their helmet. I always wondered why the headgear was of that design, now I knew! Naturally we became quite friendly with the police as we saw so much of them, so if they were having problems with an arrest we'd pitch in to help. I was a bit wary of doing this at first, after an experience I'd had in Liverpool. A woman PC was chasing some guy down Whitechapel, shouting, 'Stop him,' so I took his legs with my favourite Thai kick across the shins and down he went, out cold. The officer told me, 'I didn't mean for you to stop him like that, wait there,' and went over to check on the guy. I faded into the crowd before she could take it any further. However, relations with the police in Birkenhead were more practical. One time we heard a commotion and saw a bobby being held over the bonnet of his Panda car while two men pummelled him. Terry and I ran over, put the two guys down and held on to them until back-up arrived, which took fifteen minutes. The bobby had been hitting at the men with his truncheon, but, due to his position, couldn't generate any force.

During this time, Terry was still at the Victoriana, until it closed, then moved to the Banyan Tree, a nightclub within the famous Adelphi Hotel, near Lime Street. Gary was just around the corner on Scamps, the disco which was the after-hours adjunct to the Bierkeller in Mount Pleasant. Basically large groups of lads would get absolutely ratters on strong beer, then go upstairs to Scamps, where, if they misbehaved, a large Maori would give them a severe lesson in etiquette!

An example of Terry's frisky approach to life was at the Banyan. A large guy lumbered into reception, pursued by a barmaid yelling for the lads to throw him out. Terry moved into his path and dropped down at the guy's knees, causing him to flip right over, landing solidly on his back but with enough momentum to roll right up back onto his feet, then continue out of the club without a backward glance. On another occasion, a very big man was verbally aggressive and Terry threw three fast kicks, just clipping his ears and backing him across the hall. The guy said, 'Ah, Karachi, eh?' and departed, thanking his lucky stars.

Terry was in the Banyan chatting to a visiting Japanese Wado-ryu karate instructor who was staying at the Adelphi Hotel. A local guy wandered in and, hearing the conversation said, 'Ah, karate. What do you think of this?' and headbutted the reception desk, so hard that it bounced off the floor. The guy grinned, said, 'Want to see it again?' and repeated the butt, just as hard, then strolled off with a jaunty step. The Japanese instructor looked totally shocked and quickly went up to bed.

At the Banyan we had three Merseyside Police officers, Mike, Terry B and Alec, who worked on the quiet, midweek nights. They tended to use verbal persuasion very well and had learned how to handle aggression without violence. In those days police carried only a fourteen-inch truncheon, no body armour, and the ability to placate potential violence was an essential tool.

One night Terry O'Neill was on the door and an A Division police Jeep came roaring up. The crew asked if Terry B was in the club. When Terry told them he wasn't, they said they knew he worked there unofficially, and that was okay, but they really needed to find him; he was on foot patrol duty and had made a garbled radio transmission, with gunshots in the background. Terry jumped in the Jeep and off they went looking for him. All turned out well. Terry B had gone into the Forum cinema in Lime Street for a kip and leaned on the transmit button of his personal radio, broadcasting the sounds of a Western movie all over the force.

* * *

A few years later, Terry got a job 'over the water' at a new place called Digby's. They already had a crew; in fact the leading door crew at the time in Liverpool, led by Eddie Walker, who had a top reputation. The manager of the club knew Terry and wanted him there. Some time later, Terry asked me to fill in for him and so I went over for a night. The other bouncers started telling me about Terry. They were just in awe of him. 'That Terry, he knocks them out left, right and centre! You just stand there and watch him.' And they were the top crew, pro boxers and all the rest of it. They said they had never seen anyone like him. I only did that one night there to fill in, but I can tell you what it was that had impressed them so much: Terry standing in the middle of the floor effortlessly knocking people out.

Digby's was forced to close due to the amount of trouble there, and Terry joined us at Ruperts. Don became club manager, so, in effect, we had three doormen on the premises. The DJ was the legendary Pete Price, a flamboyant character, openly gay, who was frequently on TV and radio. One evening in the foyer, Pete was having a bit of a friendly row with his then boyfriend, Tim, and jokingly said to Terry, 'Teach him a lesson.' Always one to oblige, Terry threw a reverse round-house kick which caught Tim right in the face, dropping him unconscious and bleeding. Pete nearly fainted in shock and was in floods of tears. What had happened was that Terry had delivered the kick with perfect control, intending to pull the blow just short of contact, but a reverse kick is very confusing to the victim, who sees a kick starting on the right and instinctively ducks away right into it, because the kick crosses the centre line to strike on the other side. Anyway, poor Tim was taken to hospital, with Peter looking like he needed treatment himself.

At the end of the night, Terry suggested we pop into casualty and see how they were, and when we walked into Clatterbridge,

Peter was sitting in the corridor, head in hands. Seeing us he cried, 'Oh God, they've come to finish him off!' Actually Tim thought it was all quite funny, and next time he arrived at the club I put a bandage on his head, smeared tomato sauce on it, and took him down to the disco, telling Pete that Terry had kicked off again. After an initial shock, Pricey saw the funny side. Hitting someone unintentionally like this was known by us as a 'sorry job', and I had quite a few over the years.

One night we'd had a bit of a scrap with some locals, who legged it, leaving one of their number unconscious. A police traffic officer turned up to see what had happened. Terry had the casualty on a stool and was holding him up and making him nod, or shake his head, as the officer asked, 'Are you all right? Do you want to press charges?' It was hilarious, like a ventriloquist act.

A new club, Sir James', took over where Digby's left off, and attracted all the scallies. Billy Jones from our karate group started on their door, together with a couple of Terry's students, plus guys from other martial arts. There was a fearsome collection of nunchaku, batons and coshes stored strategically behind the door, and they got a lot of use. I said they should advertise: 'Come to Sir James' and get beaten up by the martial art of your choice.' I used to swing past to pick Billy up after he finished work, as we both lived over the water, and many times I had to leap out of the taxi and join in with a mass brawl as all hands took on a gang of punters.

After Ruperts, Terry and I worked at a new place off Argyle Street called Stairways. We had quite a bit of trouble there, but mainly with the women: fighting each other, fighting with their husbands, and fighting with us. Most doormen will agree that a woman in the full flow of anger can be a real handful. My final stint over the water was at the Chelsea Reach in New Brighton, owned by a famed Liverpool entrepreneur, Roy Adams, together with John Chase. Billy Jones was on the door with us and the manager was Paul Chase, a keen amateur wrestler. Paul is now a director of CPL, a leading company in the training of security personnel.

* * *

When not working, Terry, Gary and I all loved movies. And we'd travel quite far to see a good one. This was before videos, so you had to go to the cinema to see the film. I remember taking Gary to some inner-city area of Manchester to watch *Performance* with James Fox. We'd think nothing of going to London to visit Regent's Park Zoo, see a movie, have a scoff then catch the inter-city train home. The train service was great back then. It took two hours, forty minutes from Liverpool to London, day returns were very cheap and service was frequent. When we worked at the Banyan Tree, part of the Adelphi Hotel, then owned by British Rail, we were given free train tickets and we'd be in London all the time.

As a lad, Terry had been a big fan of the Conan books by Robert E. Howard. Later, when he got into bodybuilding, he really admired stars like Reg Parks and William Smith, who had muscular physiques. We saw *Darker Than Amber*, a fairly good thriller starring Rod Taylor, with William Smith as the heavy. Another Smith movie was *The Losers*, a dreadful tale of outlaw bikers acting as a private army in the Vietnam War. I saw it once and thought it a joke, but Terry saw it over a dozen times. Of course I gave Terry some stick about always wanting to watch movies of men with big muscles, which usually resulted in me getting a dead leg. Terry had long followed the bodybuilding career of Arnold Schwarzenegger, and when it was announced that Arnold would star as *Conan the Barbarian* in the movie, Terry was ecstatic. Imagine how he felt, then, to actually appear in a film with Arnie.

Terry had met Arnold at an airport, and kept in touch with him. He had attended a Mr Olympia contest in America, and spent time with Arnold, and they had got on well. When Arnie starred in *Commando*, Terry was invited to the set in Mexico and became part of Arnold's inner circle. He was asked if he wanted to act as a soldier in a scene, but since it was filmed by the second unit, miles from where Arnold was working, Terry preferred to hang round with the big man. Subsequently Terry did act in *Conan the Destroyer*, in a scene where he attacks Grace Jones with a stick (Terry is the one with the bad hat!). Terry was invited to Arnie's wedding, and was the only guest allowed to take photos at the reception. Deciding that he wanted to become a serious actor, Terry took acting lessons and Arnold introduced him to the top agency in Hollywood.

Another great contact was Lynda La Plante, the best-selling writer, who was starting to have her work turned into TV series. A favourite of mine was *Civvies*, where Terry had quite a big part as an ex-military policeman who has a climactic fight with the main character, played by Jason Isaacs. Terry has appeared in several of Lynda La Plante's series. I was asked to provide some technical advice for one of her projects, the TV thriller series *Framed*, and was later delighted to hear my notes on how firearms silencers work being spoken by Timothy Dalton.

Michael Caine is one of my favourite actors. I was acting as announcer for a karate tournament at the Alexandra Palace in 1967 when the organisers told me that the guest of honour had just arrived and I should introduce him. Fortunately, I was a fan of the Len Deighton books, and Michael Caine had starred in *The Ipcress File*, so I knew of his work and was able to mention all of his roles. Terry worked with Michael Caine in *Quills* and I was delighted to hear that he was a really great guy. Since Terry played his footman he was in almost every scene with him and spent many hours chatting with him. Apparently he has a terrific sense of humour and had Terry rolling up. My favourite British gangster film is *Get Carter* and Terry got hold of the paperback with Michael Caine on the cover and the star autographed it for me. A very nice gesture. Another star is Sean Connery, who Terry has worked with in *Entrapment* and *The League of Extraordinary Gentlemen*. I know that Terry really valued the time he spent on set with this icon.

One of the best parts Terry had, was when he portrayed a karate-trained doorman, with an Irish name – no typecasting there – in the series *Liverpool One*. Filmed by local producer Colin McKeown, this series really made the city centre look fascinating. Another TV part called for Terry to play an ex-military, karate-trained, detective. The fight arranger got the wrong end of the stick and brought in a mate of his to train the lad in kung fu. Terry at first tried to explain that the role called for karate, but the pair insisted on teaching Terry a sparring sequence involving blocking a kick using a set of flowery moves. Finally, losing patience, Terry told the kung fu expert to show him in real time by blocking Terry's kick, telling him, 'I'm not convinced about this stuff.' As he got ready to block, the kung fu guy asked, 'Why?' Terry blasted him onto his back with a blistering kick, saying, 'Because it doesn't freakin' work!' The fight arranger, angered, rushed in and Terry gripped him by the throat and put him on the ground too. It was all sorted out by the director, who sided with Terry, as the part did, indeed, call for a karate sequence.

Terry worked with Peter Postlethwaite on the movie *Dragonheart*. Peter, who is from Warrington, was delighted when Terry told him that he is a cult icon amongst Liverpool doormen, on account of his starring role in *The Muscle Market*, set in Liverpool's gangster scene. Another top role was in *Sharpe*, and Peter enthralled Terry by slipping into his Sergeant Hakeswell persona and reciting some of the lines.

While filming *Gangs of New York* in Rome, Terry had the chance to meet Daniel Day-Lewis. Movie industry rumour had Day-Lewis staying in character throughout a shoot, and insisting on being addressed by his movie name. So Terry went up and called him Bill the Butcher. Day-Lewis smiled, and said, 'My name's Daniel.' Terry mentioned he'd worked with Peter Postlethwaite, and Daniel, who had starred opposite him in the acclaimed *In The Name Of The Father* was delighted, and couldn't praise Peter enough. Terry said he was a really top bloke.

* * *

Back when it was still legal Gary, Terry and I were pistol shooters. Like many martial artists, Gary and Terry were good shots, but they were always at it, always joking. At one session on an outdoor range, the three of us got lumbered with target changing duty in the butts. You are in a trench, with the shots going over your heads. Terry threw Gary's ear defenders onto the backstop, then, as Gary bent to retrieve them, pushed him onto the impact area. Gary was scrabbling his legs like a cartoon dog as bullets hit the sand all around him. Terry was laughing like a drain. I could only shake my head.

At a pistol competition we watched as one shooter, a police officer repeatedly fumbled and dropped his pistol. Gary approached him.

'You're a policemen aren't you, in London, right?' said Gary. 'Jeez, the next time I'm in trouble down there I'll call a postman!'

Travelling with those two was another story. I tell a stroy later in the book about when we went to Denmark by train in 1972, together with Steve Cattle and spent the time wrestling. Gary, Terry and I regularly travelled to Manchester or London for training. On one journey, Brian Waites was with us and three of us ganged up on Gary and tried to immobilise him. Terry had a neck-lock, Brian had one arm, I had the other, and we were all lying on him too. We'd tried to do this before but he had always been too strong. This time we wore him down and had him pinned. Unable to move a muscle, Gary thought for a second then 'snotted' us, snorting mucus all over us and causing immediate reflexive release. What a player. As I've said before, he had a superb brain for combat.

The towering Nick Hughes demonstrates an eye-gouging technique.

CHAPTER 11

TRAINING BODYGUARDS

WE WOULD OFTEN have uniformed guards alongside us on events and they would ask how they could become bodyguards. We also found that several of the guys on the scene were little more than mobile barrow boys who had limo driver mates who got them into VIP protection. They were useless opportunists, always looking for 'bungs', or tips. So I decided to run a bodyguard training course, just a one-off, to give guys a way into the industry and to create a pool of trained men to replace the London wideboys. I wrote articles in Terry O'Neill's *Fighting Arts* and in a handgun magazine and was overwhelmed by the response. I quickly realised that I would have to run two courses back to back.

The training area we used was first-class. A company called Delta Training had taken over the former HMS *Ganges* naval training base near Ipswich. Besides outdoor and indoor shooting ranges, there were two huge gyms, accommodation, a swimming pool and numerous empty buildings and streets ideal for running protection drills. As training cadre I roped in Pete S, who I'd worked with on several jobs since the Doctor Sheik experience. Also lined up was another guy I had worked with a few times, Chris R, a former member of the Selous Scouts, the most feared counter-insurgency force on the African continent. Pete took me along to meet Lofty Wiseman to have a chat about the course and, to my delight, Lofty offered to join the training team. At the time he was still serving with the Regiment and was running their training area. Lofty was an amazing bloke whose skill and knowledge was unsurpassed. During his twenty-six years of service with the Regiment, he was an instructor in combat survival, was Squadron Sergeant Major of a 'Sabre Squadron', was tasked to set up the British Counter-Terrorist Team, and ran the famed SAS selection courses. He went over to America to help in the setting up of their Delta Force. Since leaving the Regiment, he had founded the leading survival school. His books, *The SAS Survival Manual*, *Urban Survival* and *The SAS Driving Manual*, became worldwide best-sellers. I can do no better than quote what the Commanding Officer of 22 SAS said to me in 1985: 'Lofty is a legend in this Regiment.'

One of the core subjects for the bodyguard training was CQB, or close-quarter battle: the use of armed and unarmed combatives for close-range confrontations. I had already trained government personnel from states such as Saudi Arabia, Nigeria and Somalia and one of the challenges was devising a syllabus to teach CQB skills, in the limited training time, to personnel with no existing skills or abilities. The requirements for CQB are:

1) Easily taught within the allotted training time
2) Ability to perform under stress of actual lethal attack
3) Ability to perform in real environments while wearing normal clothing.

Although my main self-protection training was in karate, I had come to realise that for CQB we needed to utilise a different approach. I turned to the World War Two syllabus, devised to train commandos and SOE agents by W.E. Fairbairn and E.A. Sykes. CQB training has become such a primary activity in my professional life that I've covered the subject in more detail in the chapter At Close Quarters. When I consulted Lofty on the syllabus, he told me that the SAS used the WW2 methods as the basis for current CQB, and they considered *Kill Or Get Killed* by Colonel Applegate, an American student of Fairbairn, to be their bible. So important was that topic that I named our training company CQB Services.

Again, the interview with Graham Noble bears quoting here:

GRAHAM: *The CQB you're doing now, how've you developed that, from the karate base, if you like?*

DENNIS: CQB, Close Quarters Battle, is a military term for an integrated system of armed and unarmed combatives. The different elements also have to be integrated. Whatever you do has to work with everything else. Take firearms. It's a bit of a non-subject in the UK, but in other places it's not. Your firearms training has to fit with your empty hand training. It's no use training guys with, say, an impact weapon like the PR24 in one way, and then doing something else in another way. For example …. the thing about CQB – let's take firearms training. You have a stoppage drill, your firearm stops and the guy's piling in with a knife. Your response to that – is it a firearms drill or is it an unarmed combat drill? And who should teach it – the firearms instructor or the unarmed combat instructor? Obviously, it has to be integrated. It's no use the firearms instructor telling you one thing, and the unarmed combat instructor another. It's all got to fit together – what we call the seamless transition between each of them. That's what we're after: integration.

For bodyguarding, not having firearms is not that much of a detraction, because your role is to avoid things anyway. If you're getting into gunfights, you've already got it wrong. It puts your situational awareness up as well. Putting it another way, a lot of people carry guns and rely on firearms as if the firearm had a mind, whereas it's you who's the protector.

* * *

That first BG training event, with two courses back to back, was an outstanding success. The training area was superb, the programme, devised mainly by Lofty, was brilliant and the staff all worked well together. The feedback we got from the guys was 100 per cent positive. The training days were long; we started at 7am and often were still working at 10pm. The fitness work in the gym was severe, the amount of information they had to absorb and then produce in practical drills was fearsome, but they loved it.

A couple of guys really stood out. Peter Consterdine, a member of the British karate team, I had known for many years. He was appointed OC for the final test exercise and was outstanding. Peter went on to have a long career in VIP protection and currently runs a top training company. His book *The Modern Bodyguard* is required reading for all coming into the industry. Brad had served in the Light Infantry, then done an attachment as instructor to the Sultan of Oman's Armed Forces. We worked together on several BG jobs where his fluent Arabic was an asset. He also became an assistant instructor on BG courses for us. Tony T was an old Africa hand, with bags of experience. He is still working, currently running the protection for a royal family. Ed S was still serving with the Paras and did the course as part of his pre-release training – we had an arrangement with the Ministry of Defence to provide this. We worked together on a couple of jobs with Mac and Ed is still on BG teams.

The training area was also used by sports groups, and when we held that first course, a party of Swedish volleyball players had just arrived. I was lurking about waiting to ambush the VIP party in an exercise when a group of drop-dead gorgeous Swedish blondes wandered over to say hello. I heard the car convoy approaching, so I said, 'Excuse me girls but a group of people are just about to arrive … and I'm going to kill them.' I whipped out a pistol and started firing (blanks) at the lads. After the girls got over their shock at witnessing an assassination within hours of arriving in England, they were very enthusiastic about the course and actually joined in as role players, distracting the guys really well as the staff tried to attack the VIP.

Although the training was in a very serious subject, we always had a laugh during the course of the programme. Two lads were tasked to check out a room prior to bringing the VIP there. As they approached, they saw Lofty enter the room. They came in to the rather small room and couldn't see him. There was only one door and the only window was securely latched. Lofty had immediately climbed over the door and was braced in the space over the lintel. They started searching the furniture, and Lofty almost fell off laughing as they started opening drawers looking for a 6ft 4in man. In the end they declared the room clear and escorted the VIP inside, only to have Lofty drop on to him.

Another time, Brad was acting as VIP on an exercise and, during a walkabout on the range area, was nominated to go down with a simulated broken thigh to give the lads a medic problem. Brad had actually hurt his leg in the gym and was walking with a stick, so he was a good 'training aid'. They started well, splinting his leg, then finding a plywood target-backer as an improvised stretcher, to which they strapped Brad. A lad called Neil had bought an old banger for £60 and driven it to the course, thinking it would be a good car to use in exercises, as he wasn't worried about damage. He sprinted off to get the car so that Brad could be extracted and returned, skidding all over the range, demolishing several target stands. The team tried to load Brad, trussed like a turkey, into the passenger compartment, but the stretcher was too wide. Neil had a bright idea: 'I know, we'll strap him to the roof rack.' This didn't appeal to Brad, who responded, 'You can freak off! You're not having that lunatic drive with me on the roof. Den, call Endex [end of exercise] for Christ's sake.'

We decided that the BG course was something we wanted to continue, so we scheduled a couple every year and took its programme overseas to the USA, South Africa and Europe. Since that 1985 course, which was the first ever open body-guard course in the UK, everyone and his dog is teaching VIP protection. There are several really professional outfits and a whole lot more wasters since the Security Industry Authority (SIA) 'regulated' the industry.

* * *

We presented our first programme in the USA in 1988, hosted by Evan Marshall, a Detroit Police homicide detective with a wealth of experience. Evan had been in numerous gunfights, including one off-duty encounter in which he shot two armed robbers while going to his local shop for baby food! Evan had been the primary instructor for the Detroit Special Response Team, and had cross-trained with several military special operations units. His material of firearms and tactics was top-notch and I learned a lot from him. We worked together on various training jobs frequently over the next few years. Another team member was Dave Scott-Donelan, who had served in several special force units, including the Rhodesian SAS and the Selous Scouts, before moving to South Africa as an operator/instructor for the Directorate of Special Tasks. Dave later opened a tracking/survival school in America.

Once again, the BG course was very well received by the lads, many of whom were already working bodyguards. One such guy was Marcus Wynne, who was an outstanding course member. We had chatted quite a bit during the course, and since we had both spent time in Japan, had quite a common interest. Marcus had been an NCO in the US Army Airborne Forces. Experienced in the martial art of kempo, he had sampled the Korean system while running a reaction team during his army service over there. After leaving the military, he pursued his education, graduated with a degree and entered the field of specialised security. During this time he kept up his training, primarily in the Filipino fighting systems of *escrima* and *kali*. Being of partial Filipino descent gave him a particular interest in these arts, and he has specialised in offensive/defensive knife systems. He was also running the VIP protection activity for National Security.

Marcus offered to host a course in Minneapolis the following year, and this started the first of what became several training trips to what became my favourite US city. It was a busy trip. After presenting the BG course, we did a short hostage rescue training programme. Evan provided some Heckler & Koch MP-5 subguns for the guys to use, and Lofty gave a terrific overview of the tactics and equipment options. Dave Scott-Donelan and I covered room combat tactics. The course culminated in a full-on exercise in rescuing passengers held hostage on a bus. Marcus and I played the terrorists and the class did a sound job in freeing the passengers.

One of the course members was Warren Buttler, an operator and instructor with the newly formed Federal Air Marshal Service. We became good friends and kept in touch over the years. Warren later became an instructor at the Federal Law Enforcement Training Centre (FLETC) at Glynco, Georgia, where about seventy federal agencies train in firearms, tactics and close combat. Warren arranged for me to twice visit FLETC, and I actually helped out on a couple of programmes they were setting up.

Following the hostage rescue course, we flew to Spokane, Washington, to present a course for the US Army Special Response Team at Fort Lewis. Joining us on this programme was Gary Wistrand, who had been second-in-command of President Reagan's protection team for the US Secret Service. Gary made an interesting comment. We were putting the guys through live-fire vehicle ambush drills, and Gary said 'Dennis, we used to do these drills in the Secret Service, but we never did them live. This is the first time I've seen them done with live firing.'

That was an arduous course for us. The Army ate breakfast at 0700, so we needed to schedule the fitness and unarmed combat training at 0600. Marcus and I had to get up at 0430 as the duty driver picked us up at 0500 for the long drive to the base. Following the physical training, we would be driven back and the driver would lift the rest of the guys to the base to start the lectures and practical drills. After a shower and breakfast, Marcus and I would return to Fort Lewis and join in the programme. The course finished with a final exercise, and Marcus and I acted as terrorists. We were running around the base carrying MP-5s and wearing balaclavas, and nobody took any notice!

That was an exhausting series of courses, with no downtime and long flights across time zones. But we loved it. We have continued to train guys in America ever since. On the next visit to Fort Lewis, Lofty took the class, which included twenty-year-old Rangers, for a run and came back alone. When Ev asked what happened, Lofty just said, 'The lads dropped out.' What a player, at fifty-seven years of age!

Training continued back in the UK too, and we had guys attend from all over the place: Switzerland, Germany, Belgium, Sweden and even a couple from Australia. One of these made an immediate impression, as he stood 6ft 8in tall. Nick Hughes was originally from Melbourne and was serving in the French Foreign Legion. A highly skilled Goju-ryu karate exponent, he had worked on numerous nightclub doors in Oz for Bobby Jones, the same guy Gary Spiers had worked for. Jones taught a form of Goju Karate he called Zen-do-Kai [ZDK], and ran the door crews for most major venues in Melbourne. Nick had trained in the same ZDK organization as Gary.

Though a generation later, he knew of Gary, who was still a legend amongst doormen in Australia. On a subsequent visit to Liverpool, Nick and I bumped into Gary in Chinatown, I introduced them, and they caught up with a chat.

Bobby Jones had clearly made a huge impression on Nick, as he later related to me:

Regarding his charisma, damn, I wish I could bottle it and sell it, I'd make millions. He is another one of those David Koresh, Jim Jones types. If he told all of his black belts in the day to jump off skyscrapers the majority would have done it. As a fighter, unbelievable. I am not aware of him ever being beaten by anyone, and none of the black belts from the bad old days that I know, who were there from the beginning, are aware of him being beaten either. He attributed a lot of that to being a redhead and yanked to a different school two times a year every year due to his dad's work. Everyone knows, second you arrive in the new school you have to fight to establish your position in the hierarchy so he got lots of experience early on.

His favourite technique in the street was probably headbutts but he could pull most things off. I once met two guys who were roommates of his when they were all younger (neither of them training) and they told me of his regimen while bouncing. He'd run five miles every morning, then do five hundred push-ups and five hundred sit-ups before doing five hundred punches into the brick wall on the back of their digs. One morning while eating breakfast the plaster on the inside was shaken loose by his travails outside and showered them and their cereal in stuff.

He could generate phenomenal power. One day in Melbourne, when I was down there, a black belt called Adam West was complimented by Bob on his abs, as he had been working them a bunch. Adam, buoyed by the compliment, said, 'Hell Sensei, I could take one of your punches.' One thing led to another, Adam tensed, Bob punched and Adam puked all the way to the bathrooms before collapsing in a heap. I'm also aware of some big name streetfighters in Australia that he fooked up over the years and he also dropped a Samoan the size of a house while looking after Fleetwood Mac in Hawaii with one punch, as told to me by a roadie who witnessed it.

Part of the reason for producing so many good fighters was the raw material he had to work with and the second reason was the timing. With the martial arts boom on we had literally 300 people walking into the dojo every day to join up. They tried to make space by using new students as human punching bags to clear the way for the new members. The ones that couldn't hack that environment quit, what was left were hard core fookers who, by being put through that process, and working on doors, became giants with regards to fighting.

I doubt there's going to be another period in history where you're going to have so many people trying to join at once that you can afford to bash people from day one to clear floor space. Unique man and a unique time.

The last part of it was the organization. It was a little like being in a cult and you took that name with you. When I stood on that door, wearing that cross and representing Zen Do Kai, it wasn't, 'Nick Hughes lost a fight', it would have been, 'One of Bob Jones's guys lost a fight', and there was no way that was going to happen. It just couldn't, which is why you'd get silly shite like fighting seventy-five kung fu students instructed literally to kill you, and walking out of the building having put thirteen or so of them in hospital. I could never do that, but carrying his name on my shoulders I sure could.

A while later, we were on a job in Paris and I offered a slot to Nick, as he had been outstanding on the course and was fluent in French. He was still in the Legion, so he took leave and worked with us. While sharing a hotel room, Nick produced a pair of sai, a kind of three-pronged fork with the central prong being about twenty inches long, and asked if I'd show him some techniques with this traditional karate weapon. I said I'd be delighted, but then Nick started spinning and flipping the twin sai in ways I had never seen before. In the end he taught me. I had seen many of the top weapons guys in Okinawa but Nick was the most dexterous I've seen with the sai.

We worked together, back in the UK, in Paris and elsewhere, before Nick emigrated to the USA to work on high-level close protection teams. While in the Legion he created their current Close Combat system, and Nick currently teaches this in classes in Charlotte, North Carolina, and via DVD. He invited me over to the USA in 2006 to present a series of courses. We had many hours of fascinating chats about the many characters in the security business. One story he told me was about a notable encounter with a large gang while he was living in England that perfectly demonstrated his close combat fighting capabilities. Here it is in his own words:

London, England. I hesitate to tell this story because people – mostly those with no concept of fighting – don't believe it could possibly be true. Having said that, I can assure readers that it is, and I'll even mention the name and number of the police constable present who witnessed the entire brawl from start to finish. The officer in question was one Constable Ridley and his Metropolitan badge number was 666. His nickname, he told me later at the station, was 'The Beast' due to his unusual badge number and small stature. At the time he worked out of the Kentish Town police station.

I was, on the night in question, standing outside Camden Town tube station in London with my French girlfriend while waiting for the bus. Normally I'd walk the three miles to home but she was wearing four-inch heels and walking that distance in those was an impossibility. While we were waiting for the bus, two scruffy-looking sods came weaving down the road, tipping over trash cans and rummaging through dumpsters looking for something. Eventually they found an old broom handle, which they tried to insert in the hasp of a padlock to break it open. While one worked on the lock, his colleague was launching kicks at the door.

For readers who aren't familiar with the vagaries of UK law there is a term called 'squatters' rights'. What that means is that if you happen upon an unoccupied dwelling and move in, it now becomes yours. It doesn't matter if the real owners have only gone out to a restaurant for the night, or to the beach for a vacation, you now own the property until such time as the case can be brought to court and heard. What typically happens at that point is that the 'squatters', about to lose their ever-so-humble abode, will destroy the place and vandalize everything they can lay their hands on. The law in question says that you can't break in to achieve your aims, which is supposed to protect the legitimate owner, who would have locked up before leaving. However, if you can't prove they broke in, all the squatter has to do is claim the door was wide open when he walked past.

The clowns in question were obviously looking for a squat and hoping that by breaking in to the building in question they would find digs for the night. Given that it wasn't my business and that I had my girlfriend in tow, I decided not to become involved other than letting the police know at the earliest possible convenience. Another chap at the bus stop had different plans though and asked them what the hell they thought they were doing.

They replied, as thugs often do, by telling him to shut the f**k up and began moving towards him. I stepped in at this point and said something along the lines of if you bother him, you'll also bother me. They then re-directed their attention towards me and began closing in. One was reaching for something in his pocket as he got close, so in keeping with the principle of 'attack is always the best defence', I shoved him backwards. His mate moved in at speed now and drew his hand back to punch me, so I dropped him with a hook punch to the jaw, knocking him out as I did so.

His mate started ranting that I was going to come undone because he was coming back with all of his mates. Anyone who has done security will tell you the real bad guys never forewarn you they're coming after you and that they'd rather turn up unannounced and just drill you from behind. I had heard literally thousands of such threats over the years as a bouncer so I wasn't overly concerned, and was explaining that to my girlfriend when she pointed down the road to the entrance to the tube, from where a horde of n'er do wells was approaching. She asked me if that was an example of them not coming back as threatened and I could only shake my head at one of the rare exceptions to the rule.

Running away, as some so-called experts advocate, wasn't an option here. My girlfriend had a tight skirt, four-inch heels on and bags of shopping. We had no idea, given the time for her to toss her shoes and the shopping, whether or not we would be faster than them, which could have meant fighting them while exhausted from our failed effort to run. Finally, where were we going to run to? Home was three miles away and any attempt to duck down a side street could have put us in a blind alley and nowhere to go.

Realizing that avoidance wasn't an option, I ordered my girlfriend to move away from me and, if asked by them, to say she had nothing to do with me. This group was clearly the sort who would have no qualms about bashing and/or sexually assaulting a girl during the melee, and I moved out in the middle of the street to lure them away from the people at the bus stop. I honestly thought at the time, seeing the numbers – the police officer who watched it counted twenty-one whereas my initial guess to him at statement time was eighteen – and that they were armed with bottles and lumps of wood, that I was about to perform my swansong and exit the planet. I knew, given the line of work I had been pursuing, i.e. bouncing, bodyguarding and being in the military at the sharp end, that such a demise was always possible and thought this was it.

I didn't waste time with the old adage about challenging the leader to a one-on-one. Whoever wrote that nonsense all those years ago has clearly never been in a fight with multiple opponents who hunt in packs. If they had any honour, which you are supposed to use as leverage against them by challenging them to a man-to-man duel in front of their followers, they wouldn't be out in a pack to begin with. And, I found out later, this particular group of skidmarks had been politely mugging young girls in the tube station forecourt only

163

moments before, which is why a police constable, also unbeknown to me, was down there to begin with.

The fight began and I can remember snippets of it. I dropped the closest one, who was holding a weapon, first, figuring I'd take at least one with me. He had drawn a lump of two-by-four back behind his head to swing when I hit him with a drop elbow through the cheekbone. Later at the station, while I was giving a statement, I found out from the doctors summoned to check on the injured criminals that this guy had a fractured cheekbone, broken nose, broken teeth, broken jaw and concussion from my elbow shot. The rest bumrushed me and I remember looping my hands into a pile of dreadlocks and reefing knees into the miscreant's head till he eventually fell away and I was left holding two bits of his scalp and handfuls of dreads. The others were actually getting in each other's way given there were so many of them, which is often the case in uncoordinated gang assaults, and I was able to hit bad guys at will. They, on the other hand, had to be careful where they were swinging because, if I ducked, there was a very real possibility they'd hit their mates.

The fight raged on for about three minutes in total. I remember kicking one in the side of the head right as an old woman drove through our midst and she yelled out, 'Why don't you leave him alone, you bully.' Funny stuff. Another one was screaming at his girlfriend to finish her bottle of booze so he could use the bottle on me when I dropped him and that was when the sirens could be heard and the remainder fled.

By the time the cops arrived there were three that needed ambulance transport, about eight in various stages of unconsciousness and the walking wounded had fled into the tube station, leaving a blood trail which we attempted to follow. Unfortunately that particular station has multiple lines running through, and the police dogs with us couldn't go down the escalators, as their pads would get stuck, so we had to use the spiral staircase to the bottom. By the time we got there, they had jumped one of the multitude of trains running and scarpered.

At that point I finally got a chance to talk to the constable who had witnessed the entire event. He had been called following complaints from women tube travellers who had been mugged by the gang. To avoid making it look like an act of violence, they would stand around lone females in a big gang and ask for a handout, intimidating the victim into handing over some money. The constable was doing what he'd been trained to do, i.e. be a good witness until back-up could arrive, when he saw their mass exodus and followed them out to watch the fight. He apologised to me for not stepping in to help but explained that policy was not for a lone officer to enter into a gang fray, as more often than both sides would unite against the common enemy. I told him I understood perfectly and was just glad that he had witnessed it as I didn't want to be the one receiving the assault charge.

During our conversation, the businessman from the bus stop turned up and told the constable that I had been the victim and it was then that the officer informed us he'd seen the entire thing. My girlfriend and I were transported to the Kentish Town police station to give statements and be plied with cups of tea and biscuits while doing so.

As Nick mentions, lots of people might question this story. Let me state, knowing Nick as I do, I believe it fully. Nick is currently living in America, where he trains a dedicated group of guys in his FIST System. Check out his website at www.fightsurvival.com.

* * *

After the US Army course, Marcus dropped off the radar, and it was a couple of years later that I got a call from him one Sunday evening, telling me he was in London. He was flying out but would be back on the Wednesday, and could we meet up? He gave me the hotel name, and I was waiting in the lobby when a group of the most knackered Americans debussed from their airport shuttle. This was an Air Marshal team, and they had been constantly flying long-haul routed between major European hubs and places like Karachi, Bombay and Bangkok, for several weeks. Crossing time zones and eating airline food certainly made them look wasted. Since our last training job, Marcus had been through the long recruitment, vetting and training process to become a US Federal Air Marshal. Although flights had been protected since 1961, the practice had gradually fallen into disuse, until the current system started in September 1985 launched by direct Presidential directive following the hijack of TWA 847 to Beirut. On the team was Warren, who had attended our Minneapolis course. Marcus introduced me to Scotty, Butch and Clem and the rest of the team. Warren, Marcus and I went for dinner in London's Chinatown, and while talking about training they were using terms like map of reality, reframing and eye-access cues; I queried them and found that they were using something called NLP in their training.

A while later, Marcus invited me to the secret training area, where he was running tactical training for the Federal Air Marshals (FAM). So I was able to spend time at Marana, near Tucson, a remote site where the spec-ops troops trained in freefall parachute insertion methods and 'certain interesting activities' had a training function. Marana had a number of mysterious passenger aircraft, with no markings, and an array of special training facilities. I was surprised to find that the shooting range was very basic; however it's the quality of the instruction that counts, more than technically elaborate facilities, and the FAM had the highest level of firearms training of any federal agency. Although trained under federal law-enforcement standards, the actual role of the FAM is counter-terrorism, and as such they are the only federal unit whose primary task is confronting terrorists. There are implications in this role which conflict with the thinking of domestic law enforcement. Unlike SWAT/HRU teams, which may resolve a siege by negotiation, the FAM role is reactive. Essentially, to do their job they will be shooting – without warning!

While at Marana we were accommodated at one of the best hotels I've stayed in, the Sheraton El Conquistador in Tucson. Marcus's second wife, Liz, and I had lunch one day and she explained at length what this NLP stuff was all about. She had attended a seminar on Neuro-Linguistic Programming in Minneapolis, and she made it sound a really effective method of enhancing training.

Back in Liverpool I mentioned NLP to Tommy Mac, and was surprised to learn that he had been interested in it for a while, and he loaned me some books. Following this I eventually took the full course under NLP founder Richard Bandler and have used NLP ever since. Tommy went on to become a master practitioner of NLP. Marcus also went very deeply into NLP and other advanced training technologies. After he left the FAM, we worked together presenting neural-based tactical training in Europe, USA and South Africa. He is without doubt, the most skilled practitioner of this type of training I have come across. Marcus has also become a noted writer of realistic action thrillers, with three well-received books in print to date.

What the neural-based training allows is to dramatically reduce the training time, while enhancing the trainee's ability to absorb the material. As Marcus explains: 'How do we use this stuff? A short list: To improve physical performance through the use of modelling superior practitioners and through the practice of visualization coupled with auditory and kinaesthetic practice routines. To improve mental performance through an understanding of communication, both verbal and non-verbal, and state management of one's own performance. To create useful states like "switched on" or "full attack", and to learn how to properly manage your own various states. Combative applications: using sophisticated mental deception to give you an advantage over an opponent before or during a fight. To access the appropriate state and properly manage it before, during, and after a fight. To dominate an interpersonal encounter at the psychological level so that you "win without winning". That's a few ways.'

* * *

I joined the International Association of Law Enforcement Firearms Instructors (IALEFI) and signed up to attend their annual training conference in Mesa, Arizona: almost a week of top quality firearms instruction, and with a terrific group of guys. I couldn't wait a year for the next one, so joined the American Society of Law Enforcement Trainers (ASLET), and for the next six years attended the conferences and regional events held by both these organizations. During that time, I attended presentations from LAPD, the Secret Service, Heckler & Koch, the FBI, US Special Operations personnel, and many others. I was also asked to be a guest presenter at the conferences in Tampa and Arlington.

Evan Marshall was usually in attendance at these training events, and every night a group of experts would gather in Ev's room and swap ideas and stories. I called this group Evan's Marshalls and was honoured to be included in it. It was there I first met Ed Lovette, who was an officer in the Directorate of Operations of the CIA. Ed was currently serving as an instructor at their classified training area.

Another of Evan's Marshalls was Dave Spaulding, who ran the firearms training for Montgomery County Sheriff's Department in Dayton, Ohio. I was familiar with Dave through his writing in a couple of shooting magazines, was delighted to get to know him in person, and we became good friends.

A couple of years later, Dave arranged for me to train the Montgomery County SWAT Team in close protection. Scotty, from the Air Marshals, helped me with the programme, and we were both made honorary deputy sheriffs. Dave Spaulding and Ed Lovette later wrote a terrific book together, entitled *Defensive Living*. I recommend it to all the lads we train.

I was a member of the International Committee of IALEFI, and we decided to start holding regional training conferences in Europe. We began with an event in Heidelberg, and I was one of the staff instructors. Jim, one of the guys I'd met at IALEFI, was an officer in the US Army Hostile Counter-intelligence Activity, in Frankfurt. He set up a BG course for me to present to the guys there at the huge Creighton Abrahams complex. We conducted the training in a segregated compound within the complex but used many of the facilities for various training drills. The main building had been the HQ for the IG Farben chemical company during World War Two and, because the Americans had earmarked it for their use, had avoided being bombed. It was a wonderful marble-lined building, with sweeping staircases, ideal for VIP protection scenarios.

Security boss Tony Rimmer trains on the kick pads with Dennis.

CHAPTER 12

THE QUAD

IN NOVEMBER 1986, Billy Jones called to tell me he had been offered a job on the door of a big new club in Bootle, Merseyside, and there was a place for me if I was interested. I thought it would be useful to work locally over Christmas, as bodyguard jobs are sparse at that time of year. So I went along to the Quadrant Park, intending to stay until New Year. I ended up there for about seven years.

Quadrant Park, known to all as The Quad, was a massive complex near the Bootle docks. The club looked like a set for *Miami Vice*. Uniquely, the dance floor was tiled, to allow a car to be driven on for motor shows and similar events. They had a brochure featuring a car on the dance floor, with a drop-dead gorgeous model, who later became the girl who cut my hair, draped over the bonnet. As far as I know that was the only time a car entered the club, so the whole idea was pointless. The dance floor was circular, and upstairs a matching circular hole in the floor allowed a view of the downstairs action. This void was filled with the high-tech lighting and laser gantries, and despite it being surrounded by a waist-high railing I was amazed that no one was ever thrown over in the countless fights upstairs.

As well as the nightclub, which held over 2,000 punters, there was a snooker club with twenty tables and a huge warehouse space at the rear of the building, unused at the time but which would later become a prominent part of the story. The complex was owned by Jim Spencer, a very sharp businessman who owned a steel company as well as lots of property. This was his first venture into the entertainment industry and, to be frank, he rubbed everyone up the wrong way.

The door was run by Brummie and Gibbo but they were never there, as they had their own place in the city centre. So Mickey Loup, a boxer originally from Birkenhead, was head doorman. Mickey had been voted 'Mister Macho' in a competition in the *Liverpool Echo* and he carried a clipping of this in his inside pocket. There was a record out at the time called 'So Macho' and the singer of it, Sinitta, was scheduled to appear at the Quad. Mickey pestered the management to ask her if he could do his bodybuilding routine onstage during her appearance and, surprisingly, she agreed. Mick had brought his posing briefs, got Billy to oil him up and his big moment arrived. The only problem was that bodybuilders usually do about a five-minute routine but Sinitta, who had made only the one record, just sang 'So Macho' for the whole of her twenty-five-minute slot. Mickey was knackered and had to keep stopping to get his breath back. It was hilarious but rather embarrassing.

Previously I had spent eight years 'over the water' and then had been doing so much bodyguarding that I had been off the doors for a couple of years, so I didn't know lots of the 'faces'. This was a good thing because I wasn't bothered when guys threw names into the hat. They would drop some name to try to get in free but I would just blank them. Besides Billy there was John W, a noted kickboxer, and two brothers, Jimmy and Chris M. Lots of guys came and went over the next couple of years. At the time the Quad was quite a smart establishment, disco-style, with a strict dress code. Like all doormen, we wore tuxedos. Being Liverpool we had kick-offs, face-offs, it was all part of the job.

* * *

In the first couple of years he was in the UK, Gary was always going on about some major criminal 'job' he was planning. These were pure fantasy, usually based on some thriller he had just read; and as he had usually borrowed the book from me I was wise to his schemes. He would ask me if I was interested in joining some complicated caper, and when I'd tell him (again) that I wasn't a criminal, he'd say, 'Well, when I'm driving my Ferrari you'll be sorry you missed out.' Finally I got fed up and when the latest job was mooted I called his bluff and told him I was in. The conversation went as follows:

'Okay Gary, I'll do it.'

'Great mate, the job is, we're going to rob the takings at the Grand National. You'll be in charge of the diversion.'

'The diversion, what's that going to be?'

'You're going to kidnap the Queen. Can you get a helicopter?'

'That'd be right. I'll just pop down to Speke Airport and nick one. If I could fly helis I wouldn't be working on a door.'

When Terry or myself declined to be part of his schemes to repossess an oil tanker, smuggle gunpowder over the Chinese border, or kidnap the Queen, he'd say, 'I don't understand you people. If I asked you to come with me to London to bash some blokes you'd be there like a shot. But you turn down the chance to earn serious money.' To his credit, he did have a very active business brain and made a lot of money from more mundane but legal activities. As far as I know, he never really did anything criminal, other than bashing people wholesale.

Gary did eventually pull off a major job at Aintree Race-course, but it was legit. He won the venue security contract for the 1988 Michael Jackson concert there, subcontracted from a London company. This was an enormous event, as Jackson was the biggest pop star in the world, and 125,000 fans were expected. The Digger quickly realised that the manpower required was far in excess of what any one Liverpool firm could deploy. In a move which really heralded the future, he called a meeting of the major security firms and got them all to work together under his leadership. This was unprecedented, and was the foundation for the current door scene, with properly structured companies rather than ad hoc firms.

Gary recruited a whole army of security staff. The pop festival business is notorious for rip-offs. At the end of the Aintree event a helicopter arrived to whisk Jacko away (I wonder if Gary considered offering the pilot the job of kidnapping the Queen). Gary approached the London promoter for the agreed cash. Surrounded by his crew of twenty London minders the promoter said that he'd be paid back at the hotel. Sensing a rip, Gary fronted them all. 'Michael Jackson isn't getting on that helicopter until I've been paid,' he said. He got his cash there and then.

I wasn't at Aintree because I was overseas, but heard the job was a bag of frogs! Anyway, this laid the seeds for forming security firms. A core of the Quad guys, together with local brothers Ged and Tony Starkey, formed a company called TMCS and started taking over doors in the Merseyside area.

Meanwhile Jim Spencer opened a club in Southport and Jimmy M was given the job of running the door, together with myself and brothers Chris and Gus M, who had previously run their own place in the resort and had battered everyone of note in the town. So when The Manhattan opened, we had very little trouble. Chris had been severely stabbed during a fight a couple of years earlier, with all major internal organs punctured. Luckily, he recovered. Gus was tremendously strong. A plasterer by trade, he had massive forearms. On quiet nights I would bring a spring grip trainer and we would have competitions to see how many reps we could do, or how long you could keep a coin squeezed between the grips. Gus always won. The Manhattan became the venue for several of the televised *Hitman And Her* shows. There was a stalking threat against presenter Michaela Strachan, so I used to look after her during the filming.

After a year or two in Southport things changed. The rave scene arrived and I was brought back to the Quad as head doorman. Dave, the manager of the Quad, persuaded owner Jim Spencer that rave was the way to go; and he was right.

* * *

The house music revolution was starting, and being in on the ground floor gave the Quad a big lead over other venues. Of course, House music and drugs are two sides of the same coin, and for the first time we had to consider the drug problem. I was a complete ignoramus when it came to drugs, so I asked the guys to show me the various types when they found them during our search routines. I gradually learned where drugs are hidden and what they look like. We instituted a pretty strict search policy and at first we had good results. Eventually, the drugs were brought in mainly by girls in their underwear, which we couldn't find because in those days there were no female door staff.

One evening, a well-dressed, middle-aged couple arrived at the club and one of the guys searched the man. He was carrying a large carving knife in a shoulder rig. After he was lashed, his wife had the cheek to ask for his knife back. Another time, I searched a young, fresh-faced college type. I could tell by his body language that he had something to hide. In his hand was a Balisong knife.

We began to attract quite a bit of police attention, especially from one female sergeant who didn't like the club being on her patch. I had a discussion with Spencer and manager Dave C and proposed that, since the offence is 'allowing the premises to be used for drug use', if we could demonstrate that we took every effort to prevent drug use, our licence should be safe. We would hand in all drugs seized to the police against a receipt, and keep a log of amounts. The female tried to scupper that plan by not allowing the police to call to pick up the gear and telling us that she would arrest us on the street if we tried to take the drugs to the police. Dave came to an arrangement by phoning the desk sergeant, telling him he was on his way with seized drugs, then taking a discreet route to the nick. We handed in, by official police records, an estimated £20,000 of drugs in this way.

We also tried to stop any dealing or drug taking within the dance area, but walking round in tuxedos, the lads stuck out like a rip in the picture. So I had a team of six come on duty wearing their own clothes and walk round somewhat undercover. Eventually the whole door crew started wearing informal clothes. I had been given an LAPD bomber jacket, really hard-wearing and warm, by Terry and wore that. Eventually, all the lads started wearing bomber jackets and this became the uniform for Liverpool doormen for several years. I also started wearing my covert body-armour that I used when on bodyguard duty. Many of the guys bought flak jackets, or other ex-military armour, as the threat was high in the raves.

Tony Rimmer, who was still doing karate with us, told me he had started on the Harrington Bar door, in the city centre. I never encouraged the karate guys to work the door, but since he had already started, I thought it would be better for him to work with us at the Quad. He picked up the job fast and quickly showed that he was really stand-on. Tony is now a partner in Premier Security and has become the most respected doorman in the town.

We were getting capacity crowds every weekend and Dave suggested that we run an all-night rave. Some work was needed to clean up the rear warehouse area – for one thing a security dog, a big German Shepherd called Shanks, roamed freely in there, so there was about a ton of dog shit to remove. Eventually a stage was built, a set of security doors installed,

Master Higaonna, the highly-influential Okinawan karate instructor, training with grip jars. Dennis became his first British black belt.

Dennis Martin (left) and Terry O'Neill practise karate in the sea. Unconventional methods were a feature of their training.

Den and Terry in the British karate team at the 1973 World Championship

Den and Terry on Goju course. Hard conditioning work was a vital part of their training.

Terry demonstrates his kicking ability on Dennis in front of a shrine on their life-changing visit to Japan.

From left: the legendary American martial artist Donn Draeger with Den, Terry and judo ninth dan Master Mifune.

Dennis, in the background, watches over Hofi Karlsdottir, the Icelandic beauty who won the 1985 Miss World competition.

Sharing a laugh with Miss Israel, who was seen as a potential target because of the Palestinian terrorist threat.

SAS legend Lofty Wiseman demonstrating a chinjab.

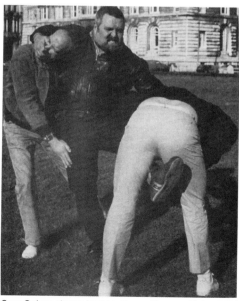
Gary Spiers shows how to dismantle a multiple attack.

Bodyguards practising an armed drill. Dennis Martin has protected princes, princesses, Arab sheiks and numerous businessmen.

Defending the principal in an attack on his vehicle in another armed scenario drill.

The formidable Nick Hughes demonstrating how to take care of two attackers. This picture was taken while he was serving in the French Foreign Legion.

Dennis with South African police officer Nonte in one of the most dangerous urban environments on earth.

Terry O'Neill and Arnold Schwarzenegger on the set of the sword-and-sorcery adventure *Conan the Destroyer*.

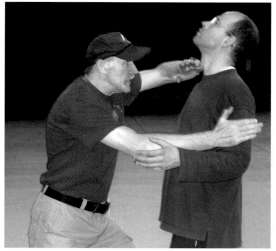

Den demonstrating an axehand to the throat at a self-protection seminar in Switzerland.

and the all-nighters were launched. One of the rave anthems was a pulsing tune called 'Insanity', and this name summed up the all-night raves at the Quad.

We used to get 2,000 people in the normal club from 9pm-2am. Then we would empty them out and they would move to the rear entrance, waiting for the rave to open. Meanwhile, ravers would be arriving from all over the city as other places closed. We would open the doors and there would be up to 4,000 punters pushing to get in. Bearing the Hillsborough disaster in mind, I drew up a plan for a steel and weldmesh cage, with staggered waist-high barriers every ten feet, to break up the crowd pressure. This would funnel the punters in an orderly, and safe, method. Spencer, despite owning a steel company, built only half the scheme and omitted the safety barriers. The result was a cage full of people being crushed, with impatient ravers climbing the mesh to drop in from above. It was chaos and the police ordered it dismantled, so we were back to an uncontrolled melee.

Inside the warehouse was total darkness, punctuated by strobe lights and filled with disco smoke. It took almost thirty minutes to get from the front door to the back of the dance floor, through the massed, writhing bodies. The bar didn't sell alcohol, just cans of cola for £1.50 a go. There was no cold water in the washrooms, to encourage the punters to buy more drinks. Spencer even made money by recycling the aluminium.

As the fame spread, we had ravers turning up from as far north as Aberdeen and as far south as Birmingham. Of course loads of locals turned up, eager to spend their night anywhere that was still open. We'd have guys in suits, attempting to smuggle booze in. Drugs were massive business and we had to front many dealers who were enraged that we had seized gear from their grafters. At the time Ecstasy was the main drug of choice, with prices going up to £25 per tablet; so when you seized a bag of fifty tablets it was a big loss to the dealers. We had five doormen stabbed in four weeks. These were actual woundings, not counting hits on their body armour. The drug culture affected the door crew, and many guys were sacked for dealing. I'm sorry to say that the majority of doormen currently consider drugs a normal part of the night out. For a time they had a local drugs advisory group working to give advice and counselling to the ravers; that is until we caught their main consultant dealing.

As a bodyguard I was trained to a decent level in first aid, but we were getting so many fights, and overdoses as well as normal accidents, that I decided we needed a dedicated medic on site. Phil J, who had worked on Miss World with us, was given the job and he coped well with an ever-increasing work-load. This sadly culminated in a fatality, when a young guy died in Phil's arms from an Ecstasy overdose. Another lad had a narrow escape when he started 'fitting' in the first aid room. His back was arching so that his heels almost touched his head. We rushed him to an ambulance and he spent three weeks in hospital.

Many people believe that we lost the licence for the rave but the truth was that Spencer came to me after the latest doorman was stabbed and said, 'The way it's going, do you think one of the lads will be killed soon Dennis?' I told him it was very likely and he voluntarily stopped the all-nighter. The rave carried on, still a full house for a while, until other big rave venues opened in competition. Gradually, the Quad declined, and I went back to Southport, until I started on the Paradox.

The Quad was, without doubt, the most demanding club I worked. It was more than a club, it was a culture, and even now Quad reunion nights make big money for hosting clubs in the town.

Dennis working club security with wrestler and cage fighter Davey Faulkener.

CHAPTER 13

THE PARADOX

FOLLOWING AN INJURY suffered in South Africa, I took a year or so off the doors, then started back at a club called the Paradox. Situated in the Aintree area, near the Old Roan in the former Vernons Pools building, the Paradox was tremendously popular. There was a main dance area – with, surprisingly, a glass floor, which often gave way – and several bars, then two smaller rooms branching off. On weekend nights there were over twenty doormen on duty. Saturday was broadcast live on Radio City, attracting a capacity crowd. The queue snaked all the way round the massive car park. Every couple of months there was a Main Event, which was usually a lockout, requiring about twenty-five doormen.

When I started I partnered with my training mate, Si James, and at first was detailed to patrol inside the club. After a while I was asked to work the front door duties. The front door crew was impressive. The three Premier Security partners, Tony Rimmer, Kev Dalley and Steve Clark, headed the team. Dave Kehoe, Joe Mack, Terry Welsh, Willy Morris and myself comprised the rest of the crew. We usually had two lads outside keeping the queue in order: Chris Armstrong and Steve Crosby, who I had worked with in Southport.

Kev Dalley was head doorman, with a great way of dealing with the punters as well as being a good man-manager. Kev could defuse aggression and reduce the heat in an argument. Make no mistake, he could do the business when it came to kick-offs, but he always tried the diplomatic approach first.

I can truthfully say he's one of the best head doormen I've worked with. Kev was also the prime mover in the pursuit of professionalism within Premier Security. We had a strict code of conduct, covering appearance, no smoking/drinking/eating on duty, and so on. Kipper, an old mate of Tony's, was in charge of the rest of the lads inside the club.

The Paradox seemed to be the place where punters from all parts of Liverpool and the surrounding area would congregate. Gangs from several large estates would try to resolve their disputes in the club, resulting in some memorable kick-offs. At the front door we had an alarm display linked to the bars and DJ, so could direct the internal teams to any fights by radio. A group of us from the front door crew would also leg it inside to assist. This was a frequent process every night, and we covered some mileage doing this. A barmaid called Sarah usually worked on Bar Two. For some reason the majority of the confrontations erupted at her bar. The alarm would sound and we'd go, 'Not bar two again,' and sprint in to find Sarah already wading in to the fight. She later worked for Premier on the doors in town.

Staff were allotted a twenty-minute break on a rota system. The front door crew had the last break period, from 1.20-1.40pm. We'd go into the staff room and eat whatever we preferred. Some would bring takeaway Indian scoffs, others would bring sandwiches. There was a repeater panel for the alarm system in the staff room and often our scoff would be interrupted by having to run to one of the bars to sort out a fight. The record for us was four fights in that twenty-minute break. Following our break, the four of us would move to a section overlooking the dance floor and each watch a different direction for the next outbreak of trouble. We would run in, deal with the problem, lash the troublemakers out, and then resume position.

While at the Paradox, Tony, Kev and Steve asked me to

give them private lessons in close combat and they also started training in the regular Gutterfighters class. When Tony had trained with me in karate he had been a young lad with a great potential. Now, after pursuing many forms of fighting arts, together with years of experience on hard doors, he had fully realised that potential, and become fearsome. In fact, all three were truly phenomenal fighters, with extraordinary levels of fitness. They were each doing up to eighteen sessions per week of weights, cardio and martial arts. We still used the Thai kicks that Gary first taught us, and although our kick pads were the best you could buy, the lads just powered right through them. We had to have them train on double pads. Working at the Paradox with the lads, I saw that fighting ability put into action numerous times.

Eventually, things escalated and gang-related violence and feuds placed a severe threat on the club. I was asked to become head doorman, and on one of my first nights in charge the Police Firearms Unit turned up and sat in their black kit in an armoured Land Rover at the front door, which was a bit of a clue as to how serious the situation was. Eventually the owners, First Leisure, decided to close 'for a few weeks', which turned out to be permanent. Like Quadrant Park, the Paradox is something of a legend, and there are now thriving Paradox reunion nights in other large venues.

Following the Paradox, which was in Sefton Council area, I returned to Liverpool city centre, requiring me to go through the badge process with Liverpool Council, which then took six weeks. I went to South Africa for most of that time, then started working in town, where I have been ever since. Since then I have worked with most of Premier's top lads: Jimmy Mac, Rob Lloyd, Sheppy, John Brady, Butch, Vinnie, Paul Smith, Davey Faulkner, and many more. These guys were not just colleagues, they were good friends that you could rely on. A guy I must mention is Mick Palumbella. I first worked with

Mick at the Paradox, then a few other places. He is a legend in the business who has stood-on in the face of some of the worst gangs in the town.

Another good, reliable doorman who is a personal friend is John Moncrieff. John served in the military and was a highly trained Commando medic. I have always placed first aid skills highly as a requirement amongst security personnel and John is one of the best. John was probably the first guy to use Quick-clot, a product designed to reduce severe bleeding in battlefield conditions. One of the staff cut himself severely and John sorted him out with the latest kit. Another time, we treated an older chap who had collapsed with a suspected heart attack. John took charge and administered oxygen, while I helped. A few weeks later the guy came into the club and told us that he had indeed suffered a severe heart attack, which required a week in hospital. He thanked us both for saving his life, but as he did he was drinking from a bottle of lager with one hand and smoking a cigarette with the other. When he went back inside, John said, 'I'll get the oxygen ready.'

Over the years I have worked with the top doormen in the business. I am privileged to have stood-on with them and have learned a lot from them. I have also worked with a number of wasters, especially in recent years, with the dilution of standards caused by such entities as the Security Industry Authority. However, in the main I have been lucky to work with the cream rather than the dregs.

Den (left) in Karoi, Zimbabwe (formerly Rhodesia) in 1979

CHAPTER 14

MURDER CAPITAL

I HAD BEEN travelling to Southern Africa for various activities since 1975. The way of life was so tremendous, the sunshine, and of course Cape Town, the most beautiful city I've been in. I just liked it. My friends there became like a second family.

In 1992, I presented a firearms/tactics course in Cape Town, which was attended by two lads who had driven the long road down from Johannesburg. Clint Oosthuizen and Gil Macquet were heavily involved in specialised security in the Jo'burg area and were very interested in our VIP Close Protection training. So in spring 1992, Clint, Gil and their colleagues Mark and Andre journeyed over to attend our course in Herefordshire. Another South African, Tim Smith, also attended. Tim now runs his own training company, Ronin Security.

In November 1993, the lads arranged our first course in Jo'burg. It was a success, and I have been returning at least once a year ever since. Gil later moved overseas. Clint, who has a background in Okinawan Goju-ryu, has established himself as the most respected CQC instructor in RSA. Clint, his wife Gail and their family live on a large rural farm with about a dozen dogs. They always make me feel at home, and they are now my second family.

Clint is currently a sergeant with the South African Police Service (SAPS) and most of the guys who attend the courses are police officers, looking to add VIP protection to their CVs. One such chap had been a member of the Air Marshal Unit and the Special Task Force, before being promoted to inspector. He was one of the best pistol shots I have met, his rapid-controlled pairs giving rise to his nickname, 'Double Tap' or 'DT'. Vastly experienced in armed encounters, DT was a member of the newly formed Highway Patrol. In America the Highway Patrol is a traffic unit, policing the freeways. In South Africa, the HP is actually the anti-hijack unit, but since a detective squad had already taken that title, the guys used the name Highway Patrol. They drove 5-series BMWs, after attending the most advanced driver training the police could supply, and a special programme at Kyalami racetrack presented by BMW. They also underwent a gruelling selection program by the Internal Stability Unit. DT arranged for me to go on ops with an HP call sign. I asked the lads:

'Do you use the Stinger?'

'What's that?' one asked.

'It's a strip of tyre-deflation spikes which can be deployed across the road to stop a stolen car.'

'No, Dennis, we've never heard of that.'

'What do you use to stop stolen cars, then?'

'7.62 rounds,' he replied. And it was true; as I found out, their SOP was to close bumper to bumper with the hijacked vehicles, then the passenger officer would lean out of the window and fire shots from a R-1 rifle into the interior of the stolen vehicle until the driver was disabled. At the time Jo'burg was officially rated as the murder capital of the world by the United Nations. As well as murder, rape, carjacking and other violent crime was soaring. It is still the most dangerous city outside of a war zone.

In 1997, Marcus Wynne came over to RSA and we presented some courses together. The MindsEye Shooting Program, in particular, was a tremendous hit with the very experienced South African shooters. Marcus did some consulting work for the SA Police at their vast Maleoskop training area. While discussing situational awareness training with the Maleoskop staff, they told him that they already had some very advanced material, but when they dug out their lesson plans, they were photocopies of an article Marcus had written a while back. His credibility soared after that.

While Marcus was over, he wanted to shoot loads of photos for various magazines he wrote for. One project was to take pictures in a squatter camp. Now, at that time even the regular police didn't enter such 'informal settlements' as the Winnie Mandela location; the rule was no soft-skinned vehicles. We hadn't made our connection with the Unit yet, so Clint decided to take us to a rural camp quite near to his plot. We walked up and made contact with the old chap who was head man. After gaining his permission, Marcus started taking photos. A young woman was sitting outside her shack with her kids running round, playing near her. The kids were entranced by us and came over with huge smiles. This woman invited us to look round her shack and despite it being made of old advertising posters and cardboard, the dishes were gleaming and the floor swept clean. The kids' clothes were newly washed and in good repair. These people, who were living on the side of a hill with absolutely nothing, no utilities, put a lot of city dwellers to shame. When we were leaving I asked her if I could give the kids some spare change to buy sweets, and they didn't rush over, begging, they lined up and received their coins with hands in the African 'thank you' posture. We all left with big lumps in our throats.

* * *

The following year we established a contact that was to continue right up to today. Clint had attended a SWAT course at the Chloorkop Training Area and had been top student, impressing the staff, who asked him to assist on future courses. They became interested in the VIP protection and other courses we offered, so next time I was over there they were in

189

the class. Colonel Erasmus was the commander, Inspector Hills the ops officer and Sergeant Piet was a tactical team leader of a unit formed specifically to conduct high-risk operations in the African townships and squatter camps. Initially known as the Internal Stability Unit, it went through several names, such as Operational Reaction Service, before the current title of Crime Combating Unit. I'll just use the term the guys themselves use: the Unit.

Potential members attended a special programme at Maleoskop called by the amusing Afrikaans acronym of OOPS, which covered intensive operations, high-risk tactics, public order policing, raids, house penetration and counter-ambush drills. Operationally, they used armoured vehicles such as the massive Casspir and the more manoeuvrable Nyala. Their weapons array was impressive; there can't be many police units that issue M26 fragmentation grenades! R-1 rifles in 7.62mm were available to augment the general issue R-5 (5.56mm) assault rifles. In the armoury at Chloorkop they even had belt-fed machine guns. One of the sergeants told me, 'We have to fight a war to get to the riot!'

Kobus, Hills and Piet loved the training, they were both excellent shooters – Hills was the best operator of a pump-action shotgun I've ever seen – and vastly experienced in armed confrontations. They invited me to become a visiting instructor for the Unit, presenting topics to Unit members as well as giving a presentation on SWAT courses for regular SAPS officers. They were prime movers behind the first CQB instructor programme we ever held, and we used Chloorkop range, with Unit officers as role players. That first course was all SAPS guys.

They also arranged for me to go on operations with the Unit. Their remit was to conduct raids in the most dangerous areas. In the past they did a lot of anti-terrorist work; Kobus and Hills told me about fast-roping from a helicopter onto a target, operating with the military Special Forces, who made an explosive entry to arrest a terrorist leader.

The first op I worked involved about 200 officers, the Air Force as well as Army Commando personnel. The element Clint and I joined was tasked to perform 'chopper drops' – helicopter insertions – using the troop-carrying Oryx aircraft. After being briefed and carrying out rehearsals, we deployed in sticks to be inserted in surprise tactical locations, until ground based units could take over. The first drop we did was near a busy junction, and the sight of the huge heli suddenly landing caused a minor car pile-up! After another drop, near Kyalami, I realised I was thirsty. It was two o'clock in the afternoon, and we hadn't eaten or drunk anything since breakfast at 04.30. Wearing a set of assault coveralls with heavy armour, plus other kit, in the African sun, carried the risk of dehydration. We sent a couple of the Commandos to a distant shop to buy water; and following that whenever I worked with the Unit I carried water in my coveralls.

On a subsequent operation we were tasked to conduct a raid to arrest a gang of armed robbers in Tembisa, a vast township to the east of Jo'burg. The Jo'burg-Gauteng area is the murder capital of the world, and God knows how many killings there are in Tembisa. It is one of the two most violent places; Hillbrow is the other one. We deployed in a four-car convoy, and in the briefing I was surprised to learn that only one other police vehicle was on duty in Tembisa that day. Seeing that at least two million people live there, and there is only one police station, it was, to say the least, high risk. It wasn't a riot situation, so we didn't use the big riot vehicles. We were basically in a Jeep, though we did wear bulletproof armour. It was a raid on premises, looking for these robbers. The week before, two of the guys from the unit had gone in to buy food and they came out with their arms full of pies. They weren't wearing their bulletproofs and they got killed.

The briefing was that the gangs in Tembisa had declared war on public order policing, but most of the briefing was in Afrikaans, so I didn't understand it – though they did take the trouble to translate that bit for me. If we got into trouble there was no one to bail us out, because the Unit is the emergency reaction force, and we were the ones deploying. Sergeant 'Batys', who had attended our course, was tactical leader and I was honoured when he nominated me to be a member of the primary entry team.

Over the years I got involved in a few potentially dangerous situations in South Africa. I had been there during the riots in 1976 and saw a lot of people being severely injured and killed. It has calmed down since then but it's a different kind of violence now. Then it was politically directed, now it's crime. Some of the things we encountered really made you shake your head. On a roadblock operation we were searching a taxi, which in Africa tend to be twelve-seater minibuses. I was amazed to find that there was no steering wheel, just a monkey wrench. Even worse, the fuel supply was a can of petrol inside the passenger compartment, with a rubber tube leading to the engine and with passengers happily smoking cigarettes around it.

There was a lot of violent carjacking. Most people who are carjacked are on their own, whereas I was always with someone, but even then we had 'the look' a few times. Particularly taxis with smoked windows: if they pull up alongside you go to red alert. We've had the severe look, when they're looking at you like food, and we just looked back at them. The taxis are just a cover for their activities. When you're out with the police, if a taxi pulls up near you, you always tell the guys to watch the taxi.

A typical case: a woman stopped at traffic signals. She must have left her doors unlocked. She had a nice car. And a guy got in, quite well dressed, had a briefcase, mobile phone, told her to drive. I don't think he even produced a weapon, though he may have shown her a gun. And he got on his mobile phone, spoke to a guy and said 'It's a dark blue Mercedes 300SL. Are you interested? No? Okay.' Then he told the woman to pull over, said, 'Have a nice day,' got out and off he went. But then you get the others who'll just open fire on you. There have been some bad ones.

Over the years I did lots of training for various SAPS groups and continued to go on ops with the Unit. Clint and I also did a VIP protection job. Piet had left the Unit to become operations director for a major security company. They sent their personnel to us for BG training. Clint was often asked to recommend guys for jobs, and a job came in one weekend when all the guys were already working, so Clint asked if I'd be interested in going operational again. We protected two visiting business executives, who were under threat from a disgruntled former employee, for a week around the exclusive Sandton City area.

* * *

As mentioned above, the first CQB instructor programme we ever held was at the Unit's Chloorkop range, with Unit personnel as role players. That first course was all SAPS guys. On a later course we had Rich, a former member of the Rhodesian SAS, who went on to work several tours of Iraq and Afghanistan. This was a popular means of employment for our course graduates, with several of the police guys taking a few months leave to work in Iraq, earning high-value currency. Recently the ANC government enacted legislation making such overseas security work illegal. However, it is permitted to join a terrorist organization overseas!

'There's more than just the tsetse fly gets into your blood in Africa,' said hunter/writer Peter Hathaway Capstick. In my case, one of the things that got into my blood after all the trips down to the Southern Constellation was a love of the *braai*.

This is the Afrikaner's version of the barbecue, truly the meat-eater's dream. Among the best cuts to cook are T-bone or ribeye steak, chops, or even chuck (Clint has a way of making this rather cheap meat absolutely delicious). Boerwors or similar quality sausage (not our 'emulsified high-fat offal tubes') also braais well, as do some types of fish. Of course in Africa venison is prime meat to braai. I can say that nyala is the best meat I've ever tasted, followed by eland.

At a family braai the girls will prepare numerous types of salad, as well as a display of breads and rolls. The guys see to the meat. However, at an all-male event, such as some post-training braais, it's usually just meat. I remember one such scoff at the end of the counter-ambush phase of the BG course at the Suikerbos Range. We used pieces of the targets as plates and Leatherman tools were the cutlery. Eating that sizzling meat while watching wildebeest at play in the valley, following a day of hard range training, was marvellous.

At the Unit, the base of the braai is a fuel drum for the helicopters, cut in two, while the grill is the mesh from a riot vehicle. One of the senior guys had a braai built into the tailgate of his truck. We were doing house-penetration training at a remote location and as the lunch break approached the mouth-watering smell of the braai signalled we were in for a treat. When over in RSA I always stock up on various spices to sprinkle on the meat. Everyone has his or her own secret recipe, and experimentation is good fun.

* * *

Clint established a relationship with the SAPS SWAT Training Centre, at Appingham Dam, way north of Jo'burg. This centre specialised in training Spoorsny (trackers), using techniques based on those used by the Selous Scouts in Rhodesia. The Spoorsny course was an arduous six-week programme, rated one of the hardest police courses in the world. Clint developed a CQB package within the Spoorsny, Advanced Spoorsny and Tactical Police courses. The feedback from graduates was very positive. I went up to Appingham a couple of times, and the training and facilities were superb. One graduate of this program was Roelf, who was, at the time, a dog unit officer with Erkhuleni Metro Police. Roelf then attended our VIP Protection course. He is currently a senior instructor with the Metro.

In 2007 Clint was tasked with developing an official CQB instructor programme for the police. I flew out to lend a hand, and Mika, our guy in Sweden, also helped out. We had fourteen officers from SAPS and the Metro, ranging from constable to captain. On the first morning we did 100 push-ups, 100 sit-ups, 100 squat thrusts and 100 star jumps – then started training! It was a three-week grueller, and the physical standard demanded, and reached, was awesome.

The programme included a substantial firearms package, held at JakkalsDans SAPS training area. I presented the MindsEye shooting module, based largely on Marcus's research, as well as weapons transitions and Extreme-Close-Range Encounters. Robert MacBride, the Chief of Erkhuleni Metro, visited the training several times, and gave the programme his full support. In 2008 CQB Services South Africa was officially appointed as Close Combat Training Providers for the entire South African Police Service.

Dennis demonstrates close-quarter knife techniques

CHAPTER 15

AT CLOSE QUARTERS

GRAHAM NOBLE IS a noted researcher on the history of the martial arts. He wrote several highly regarded articles in *Fighting Arts* magazine. He has also interviewed several personalities, including Jon Bluming and Peter Consterdine. In October 2000 he conducted the following interview with me.

GRAHAM: *You originally met Steve Morris way back in 1966?*

DENNIS: Yeah, I don't think I actually met him, not to say hello to. It was 1966, the second All-Britain Championships, and we went down from the Red Triangle to compete. We fought the Kyokushinkai team, very good guys. People like Joe Claronino were on the team.

Brian Fitkin?

Brian Fitkin was a green belt. It was him who put me out of the thing, so I was one of the first to realise what great potential he had. He was obviously a lot better than his grade. But they all had black eyes, lumps on them, all the corners knocked off them. They'd been over to Holland to train with Jon Bluming, and of course, Jon Bluming had been teaching karate for quite a while and his guys were a high standard, and they were all big guys anyway. And they'd battered the Brits quite soundly, all except for one white belt on the team who'd put his Dutch black belt opponent in hospital with one kick, and that was Steve Morris. I didn't recognise him until I saw his passport photo in 1972, and then I said, 'Ah, I remember you from 1966'.

And the next time you saw him was when he came back from Japan?

He came back from Japan and gave a demonstration at Crystal Palace with Brian, tested his Sanchin and smashed wood over him. I don't keep in touch with Steve as such, but we speak every now and again. I have a lot of time for him, his ability and knowledge.

Did you train with Steve in the early Seventies?

No, I trained with Brian. Steve came to Liverpool, did a demo for us of seisan kata, but I can't recall being in a formal class with Steve then. He was in Liverpool a few times. He used to come and see Terry, and we hung about and he'd show me stuff, techniques, and that was it. And then years later he came and did a class for us in Liverpool, and that was the only formal class I did with him.

Terry asked me to be the model for a series of technique photographs, with Steve demonstrating. We turned up at the photographer's studio and Steve went to the toilet, and Terry said, 'He's been showing me some of this stuff last night. It's fearsome.' So the first thing he did, I just had to stand there and he dashed in with an oi-zuki kind of thing, which almost drove all the air out of me.

What Steve would probably call control, most other people would call full-on. In all honesty it was a hard punch, but he wasn't intentionally trying to [hit me]. It was just the way he did it. Quite a lot of people are ... enthusiastic. It certainly didn't injure me but it wasn't a pleasant experience. And then he did various techniques. And he did a neck lock that felt about a centimetre away from dislocation. That felt the nearest he came to actually killing me. But it was very close. Either he knew a lot about anatomy, he knew the limits, or he wasn't that worried! But Steve is always an enjoyable guy to knock around with, and you pick up so much from him.

I would sum up Steve's technique as power – power personified. When he came to our dojo to do the course, I urged my black belts to partner him. I said, 'You've got to feel this. You can't talk about it. It's something you've got to experience. Someone else can't tell you about it.'

I know you were impressed by Joe Lewis (the legendary American kickboxer and point karate fighter) when he came over here in 1981 and did a course for Terry in Liverpool.

I was, very impressed by him. He was my first experience of American karate, totally different to the British style. I think I was quite open-minded, even in those days, and a lot of the guys weren't. A lot of guys couldn't handle the fact that he didn't want to bow, he wasn't wearing a conventional white gi, he was wearing a black gi, and he even had to borrow that because he didn't have one with him. But I think the majority of the guys on the course looked past that at what he had to offer, and at that time. I think a lot of what he was teaching was Bruce Lee type stuff. He was a natural instructor, had a flair for it. He had a few instructor tricks to get the material over well. We went for dinner afterwards, and I thoroughly enjoyed it. The only thing was, I didn't enjoy the movie he was in, which I went to see as a result of meeting him. *Jaguar Lives*. It was one of the worst films I've ever seen.

I thought Joe Lewis would be a power-type guy, but he was very sharp, wasn't he?

Very sharp, absolutely. Obviously, he'd done a lot of things in his background. He'd done boxing, it came out in the class and at dinner afterwards, and he was quite honest, he said he'd had to learn how to survive in the boxing ring, get his skills up that way.

How many knockouts did you see Terry do with the roundhouse kick?

I know his record for a night is eleven; mine's eight. So, he worked busy places for many nights, for many years. And I worked with him a lot of years. And then there'd be all the other fights before I was there.

What was his reputation like then?

Among doormen? I first really knew him when I was on his team. I tended to expect it of him, that the fight would be over when Terry arrived. Other doormen, at that time there really was a big gap between the martial arts guys and the old school. We didn't tend to work together much; Terry tended to work with people he knew.

Everybody says you shouldn't do high kicks in the street.

Well, they're right basically. You wouldn't teach it to people. There are good kickers around, but there's not that many who can do it in the street. Certainly there's no one else done it like Terry, no one. So he is the exception, he really is. And if you don't know him, you can't tell people how good he was. I mean, people who've never seen him at all, because they just don't understand it. They'll say, 'No, high kick are no good. I'd do this, or that'. But you just had to have been there.

Tommy McNally told me that he felt safe on the door when he was working with Terry, and he said the same thing about Gary Spiers.

Oh yeah. Terry was always the head doorman wherever he worked. I'll tell you a story from Tommy. He was on the door at one place, and Terry was elsewhere in the club. Tommy had a confrontation with this big guy, a monster. So he asked one of the barmaids to go and get Terry. She got him on the internal phone and told Tommy, 'Terry says do it yourself.' But what Terry had done was put the phone down and he was coming, running down. But Tommy thought he was on his own. So he went down to do a single leg dive on the guy, and when he's going down, this foot goes over his head, hits the guy with a sidekick, and there's an imprint in the plaster wall of the full diameter of a head. It was there forever. The guy was out for twenty minutes. I think he had interrupted Terry's burger or something.

What did you learn on the door, in martial arts terms?

A lot of the stuff that's taught in the martial arts, I never learned in the martial arts. You'll probably find this surprising, but you know, 'The mind like the moon' and all that? I got that from a book on shooting written by a guy called Brian Enos. He wrote something, and I thought, that's what they mean by mind like the moon, mind like water. He explained it, but he didn't use those words. That's the first time I understood what it was. I never got any of the mental side from formal martial arts.

You mentioned Tony Buck earlier.

I never worked with Tony, but he was someone all the guys respected. A tremendously strong guy. Tommy McNally, a great friend of mine; tremendous way of handling people. A lot of doorwork isn't about fighting, you've got to be able to do the physical stuff, but it's a people business. A lot of the good doormen are good at handling people, reading people, and getting people to do what they've got to do without animosity. I learned a lot from the job. From Terry obviously, but also from people like Tommy, who was a very good doorman.

What were your worst situations on the door?

Boredom!

Did you ever get hit?

Oh yeah. I had to go to hospital afterwards, but it was only minor stuff. I got hit with a chair. I've been lucky: I've never been seriously injured, and a lot of it's due to having worked with good guys. I haven't really got bad experiences to recall. I'd say that the downside of the doors is quiet nights. I like busy nights. We all do. We all enjoy busy nights when it's buzzing, there's lots happening – I'm not saying lots of incidents, just lots happening. You're needed; you're doing your job. The worst is when you're just sitting there – and of course, that's when it kicks off. You know, when there's only two people in the place and they decide to have a fight.

So did Gary go on the doors as soon as he came over?

Almost as soon. He didn't intend to, but we were going out to the club, and it just became natural to come along, and there was a night we needed guys, so we said, 'Why don't you do it?' So he put on a tuxedo – and he was in his bare feet. I can remember at a club where they had a strict dress code, Gary said to a guy, 'You can't come in. You haven't got a tie on,' and the guy said, 'But you haven't got any shoes on!'

I'd say Gary had two main things going for him. He could use karate very effectively, and he used techniques that don't tend to work for a lot of people, like front kick. I can remember one big mass kick-off. I ran through the door to get to the fight and there was Gary with a huge grin on his face, gathering people into an arc in front of him and kicking them with his bare feet and putting them down. So he could use things like front kicks, but he was also physically strong in things like grappling, grabbing; I'm not thinking of things like joint locks, but just grabbing them.

He's big. As he says, 'I'm big, see,' and he uses his size to advantage. In the early days, there'd been a big kick-off, and we'd thrown a guy out. We were standing by a door stopping him getting back in, but there were people in front of us still wanting to argue. The guy was standing behind Gary trying to get back in. Gary went, 'Leave it mate. You're out, now stay out.' About three times he went, 'Leave it,' and then after the third time he did a back head butt, which I've never seen anybody do before or since. He snapped his head back, the guy went horizontal in the air before he hit the ground, and then we shut the doors. And then when we reopened the doors, he'd recovered. He had been unconscious and there was teeth, blood and money on the floor; his change had fallen out of his pockets. That was memorable, because he didn't aim it or anything, he just did this instinctive head butt.

Another one I heard about from a guy who was there was where somebody jumped on his back in a fight and Gary just grabbed him with one arm and just continued putting people down until everyone else was down and then he just held on to the guy and went over to one of the other bouncers and said, 'Give this bastard some in the kidneys.' Just held him there while the other guy hit him. The moral of the story is: Don't jump on the back of a twenty-stone Kiwi. Gary has one of the best combat brains I've come across.

You mentioned that thing about Lajos Jakab earlier, when Gary first came over.

Yes, we were looking at *Karate and Oriental Arts* magazine on the train and there was a guy at that time, Lajos Jakab, who all the karate people considered to be a bit of a kung fu charlatan. And Gary just looked at it and said, 'He's got some forearms on him; wouldn't like him gripping me.' And I sort of re-evaluated him [Jakab], looked at him and thought, quite big arms. Gary had just looked at how the guy appeared, without taking his background or style into consideration, and that wasn't a bad thing to do.

Backtracking a bit to Terry, you said when he'd kick you he'd do it from impossible angles.

So it seemed, yeah. As you know, Terry's kicks are very classical and he's tremendously flexible – and he used to wear clothes that would allow that flexibility. His knee particularly seemed to reach a tremendous height, and then the kick would come from that angle. It was always at an angle that was very difficult to block, and I'm talking about people who knew karate. It was presented at an angle that made it difficult to block, plus the speed, tremendous speed, and he didn't telegraph it at all.

He was physically strong too, wasn't he?

Tremendous. Integrated strength: his whole body used to go into it.

Did you ever have to deal with knife attacks when you've been on the door?

Not really, in the sense of somebody pulling out a knife and screaming and coming in at you. Someone gets stabbed and we have to go in and sort it out. There have been incidents and quite a few knife disarms. But remember, your edged weapons are not just knives: there's bottles, glasses, stuff like that. If you get a bottle in your jugular vein, it's just as dangerous. I was head doorman at a place and we used to have a search policy, and the guys were searching these lads who were coming in. I used to overview, watch the body language. It was a bit busy, so I said I'd search this guy. I went over to search him and, as I'm searching him, it's classic the way he has his hand. I know he's hiding something in his hand, so I grab his hand and he's holding a balisong. So – it was like a scene from *The Exorcist* – I slapped him so hard his head turned round.

You said that in the old days, you used punches, but you don't use punches now. In fact, you don't do karate anymore.

No, I stopped teaching karate for reasons of logistics. I was going away, working on bodyguarding, and it just wasn't feasible. At the same time, I thought I'd like to do other things. I wanted to continue training, obviously, and I was keeping my dojo just to have a place to train, although that wasn't economically viable. So I stopped teaching karate, and then I took up some of the Filipino stuff for my own training, and other things. But getting back to the punches

– although snap punches worked quite well for me, they didn't work fantastically well.

You were talking about range before, going into trapping range and stuff. I've seen people explain up to eight different ranges that exist, but in my view, range doesn't exist at all. It's a hard thing to explain in an interview, but if you take something like the Ultimate Fighting Championship, just as an example, it's noticeable that the grapplers, the good grapplers, will start from the longest range – outer range, where you can't kick them – and they will take you to the ground with a leg dive, instantly. So they go through every range instantly. Simon James and I demonstrate this in classes. He comes in and takes me down – so what happened to all those ranges?

I've thought exactly the same thing.

So as a concept it might exist, but functionally it doesn't. As my friend Simon James says, 'In a sparring situation it exists, because you're practising techniques, whereas in a real situation people are angry and they just steam into you, or you steam into them.' The only range that exists is the one you're at, and that's it. All those intermediate ranges are an illusion, they don't exist functionally. We can practise at those ranges as much as they like. It's a good idea to do that, but don't expect to impose your ranges on someone else.

You taught knife defence today, but in fact ninety per cent of the course is about the use of the knife. That's intentional, obviously.

Definitely, yes. I actually started the training programme quite a while ago, and it didn't have the knife defence part, because at that time, I hadn't been exposed to a system that I thought would work, or was teachable. I used to teach knife awareness and knife threat. I was very much into showing how dangerous the knife was, to more traditional martial artists. It went down really well. Then, once I'd trained in a system called the GUN system – Grab, Undo, Neutralise – I was happy to teach that, and we added it to the syllabus. But it doesn't take a great deal of time to teach, as you saw.

Is there a problem with self-defence teaching that you can sometimes have too much technique? That came up when I was talking to Pete Consterdine: too much technique can get in your way.

I think Pete's analogy of the hourglass, or the logjam, is probably the best description there is on that. He put into words what the truth is. So yeah, our saying is, 'Less is more.' I want to learn less than I'm doing now. I really do.

The guys you work with train regularly?

Most of the guys we work with train a lot. They're very serious trainers; cross-training, multi disciplines. At the same time, you have these limitations on what you can do, so the guys' attitude, they tend not to be hot-headed, they've got self-control – just because, if you're in an incident, they can take your badge there and then and that's it, you can't work. There's no way round it. The clubs just can't employ you, it's their licence that's jeopardised.

Doesn't this make it all more difficult, in the sense that people think they can get away with more?

Definitely.

So what do you do?

You've just got to – well, we call it, lash them out, and just get them out of the club. The sanction you've got is that, if it's a popular club, they don't get back in. Obviously, self-defence is still justified, if a guy makes a physical attack on you, and then the cameras work for you.

You teach about knives. Are more knives being used now than when you started?

Definitely. I remember when I started there was a guy who's stabbed somebody and he was like a legend in Liverpool. He was feared. He was just a little rat, but he was feared because he'd stabbed somebody. Now, everyone and his dog is carrying a knife. A lot of the kids carry knives because they're scared of the other kids carrying knives and it escalates, particularly when you add lager and speed into the equation. One of the places we worked had five doormen stabbed in four weeks.

Were any of them seriously hurt?

No, not seriously. One was fairly bad, a torso stab. Two were stabbed in the thigh. And interestingly none of those guys saw a knife, not one.

You were telling a story on the course about a friend in South Africa who'd used a knife in self-defence.

Yeah, Les, a guy who'd been on our course. He was a very good operator, he'd served in two special forces units. He was going into a shopping mall, concentrating on getting his shopping list out of his pocket, and inadvertently he bumped into this huge guy, who was probably around six foot eight. Les apologised, but the guy palm-heeled him to the head and knocked him yards back over a bench, and then came in, yelling at him that he was going to rip his head off. Les produced his knife – he has a firearm, could have shot him, but chose the lesser option – pulled out his Spyderco civilian and did a 'defanging' slash to the guy's leading arm – which stopped the guy in his tracks. The guy screamed so loudly that even Les just froze. Blood was pumping everywhere, up onto the advertising posters. The security force came and arrested the guy. It turned out that he'd been molesting staff and throwing his weight around generally. But it was a perfect, textbook technique.

And that was all right in South Africa?

Yeah.

But it wouldn't be okay over here?

It probably wouldn't. You certainly wouldn't be carrying a Spyderco civilian around in the UK anyway.

Going back to pick up a few loose ends, you didn't seem to get involved in tournaments much in your karate days. Was that because your interest was always more in the self-defence side?

Yeah, I think it probably was. Like most people who come into karate. I never got wooed into the tournament side much. I was never that good at it anyway, to be honest. I did used to write a lot of reviews for tournaments, but I very quickly ran out of ways to describe a snap punch.

Some good karate people, maybe like Andy Sherry, Bob Poynton, they concentrate on their karate and don't seem too interested in the self-defence side.

I respect them because they're honest about it, and they're brilliant at what they do. A lot of other competitors are, and I respect and admire them for that. The problem is that other people quite often offer self-defence-type training and they're still teaching what is sports-type training, and I think that's wrong.

In terms of using martial arts for self-defence, you and Terry and Gary were on the doors back in the sixties and seventies. Do you think you could have pushed that kind of teaching then – like Geoff Thompson did about twenty years later? He promoted that and he seems to have done well out of it.

We probably could. I'm not sure I would have been able to produce as many books as Geoff, mainly because I'm lazy! He really is prolific and very, very industrious. He and Pete [Consterdine] really have defined this business in many, many ways. They're certainly good role models for it.

We were talking about head butts, and we agreed that the guys on the American tapes don't seem to get it quite right, and that's probably because they don't have that footballing tradition of heading a ball.

Terry worked with a guy, he was called Les, and Terry said that he could head butt like you'd jab. He'd throw a series: ba-bang! ba-ba-bang! – just like a boxer could jab. A doorman in London knocked two guys out with his head. Bang! Bang! I mean anybody can go Whoo! like that [mimicking a ponderous head butt], but a guy who can leap up in the air, take a ball coming at eighty miles an hour this way, a heavy leather case ball soaked in rain, and direct it to that corner of the net and doing that every day of the week on a field somewhere growing up, that's how you get the skill.

We were talking about grappling being such a big deal. But, when I see self-defence techniques being shown in magazines I sometimes wonder if grappling moves are put in needlessly.

I think that's a fair comment. The UFC is probably the epitome of [the use of grappling]. The NNHB, as I call it; the Not No-Holds-Barred – which I love, and which I really enjoy watching – when it came out, the first thing which was no surprise to me was that the grapplers won, because I always thought in that sort of situation the grappler would do well. And I was very impressed by Gracie. But the downside of it was the explosion of grappling-type training to the detriment of the logical training for self defence. Grappling is an essential skill, but it's like first aid, You wouldn't cut your wrists to be able to practise first aid. Similarly, you don't go to the ground. Tommy McNally trained with a guy who was the wrestling instructor here, a guy called Johnny Mack, a well known guy in Liverpool. And his advice for the street was, 'Keep off the fucking floor.' Train, wrestle, but keep off the fucking floor. And yet they're teaching cops now the mount and guard.

And why's it bad to go on the ground in the street?

It's all the B's: blades, biting, blinding, buddies. A guy can produce a blade, biting can defeat grappling, [though] you never see it in the no-holds-barred contests. Blinding – the eye attacks. Buddies – there's usually more than one of them. They're the reasons to avoid the ground like the plague. Quite a decent wrestler near where Simon lives, working the door, he got attacked by a few guys and he ended up bitten, like a dog had bitten him – biting his back and everywhere.

Did you see many examples like that when you were on the door – people going down and getting badly hurt?

I've seen lots of people go down and not get up. That's the thing. There seems to be a thing that once you're on the ground, you become everybody's football: people who are not involved at all will have a go, just for the fun of it. I don't personally know anybody who favours going to the ground. You've got to know it. There's a guy teaches the cops in New York and he has them wearing a pistol in the centre, because if you inadvertently go down, it's very useful. Things like that I agree with. But to go to the ground as a strategy? Definitely not.

Did you train specifically for bouncing, Dennis? We were talking about that drill where Terry would take weights and throw them against a wall, but he also told me he'd get people to rush at him, things like that, and he'd practise turning people, specific bouncing techniques, if you like.

Quite a bit over the years, with different people. Picked up quite a bit from Gary, from Tommy, and of course Terry. I did a lot of grappling with Terry, by the way. That's where I probably refined most of my grappling. I did judo originally, then Terry and I used to grapple, go to the park and do some wrestling on the grass, sometimes for hours; it was very arduous. And I learned a lot, because obviously he outweighed me a lot. I think a lot of people have given me knowledge on door strategy over the years.

You said Tommy McNally called a lot of the old style bouncers 'Ale Tanks' – they were there because they got free beer.

Yeah, a lot of them were, but, as I said, I tended to work with a specific crew in the early days. We were the outsiders, really, the martial arts guys.

Gary Spiers demonstrating his own super-
aggressive version of self-defence. *(Photo by
Arthur Tansley)*

CHAPTER 16

GARY SPIERS

Part II

WHILE TERRY O'NEILL and I pursued our own varied careers, Gary Spiers was taking his Aussie mentor Bobby Jones's model, training a group of lads in what he called Applied Karate, then using them as his soldiers to man the doors in Liverpool, Southport and Blackpool, as well as at raves as far away as Watford. He built up a formidable team and an equally impressive list of security contracts around the north-west of England. What follows is his story in the 1980s as he told it to Terry at the time.

TERRY: *For a time, Gary operated several successful karate dojo and even earned a placing in the all-styles British karate team, which he represented in the heavyweight division in Europe. However it was not long before this powerful karateka's ability at quelling disturbances and sorting out previously 'unsort-outable' thugs and villains, earned him a quite formidable reputation. This in turn led to an increasing demand for his services in and around Liverpool, a city that unarguably has more than its fair share of hard cases; even the Scousers who can't fight want to! Gary has consequently become more and more heavily involved in this dangerous vocation, which he terms as a professional security advisor: 'Bouncers are bra-less ladies out jogging, aren't they?'*

He still practises karate (and teaches several small groups of students) but it is now a work-related karate. That is to say, it's not the usual balanced blend that most other practitioners of the art adhere to. From the first rei (bow) to the last rei of the practice, Gary specifically gears his training to his line of work, which is close-range personal combat in live situations. As a consequence, his karate is actually a lot better than it looks. The style and correctness of form that earned him his fourth degree black belt from Master Yamaguchi in 1975 have deteriorated, but commensurate with this loss of appearance has been an increase in the knowledge, ability and general street savvy that keeps him, most of the time anyway, in one piece. Paying scant attention to finesse, his 1986 brand of combat karate (my description, not his) is crude, limited in repertoire, often messy and always vicious – but then the people it is designed to cater for all have that last commodity in abundance.

Whatever qualities it lacks though, effectiveness is not one of them. Over the years, a number of people have attempted to stab and slash Gary with assorted blades. Some have succeeded, as is evidenced by an interesting collection of scars interspersed between his even more interesting network of Maori-style tattoos. He has been hit with clubs, barstools, bottles and some objects he didn't even see, just felt, and been the subject of gang attacks, some spontaneous but others specifically orchestrated with him as a target.

I also personally know of several quite hair-raising encounters that the interviewee has had that he most definitely has no wish to talk about. All I will say about them is that Gary was never the instigator, but the people who were suffered considerably, and deservedly so in my opinion, but the authorities, who became involved, saw only the final results, so that will be all on that subject. The point is, how he managed to survive some very nasty attacks in the manner in which he did, amazed even me – and I did the same job for seventeen years. Whether or not you agree with what Gary Spiers does for a living or whether you find his attitude, views and behaviour harsh, or in fact question the rationale that motivates him, is not of prime concern to me. What is, is that readers find his story interesting. I hope you do.

You have agreed to describe some of your experiences, actual fights *that you have been involved in over the years.*

GARY: Yes I will but you must edit out or change any names and places that might lead to any future embarrassment for me and you know what I mean by that. I won't be too rapt if I get landed with some police or civil action as a result of this magazine story.

It's a deal.

Okay. Where to start? These will not be in chronological order you know – there has been that many of them. You'll go two weeks with nothing to do, just the usual drunks and 'domestics' to split up, and then you can have three major incidents in the one night. The place that I look after now, for example, it's been nice and quiet recently, just some threats from assorted idiots whom I refused admittance to. But then just the day before yesterday, I had to 'get into it' with three right bastards, a father and two sons who decided to kick the shit out of the disc jockey because he wouldn't play a record for them. Now the reason for it is of no interest to me, I just added it for your readers who might not be able to comprehend some of the behaviour of a particular section of the community that I come into contact with.

Doesn't alcohol or rather the over-consumption of alcohol in pubs and clubs have a lot to do with the violence that you are involved with?

Yes, booze does promote that kind of foolishness but there are a lot of people around who don't need any outside factor or excuse to make them degenerate into violence, it's just them, they enjoy it – until they meet someone like me.

Let me take it further. If nice people didn't go to pubs and clubs then they wouldn't get butted, punched, kicked, glassed or stabbed, would they? The reality is that people need to have places of entertainment to go to to relieve the frustrations of society. Day-to-day living would drive them mad if they couldn't go somewhere to unwind. It's just an unfortunate fact that they need protection against the mindless element but then that's what keeps me employed. The mentality of these types is unbelievable. I have had a fight at eleven o'clock in the bloody morning and then another one in the middle of the night, at 3 a.m.

As part of my duties, I oversee an amusement arcade at a popular seaside resort, and just before lunch one day I'm called to an idiot who is kicking this bingo-type machine to pieces. He had lost 10p in it. I offered to open the machine and give him his 10p back. No, not interested, he'd 'open' the machine himself, with his feet, and I'd better 'freak off'. He saw fit to reach out toward me as he was saying this, so he ended up missing his lunch, because I'm sure he wouldn't have felt much like eating after the front kick I put into his guts. He also lost his 10p, plus other assorted coins that fell out of his pockets as he bounced off the machine behind him. Fifteen hours later, I had a more serious problem with a fellow who came to the nightclub gunning for me with an iron bar, and that was all because I would not allow him to come in the place at 7 p.m. Now I hadn't touched him at all but he decided, in his wisdom, over the next six hours, that it was worth coming back for me. And I found out later, when the police were making enquiries as to how he had ended up in hospital, that this was a man with three kids. How would you go with morons like that bringing up children?

I had a rugby captain follow me on to an Indian restaurant after I'd locked up the club for the night and gone for my supper. I did give him some stick, I'll tell you – I dropped my knee into his kidneys several times – because he deliberately came looking for me and had gone to the trouble of finding out where I ate after work. He stormed in to the restaurant, a real big guy, and shouted 'Right, who is the *** who ***'d my mates?' He must have really fancied his chances to come on his own to settle up with someone who had just polished off two of his teammates at the club during a disturbance. The little Indian waiters nearly had a fit, they thought their place was going to end up in splinters, but we went outside. It didn't last long and I talked to him during it. I was never in any trouble at all but he was, right from the word 'Go'. I told him, in between bashing him, that he should stick to his rugby because he wasn't too good at this stuff!

Aren't you dramatising things slightly when you liken these nightclub fights to life-or-death situations?

No, I don't believe I am. A number of people, both doormen and customers, are actually killed in nightclubs, bars and pubs each year, or else they die later from injuries received at such places. A great many more are left for dead and it's through no fault of the people who attack them that they survive.

I have been involved in many very nasty situations in which I and other people could very easily have been finished off. At one particular 'fun place' here in Liverpool, there was that many incidents of people being glassed over a two- to three-year period – very few even made it into the *Echo* [the evening newspaper] – that the police made serious attempts to close the place down. They were unsuccessful only because of the size and power of the organisation that the place belongs to. I actually was working in a different venue at that time but it was only a sub-division; both places were owned by the same people. So I was often called upon to 'perform' there and you would not believe, until you saw it, the amount of blood that comes out of someone with their jugular vein cut open. On two occasions that I know of, and I'm sure there were similar occurrences before I worked there and since I left, people had their throats cut by beer glasses that were thrust at their faces and then, when they pulled back, it got them in the neck instead.

There was a guy kicked to death outside one nightclub – not one that I was looking after – at a seaside resort where I was employed. Now it was in the newspaper of course, the fact that he had been the victim of a gang attack and been kicked to death, but they glossed over the actual details by describing them as 'frightful injuries'. I'd certainly call them that all right: his head was kicked off and I mean 'off'. I was told by a reliable source that when they tried to pick the body up, his head came off at the neck.

I was the security adviser for a major entertainment company in a particular seaside resort for two-and-a-half years and during that time I was involved in some of the most dangerous situations I have ever been in. Vast amounts of people – several thousand a night on weekends – would use this place and you will always get a percentage of them that are there for nothing but trouble. There would be, at the most, ten of us working there and we would have to block sometimes up to five coachloads of people from one suburb of a city or from the one village from coming in. They would have been drinking all day and early evening and would, by the time they showed up, be in no fit state or attitude to be admitted to the premises that I was looking after. Sometimes they would have been crafty and tricked me by drifting in in twos and threes, until there was a sizeable contingent inside. Then as soon as they started performing, we would have to go in and get them out before they wrecked not only the place but some of the decent customers along with it. Now no matter how good you are, when you have to approach a large partisan group of people – drunk, belligerent, nasty, possibly armed and not caring how much damage they do to people because they are from out-of-town and once they are back on their coaches, that's it, they have disappeared – you have got a really bad job on your hands.

There was one incident, the second year I was up there,

when a doorman friend of mine had an axe put in his back by just such a team. Now what in the name of Christ are you doing, getting on a coach for a day out at the beach with an axe? Now a lot of people will just say, 'Well, that's what the job is, you do it and you take those chances.' That's fine but the penalties that the courts dish out to people who do this type of shit, who take up weapons and deliberately go out to damage citizens going about their lawful duties, is ludicrous. I do it right then and there on the spot and I'll tell you something, it 'cures' them immediately. I don't know about the long term but it certainly puts an end to their violence at that point in time.

Have you had many other people use, or try to use weapons on you since those incidents you have just recounted?

Oh yes, I've been stabbed three or four times since I have been in this country.

How do you teach your karate students to react to people who use weapons against them? What sort of a response do you deem adequate?

Do you want me to tell you the truth now or something like, I advocate trying to disarm them without causing them undue damage?

The truth of course.

Right. For anyone who attempts to use any sort of a weapon on me, particularly a blade, which I have a thing about, I try, to the very best of my ability, to cause them as much damage as I possibly can. It's like I have often told people who have threatened me, on the telephone or through messengers or from a distance, with what they are going to use on me. I tell them, 'You'd better like the sight of blood and lots of it, because whatever you pull on me or manage to cut me with is going to end up sticking in, out, or up you!' And that's it. As long as they are prepared for that – but you know, 99.9 per cent of them aren't. After having gone to the trouble of purchasing a suitable knife or razor, or chisel – I have had would-be carpenters pull sharpened chisels and files on me – and being unable to put me away with it, they then want to call it a day, squawking and crying that they are sorry and if I'll just not hurt them, they will never do it again. I have seen them wet themselves with fear, once the tables are turned. Yes, unbelievable isn't it, an instant change of heart.

Now I suppose some people might expect me to just put a nice, come-along hold or restraining lock on them at this point. The day I am inclined to be merciful to someone who has just tried to open me up like a melon, is the day I stop doing this kind of work and join the church or something. And I'll tell you another thing: I'm not in the forgiving business either. If I could meet up with my friend from twenty-odd years ago who presented me with this nice memento (pointing to his facial scar), I'd have some more business with him right away.

As for training specific responses, I never have a preconceived idea of what I'm going to do in any given situation. You see, in the time it takes to close in on an incident, an on-going fight or one just about to commence, the participants have changed their positions. So what were possible targets for particular techniques, be it groins, knees to kick, legs to sweep or arms to bar, at say five yards, are no longer accessible. Also, by the time it takes me to get across a crowded dance floor or the lounge of a hotel, one or more of my imminent opponents may have produced a weapon from a pocket or even 'manufactured' one – pulled the leg off a table, broken a bottle, picked up an ashtray or whatever. I have not been conscious, for several years now, of making the decision to 'go'. I used to deliberate – shall I … what if … he's screaming and swearing at me … is it too soon? – that sort of thing, but nowadays it just happens naturally. I do my best to constantly condition my mind to react properly. And this ability has enabled me to beat younger, fitter people who are constantly training. You must always go deliberately to finish an incident, once you have realized that it is going to become physical, as quickly as possible, because you have no knowledge of who else will become involved.

To give yourself the best possible chance of winning in a street situation, you must develop the ability, both physically and mentally, to explode, to switch on instantly. It has got to become as natural in your psyche as changing gears or applying the brake in a motor vehicle. You have to suddenly shift into overdrive. Any martial arts person who is going to put himself on the line must be able to switch on from a state of nothing to one hundred per cent 'go' instantly. An instructor must instil the attitude, 'My life is in jeopardy here, I must finish this man (or men) here and now.'

As for actual techniques, I'd say that over the years I have put people out of commission with practically every martial arts blow known to man. At one place I was working, shortly after first coming to Liverpool, I even used an *ushiro kubi-tsuki*.

What's that?

A rear headbutt; the Japanese term it a head punch. You were there actually. Don't you remember when that fellow grabbed hold of me from the back?

Yes, I do remember, it was just the term that I was unfamiliar with.

Anyway that worked spectacularly, the front of his face looked as flat as a pancake afterwards. In fact I just love people to grab me, you know; I'm right into that. It's rather a speciality of mine. I think it's hilarious whenever someone lays hands on me. I have even had a few try to put holds on me. It's often happened in incidents that have escalated into brawls, with a lot of people packed in close together, like on a dance floor of a discotheque. As soon as someone tries to grapple with me, I think to myself, that will do me, my dear, you're about to be really, really sorry you left the house this evening!

Gary, let me ask you at this point just how far you go. I want you to be truthful again here. By now the people reading this story will be aware that you do not cause these altercations, but you are a huge man with a vast amount of martial arts training and combative experience. How hard do you actually hit these people? I mean, on two occasions I have really thought you had killed your opponents. One was that monster black guy, the one from the American base.

Yes, that was a beauty, wasn't it? I did catch him with a couple of really good shots. He was halfway out of the game from the side thrust-kick I gave him in the ribs and then he turned right into that right cross and that was that, period. Whack! I got him right in the temple with this here (Mr Spiers tapped the oversized second knuckle on his right hand, a result of strenuous toughening on the karate *makiwara*).

Do you still hit people as hard as that today?

Well it all depends on the situation. My mind is tuned to react accordingly to whatever they decide to do. For example, I always watch very closely for the appearance of weapons and I have already told you how I feel about weapon-users. You see I do not start violent confrontations, but I do stop them – real quick. I have no intention whatsoever of being crippled or killed by some pathetic moron who has decided that I will look better with a knife in me or with an iron bar over my head. If somebody is going to have to put in some hospital time, then it's going to be them, not me. So I can summarise that for you: if we now have a fight in which I have less than a few seconds to evaluate the potential danger, then I hit man, woman and dog with the same level of every degree of physical power that I can generate. Because if I don't put my opponent away immediately, I have no way of knowing how many others are going to join in on the attack.

Are you not scared that someday you will kill somebody?

I have thought about it. What can I do? I have never initiated an attack. The options are always there for the people who start it. Let's put it this way, I certainly have no wish to kill anybody but I'd rather be the accused at someone's murder trial than be the main star.

Have you ever hit somebody really hard with what you considered a good shot and it hasn't had the desired effect?

Yes, I did that years ago and the first time it happened I was actually physically shocked. I hit an Irish immigrant fellow with what I thought was a real good right-hand punch on the side of his jaw, the timing was right, so was the distance and so was the placement. I hit him as hard as I possibly could and it didn't even faze him, his head moved but that was the full extent of it and he promptly hit me back. And I was astounded. Prior to that, I had never had anyone take such a beautiful shot from me and just shrug it off.

And then what? What was the eventual outcome of that dispute?

I beat him in the finish because I took his leg from under him and dropped on his groin with my knee. It didn't knock him out but he couldn't get up. So I dragged him by the ankles down the stairs of the place I was working in and dumped him in the street, still doubled up and gargling. I did learn from that though, and since then I do follow up with a second and, if I have the time and somebody else doesn't need some attention, a third blow.

You do enjoy it don't you? It's very obvious to me, not only from your enthusiasm in re-living these fights but also by the fact that you have stuck at this line of work for so long now, that you get a certain pleasure out of putting people 'out of commission', as you put it. Can you deny that?

I couldn't say that I don't enjoy it because I have spent my whole life in gymnasiums training for just this type of situation. If I had spent the same amount of time working on motor vehicles, the engineering, performance and driving side, then I'm sure I'd really enjoy the handling and racing of them. And it's the same with me and fighting, I suppose, if you can follow my drift. When you see the opponent grab the bottle off the bar or reach into their pocket or shift their bodyweight to throw a kick, then I feel more comfortable in that situation than in ninety per cent of other situations that I live in, day-to-day.

I'd like you to recall some more incidents, fights that you have been in, during your many years spent working the clubs here in northern England.

All right, but here particularly I want you to change both the locality and the names of the people involved. I'll tell you all the details of who, how, where and what happened on the understanding that I will be suitably covered against any resulting flak. In other words, should any authorities become interested in me, you made the whole story up.

Who is to say that I didn't?

Fair enough. We can start with one that I was particularly pleased with at the time. In fact, come to think of it I'm still very happy about that performance. Remember I told you some years ago about the team from Scotland I got into it with in that club in Southport?

Was that the boxers, the time you had two really bad black eyes?

Yes, that was it, but I'll tell you what, that was nothing compared to the state that some of them finished up in. As to them being boxers, well, that I can't vouch for, but they were all handy. A few of them were big strong lads and they could certainly dig. They gave me some really sound smacks in the face and back of the head. As it turned out, this particular team had been demanding, and getting, a certain amount of protection money from a few local establishments. Now I happened to be part of a wedding party at one of these establishments. I had taken a night off from the club I was working at the time to celebrate a friend's 'demise' (his wedding). At that time I had not heard of these Scots, nor was I aware that the place was being 'minded'.

Anyway, at one point in the evening some drinks were taken from one of these fellows' table, by mistake I'm sure, because the people I was with were not the type to do that. Well an altercation started and several members of the wedding party, who were not fighters by the way, were attacked and injured, including the bride, who was knocked out. So of course I became involved. We had a very severe fight which got that 'busy' as it went on that, during the worst part, I only remember doing two or three distinct things. I used knee kicks several times and various elbow strikes.

How many of them were there?

I don't know exactly. I was told later that there were at least seven of them but there might only have been five. I didn't have time to count them. I was too occupied blocking and covering up because I was in danger of being put away. They were all a bit useful. Every time I saw a vulnerable point – a throat, an eye, a joint or a groin – I hit it. I was not put on the ground at any time. There was a lot of blood from a cut over my eye but that's all. I was hit in the groin but I'd taken lots of that during my time in Japan, doing Goju-kai karate. That was a favourite pastime of some of my little 'yellow friends' – kicking each other, but particularly big foreigners, in the balls, so that didn't bother me much. All the other shots they had got into me left marks but no impression, if you know what I mean. If I have to, although it's not one of my favourite pastimes, I can take a lot of stick and still perform. One of them gave me a pretty good kick in the back. It missed the kidneys though, which was fortunate for me and very unfortunate for them. As it went on, they must have been getting more and more disheartened and I was getting more and more into it.

So I got out of that fight without any severe injury as a penalty, whereas they all went to the hospital. Some of them just needed patching up but some of them, I'm very pleased to report, had to be booked in for several days' stay in the place. And one of them, who I later was given to understand was the 'main attraction', the biggest hard-case of the crew, had to have an extended rest and extensive treatment. I do remember him because it was right at the end, it was all over actually because there were none of them standing. I was just darting into the washroom to swill off, because I was covered in 'it', before I left the place. I didn't particularly want to be there when the cavalry (police) arrived. Just as I pushed open the door, out comes this big one, shouting something garbled at me and pointing to his face. I thought it was me that had gone partially deaf, from one of the punches I'd taken in the ears, and it occurred to me that he was saying something like, 'Try me on!' So I promptly gave him two really good shots in the head: a right-hand palm-heel strike and, as his head bounced off the door frame, I followed it with a right-hand elbow in the face. Well, you'll laugh at this, I practically wet myself when some of the staff told me about it later. I had apparently already broken his jaw early on in the proceedings and he had been in the toilet, trying to line up his mouth and teeth. Then he'd come out, bumped into me and been trying to say, 'Look what you have done, you bastard.'

Anyway I certainly 'cured' him. One of my associates was interested enough to telephone the hospital, where he was still in residence five days later, and they told the 'interested relation' that his condition was 'still poorly' and that he was still in considerable discomfort after his operations – plural, if you don't mind. This 'gentleman' and some of the rest of his crew may well have had doubts about their future in their chosen line of work.

Have you had other incidents like that one where you have been severely outnumbered?

Oh yes, quite a few times. When I was stabbed in the knee – that was a gang attack. You will probably remember that I was limping for bloody ages. There was a young chap who was attacked and very nearly killed – I do seriously believe that if I hadn't been there he would have died – because he had a different accent. He was ridiculed, pushed around and then eventually slashed with Stanley knives, or 'Stanley'd', as it's popularly known in Liverpool. These weapons are used that often in the city and its surrounding areas, I think of it as the modern-day equivalent of the Japanese katana (long sword). By the time I was brought up a flight of stairs and had got into the function room, where it was all happening, there was blood everywhere, on the floor, on tables, up one wall, and it was all coming out of this one kid. A team of about eight 'heroes' were into him and even with those odds, at least two of them were stabbing at him and slashing him with those little razor-sharp knives. His girlfriend was standing on a table screaming hysterically and everyone else had instantly vacated the area. None of the other customers and bar staff had any intention of intervening.

Now I made a tactical error here and I paid for it. Which is correct: if you drop your guard in a proper dojo you should get whacked for it, and if you don't then you are not being taught proper karate. I should have got right into them immediately. I reckon I could have polished off three or four of them before they knew what had hit them, because I was coming from their rear. But the kid was in such a state that I just dashed through the middle and only threw and pushed them out of the way, so that I could get to him. You see, as they were stabbing at him, he had his hands up in front of his face, their main target, and both of his wrists had been slashed, one of them through to the bone. The blood was pumping out of him that fast that I went straight for him and grabbed his wrists. I thought if I didn't stem the blood real quickly, he wouldn't be with us too much longer. It did take me a few seconds to secure proper grips on him, his wrists were that slippery, plus he had lots of other cuts on his hands to down past his elbows, they were really into carving him up.

Anyway no sooner had I grabbed him and begun running toward the door, dragging him with me, than I became the subject of attention. I was hit by a chair first, felt a few kicks and punches and then I was stabbed in the side of the knee, a real beauty, by someone behind me. Now this was a deliberate attempt to cripple me. You should have seen it, my leg just opened up like a mushroom. It did not totally succeed but it did reduce my capacity, I'd say by about sixty per cent. I didn't feel any pain but within fifteen seconds I lost the use of that leg, it just wouldn't work. So from then on I had to go on the defensive. I knew if I had attacked at that point in time, I would have definitely gone down. And if it hadn't been for the intervention of two friends of mine who had followed me up the stairs, I believe I might have been killed in that place, because when they saw I couldn't move too well they were coming on to me like a pack of dogs. As it was, the team was broken up by my friends hurling two of them down the stairs. The rest of them paused for a few seconds and that was enough for me to be able to turn it around. I had let go of the kid's wrists – I believe someone else then took over that job – and when I started on them, they turned and ran. I snatched one and dragged him in real close – I believe I had my teeth into his nose and cheek at one stage – and, using him as a support, I side-kicked one of them in the ribs, a real close shot which smashed him up against the bar. And then I just tore into them and they turned around and ran for it.

At that point I knew I had been 'stuck' again – knifed – and I wanted to kill them. And they knew it. That's why they ran. They all got away, except for the one who I believe stabbed me. I'm not a hundred per cent positive it was him because I was stabbed from behind, but he was definitely one of the two that had a Stanley knife.

What did you do to him?

Lots. And that's it on that one, thank you. Next.

I recall an incident, a couple of years back, where some people came back to a club you were working at, specifically to sort you out.

Well I have had a few of these over the years – they have been hugely unsuccessful to date, I may add – but I know the one you mean. It was at a club on a seafront. There was only the boss and I left there – we were just at the door locking up at about 3 a.m. Now I never found out if it was him – my employer, me or the takings they were after. Actually all the money had been locked away in a safe but they weren't to know that, so it may only have been an attempted robbery. Anyway, whatever it was, it was planned. There were four of them and they must have been hiding in this nearby hedge. The first we knew was when they came running across the road, complete with big fence-pickets and clubs. 'We've come for you mate!' shouts one of them. 'Good,' I said and I charged at them. Now it did become rather severe because they all had weapons, I had none, and they did intend to do the business on me. I was fortunate in getting away from that one without having my head bashed in. My forearms got some real nice lumps on them though from blocking their staves. Unfortunately one of them had one of his eyes almost popped out on his cheekbone, which sounds a horrific thing if you are a normal, moral, civilized character but then civilized people do not leap out of hedges in the middle of the night and start trying to open up people's heads with assorted clubs!

How did the other three fare?

On the first contact, I blocked a stick aimed at my head and got that first one with a front kick which put him right on his arse across the pavement. One was foot-swept and heel-stamped in the groin, which finished him. One of them got his head wedged in between two phone booths. He must have thought that all of him would have fitted into that space, thereby giving him some protection, but as it happened he couldn't get his shoulders in, which was unfortunate for the rest of his body. Sadly, one of them got away. He abandoned the enterprise completely, dropped his club – which I picked up, thank you very much – and took off at a great speed along the promenade. Now I'm not built for running and I had no hope of catching him, although I did hit him in the back with the stick, which I threw at him. This did upset me, him escaping, because I felt he should have had an equal serving along with his colleagues. I'm sure that, had it gone the other way, they would all have been very busy bashing the shit out of me.

Does it ever occur to you that you might get killed?

I have thought about it, yes. But, see, it is what I choose to do. I have done this work all my adult life. I love the martial arts, and being paid for the abilities I have gained through their practice and for the heaps of experience I have had in dealing with the scumbags of society enables me to live solely in a combative field. Like anybody else, I only have so much of a useable life, so of course you are constantly having to negotiate your wages up to a high level of payment in keeping with the dangers and demands of the job. I provide what I consider to be a really good service and I now get more offers of work than I actually have time to do. But if it is worthwhile, by which I mean that the finances are right, then if I can't be there all the time myself, I can usually provide competent, qualified students of mine to look after the places and I then oversee the premises and personnel.

In one big club that I was employed they had had seventy-two incidents in which police had been called onto the premises in one season. I was hired to control the security and the following season they had just one such incident, and that's a fact. So everybody was happy, except the idiots who I had disputes with. They weren't too overjoyed but who cares about them? I'm really glad they were around actually, they made me a lot of money.

Do you still get scared when you know 'it's about to start'?

Of course. But you need that, you always go better when your nerves are on edge, when there's some fear. But I'd have to say that it doesn't get me as much as it used to when I was younger. The older you get, how can I put it, the more interested you become in survival. Take dogs for example – perhaps it's the same with other animals, I don't know – the most dangerous in a group of dogs is generally the old male. He has the experience, the cunning, and his attitude is harsher. He takes life more seriously because he hasn't got that much of it left. I take less chances now than, say, seven to ten years ago. At the slightest hint of it turning physical, I'm all over them like a rash.

Most self-defence classes promote waiting until the opponent makes the first move.

Well, legally I suppose it then allows you to defend yourself, but practically it's a different matter. Did you ever wait for people to start the proceedings if you knew they were going to perform?

I'm interviewing you!

I'll put it this way, I have scars all over me from bastards sticking things in me over the years and I sometimes get splitting headaches from the shoes, fists and assorted wooden objects that my head has stopped over a period of time. I try not to allow them even half a chance. If I kick-off it's because that is what it takes to do what I do for as long as I have successfully done it. Experience is a huge asset in this work. After twenty years, I can spot 'them' from a great distance off. Sometimes I'm wrong but more often than not, I'm correct. And of the times when they don't perform, a good percentage of them had every intention of, but something they see or sense in me persuades them to change their mind. Remember, I have worked in many environments around the world where I did not speak the language. To stay in one piece and keep hold of what belongs to you, you have to develop a sensitivity to attitudes and intentions of the people around you.

What sort of opponent do you find the most dangerous?

Well, they are all dangerous to a greater or lesser extent, but I know what you mean. It's not physical size nor actual capabilities that is the most important factor in my book, it's who is the nastiest and most cunning. That's the worst kind. Very often it's the small guys who turn out to be most vicious, probably compensating for their lack of size. Then there are always exceptions like Mr. Farmer [we can now reveal that Gary was referring to Eddie Palmer here – D.M.], who you may recall I had a major difference of opinion with.

He's dead now isn't he?

Yes, but he was very much alive when I fought him. Farmer was, as you know, a notorious hardcase with a good twenty years of reputation preceding him. He was widely known throughout his home town as the 'Terror of Toxteth' and that's what the national newspapers called him when they reported his death. He was around 6ft, usually over eighteen stone and he had been, in his time, a very able and hard heavyweight boxer, and he was quite willing to fight anybody. Very few people liked him but hardly anyone would tell him to his face, not even the other hardcases, because he had battered a large percentage of them. Some of them had had several return matches with him and they had still ended up out of the game. He hadn't taken many 'seconds' in his fighting career. We are talking about a proper determined man who made a vocation, in between his prison stretches, of going around intimidating other people and, as often as not, giving them a really good bashing. Anyway, a couple of years before he was killed in a street fight, me and him had a severe 'do'.

Let's have the full story

How it got started was that he had knocked a girl unconscious on the dance floor of a place that I was working in.

Why?

She had refused to dance with him. Lots of these people don't need much reason to start performing. Anyway, I don't exactly know what had gone on prior to that, all I was told was that Farmer had kicked off upstairs. By the time I got up the two flights of stairs, there were two bodies stretched out on the floor – the girl had been joined by a little Indian doctor. He must have been all of five foot but he was the only one in the room that had the guts to go over and re-monstrate with Farmer over punching the girl. He had also been treated to a right-hander which had broken his glasses, his nose and also removed a few of his teeth.

I did not touch Farmer at that stage, simply because I did not know then what had happened, I only found out later, I just said to him, 'You have got to leave, boss.' Now, even though I'd been told many times about how fast this fellow was with his hands, I still got nailed. He caught me with a real nice hook, right in the jaw. I have to be honest and say that I did not see it. Boom! It was perfect.

Did it put you down?

No, it did not put me down, probably due to a combination of my rather large bone structure, the way I'm put together, and to the fact that I'm not in the habit, mentally, of being put on my arse by people. It did shake me though and I lost time, fractions of activity, but I was still able to take him to the floor. He should really have followed up on his lead with another shot but he was probably so used to sparking all and sundry with just the one shot that he wasn't geared to putting a com-bination attack together. I ducked low, grabbed him behind the knee with one hand and pulled his foot out from under him and drove my shoulder into his groin. Down he went and I was right on top of him. I automatically had him in a half-strangle, just a reflex action.

At that point I could have finished him there and then. I would have strangled him properly, wrenched his neck out or gouged him, or maybe all of those things, depending upon how well he stood up to a bit of treatment. But he had a little crew with him who were justly famous for their willingness to get into people with their Stanley knives. They were nicknamed 'the Stanley Boys'. Obituaries have even been placed in the local newspaper for people who were alive, designed to upset them, reading their own death notice in the paper signed, 'Love from the Stanley Boys.' Now I believe you have to show a death certificate before they will publish the notice but you didn't have to do this till recent years. I knew that, had I started to do the business on Farmer, I would probably have been cut to pieces. Remember he was still conscious underneath me and I had not yet recovered from his punch. So I let him up, much against my wishes – and he promptly challenged me to a straightener outside, just him and me.

Rather than get involved in what possibly could have been a massacre – of me, because his mates were all around us – I agreed. I don't like going outside the premises, there is much more chance of police involvement and also I knew that there was a possibility of my ending up on my own on the street with him and his pack. Even though I was working with people – there were other bouncers on with me – one never really knows what people will do in serious circumstances that just flare up instantly. Conditions can change, even amongst trusted colleagues, and if for some reason your friends, whom you are relying on to hop in, do not come to your assistance right away you could easily be killed. Something that's gone wrong at home, even a silly argument with their wife before they come to the club that evening, can change a person's mind about the determination with which he will do his job. The fear of physical reprisals and/or legal repercussions can also alter a man's commitment to 'performing'.

Have you ever had people, other bouncers, desert you in similar situations?

It has happened twice now in my life. I haven't had it occur much, because I do take it very personally. We went outside and I agreed not to kick him. Somebody had obviously informed him of my pedigree; he wanted 'rules', which to me is so much bullshit. When you fight, you fight, and that's it. Anyway his people were there with him and several of them already had their hands in their pockets, obviously holding their working 'tools'.

So he says, 'We won't kick.'

I said, 'That will do me, let's go.'

So we started and as I charged, he punched and we ended up with my right forearm in his mouth. He bit me almost through to the bone whilst I held my right fist with my left hand and started smashing his head back against the wall behind him. His teeth were hurting me a lot but at the same time, he was nearly choking on my forearm. Well, because he was biting me, he could not let go and as I was trying to knock the wall down with the back of his head, I instinctively put my knee into him twice, once in the stomach and once in the hip. I'd have had him in the groin properly with the next one. You see, I'd used a left and a right knee strike to get a fix on his position and the third one would have crushed 'them' for him. But my knee attacks brought savage threats from his gang, who by this time had apparently pulled their knives out. My colleagues had thankfully chosen to come out with me, for which I am eternally grateful, because even if they hadn't, I'd have been obliged to go out anyway. I wouldn't have particularly relished the idea but neither would I have backed down from this pack of shit. I'm certain that it was only my people's presence there that prevented the other team from tearing me to ribbons.

I also gave him some elbow smashes in the gut with my left arm but because of the way our bodies were locked in, I couldn't get any real heavy shots into him from that angle. Now I was not able to knock him out. People have told me that he had been kayo'd but I have never met one who had actually done it. As it was, though, he wound up that exhausted he was unable to continue, whereas I had loads left in me. Now I had great difficulty in restraining myself at this point from finishing the job off when he was in this state. It flashed through my mind that if I did drop on his throat or his spleen with my knees, as I wanted to, or stomp him with a heel-kick, that the incident would immediately escalate. So I left it at that. But he was well fucked.

What's with this dropping your knee on opponents, you seem quite fond of that technique?

Oh I am quite fond of it, as you put it. I think it's a very valid technique. If you do it properly, you have every chance of breaking something on them. At the very least you severely wind them. I'll tell you this, I have never done it to anybody and had them get up after it, at least not for a while and then not under their own steam. They have had to be carried away.

Did you have any further trouble with Mr. Farmer?

No I did not. I did tell him that if he came back for a return match, I would have to seriously consider crippling him permanently. Whether he believed me or not I don't know but he never again performed in a place that I was looking after. Several years after this, he went too far with someone and they killed him. The story I heard was that he was busy engaging in one of his favourite pastimes, intimidation, and someone decided that enough was enough and, whoomph, there you are, a carving knife right under the arm and through the heart, and that was that. Period.

Have you ever used a blade of any description against people?

No ... well yes, I suppose I have, but it's just the way you put the question on me. It could make me sound really violent.

Oh, Heaven forbid that you should come over in that light, Gary. Actually, it was a loaded question because I know for a fact that you have used a katana [Japanese longsword] at least once.

Twice actually mate, but I never actually used it on them, although at the time I certainly was prepared to do that, otherwise I wouldn't have pulled it out. The first time was against an idiot who threatened me with this stupid little Stanley knife. Now I had been practising on the premises during the day with one of my students who was interested in learning how to use a sword. I'd done some of this in Japan during my stay there. So this character had been refused admission by another member of staff at the front door. He became very abusive and by the time I put in an appearance, he was like a raving lunatic; I thought from the look of his eyes he was on drugs. So he pulled this knife out and began brandishing it, along with all the verbals, we were all going to be cut up into dog meat, etc., etc. So I told him, 'Here you are, sport, I've got one of these myself,' and I produced my four-foot version and went at him. Well he wasn't that much out of his skull that he wanted to play an Errol Flynn game and he took off in the opposite direction to annoy someone else, I suppose. I did pursue him because he had disturbed me and got me switched on but once again I had no luck at catching them.

The next occasion I had to take this same sword to work with me could have developed into something a lot more serious if the opposition had had the bottle to get into it. I was committed to it and so were they, they said, but when it actually came to the crunch, they 'turned their arses on it' (went in the opposite direction). Now this was a racial-motivated situation and I do not know what had led up to it, because I was brought into it halfway through. A group of people who had been chosen for the job on the strength of their physical abilities and nastiness turned up at a place one night and wrecked it good style. A couple of women had bought tickets, gone in and then opened the fire-exit doors. In came the team and people inside the place, customers, bar staff, manager and bouncers, were indiscriminately battered. Several were stabbed and slashed with all manner of weapons. The place was smashed to bits and a promise made that they 'would be back' the following weekend.

This one incident suitably terrified everyone connected with the club, which up until then had been a very popular country club with a nice clientele. Now I was immediately contacted by the company who owned the place. They were properly sick about the whole affair and I was asked to straighten the problem out. So I made attempts to defuse the situation by letting it be known on the nightclub grapevine that everyone at the club was very impressed with the gang's performance but that if they knew what was good for them, they had best not come back, not unless they wanted to become permanent fixtures in the place.

They chose not to take this advice – which was really sound advice – and they did come back. I was of course waiting for them. I had made it my business to be there every night since the attack. I was alone but I had with me the sharpest katana you could imagine. You know how well I used to sharpen my butchering knives for my slaughtering jobs in the meat works, well I'd done as good a job on my old katana. I copped for them in the car-park of the club. The instant they switched off the engines of their vehicles – there were three car-loads of them – I was on them. And I slashed most of the tyres on all the cars before they even knew what had hit them. I wanted to make sure that they stayed around for what I had in store for them. But their bottle went and they chose not to get out of their vehicles, despite the fact that I saw at least one hatchet and a few baseball bats through the windows. The windscreens were going to go in next, as I intended to do as many of them in as I possibly could before they even got out from their seats. I'd have had to, you see, because of the amount of them. Anyway, in between screaming and blubbering, the drivers switched the engines back on and took off on the rims of their wheels rather than participate further. I should add that this lot were not kids, they were all adult males of a particular ethnic group and they did mean business, make no mistake about that. Despite threats of, 'It will be shooters next time,' this group has never returned to that place since.

So yes, I am worth the money that I get paid for this job. And it is a service that is very much needed. If a club owner wishes to build up a good business, he has to not only put in a nice décor, lighting, sound system, etc., he also has to make sure his customers are going to be protected against society's lunatic element. Now, I work on the basis that if people come to a place to participate in aggravation and violence, then the only way you can cope with it and at the same time preserve the behavioural standards of the decent people in the place is to display better physical capabilities than the thugs. Which I can do.

Are most of your opponents really tough, or do some of them merely talk a good fight?

Over the last three or four years, with a few notable exceptions, I'd have to say that the individual levels of the people I have fought has been quite abysmal. Whilst they have been very willing to get into it at the onset, once I got into them it has only been a matter of seconds before they have wanted to call it quits. So, as fighters, I have not rated them at all. Firstly, because wanting to throw the towel in so soon means that their minds are not tough enough, and secondly, the amount of medical attention they often need after the event shows that their bodies weren't much good either!

Do you have any advice, fighting savvy that you could pass on, as to how you see the best way of handling a good puncher or someone who wants to grapple?

Well, if you have the time to assess a potential opponent, you must then be cunning enough to completely oppose him with a totally different method to that which he is used to. So in other words, you'd try to get a boxer on the ground. If, on the other hand, you knew your opponent to be a wrestler or a judo man, you'd try to kick pieces off him before he could get a hold of you, because if he does and he is good at his business, you have every chance of being beaten by him.

Of course, the distance between you is very important. I've had good success against boxers by smashing up their knees, going for the cartilages on their leading leg with joint-stamping kicks. With one, or preferably both, knees gone they are usually not too interested in continuing. Now if you are in close with a boxer, it's of little use trying to out-punch or headbutt them, because that's their game. Use a takedown on them, like I did with Farmer. If you are unfortunate enough to be real close to a wrestler, you'd better go for his eyes, ears or his balls before he secures a proper grip on you. And if you don't do it right the first time, you're unlikely to get a second chance with a capable wrestler because those fellows are bloody good.

Yes, I also rate wrestling highly, although on the negative side it is geared to a one-to-one situation, whereas karate for example, does teach techniques and principles against multiple opponents.

Yes, well I'd rather not go into the relative merits of karate or kung fu, with regard to street fighting, if you don't mind.

What do you mean by that comment? You don't sound too complimentary in your evaluation of karate's effectiveness in the street.

It's not the actual karate that I don't rate, it's the majority of the people doing it. Not all of them, of course, because some are really useful. But I have been around a great many karate people in my time and to be perfectly honest with you, no, I don't rate them too highly for the real stuff. I wouldn't put my money on ninety per cent of them. They don't really have the mentality for it.

What do you put that down to?

Well, a lot of it has to do with the training, that's the way I see it. The continuous teaching of no-contact and the teaching of long, strenuous exercise, conditions the karate student's mind to (a) miss the target or else merely touch it, and (b) place too much stress on fitness levels rather than getting used to avoiding and/or absorbing a certain amount of pain and physical discomfort. Even after years and years of training, most of them have never been bitten, never had their eyes scratched, never been repeatedly hit hard, perhaps winded and then kicked when they are on the floor. A fellow who plays rugby, that's one of the first things he's going to do to you, smash into you with his full bodyweight and take all the air out of your body. A wrestler is always being put in nasty punishing holds that he has to fight out of. A judo man takes heavy throws, is arm-locked, dragged to the ground and strangled. Boxers get the shit punched out of them on a regular basis. You know what I'm saying; they are all used to being knocked about. And that is what's going to happen to you when you start getting into some street activity. Now if the first shot stuns and stops you in your tracks, if you are not conditioned to recovering from hard physical abuse then you are going to be in great trouble. Whether it's a lucky shot or a planned deliberate technique doesn't matter if your opponent has got the courage to finish the job off once you are temporarily out of it. That's you, thank you and goodnight! I think that the constant practice of deliberately not hitting each other in the karate dojo makes the participants more vulnerable than any other combative art.

I understand what you are saying. But the technique you rely most heavily upon in your fights is karate, so it's never seemed to hinder you. Also, I know of other street-competent karateka.

Yes, but they have to be brought out of the no-contact system. As you get higher in the grades, the contact has to be taught to you. You have to learn to take an elbow in your ear, be kneed in the stomach. You can teach a hundred people to get the best level of competence that they possibly can by driving them through constant repetition of technique but you cannot teach the ability that gives them the edge, so that after he or she has been severely hurt, by a weapon, a blow, a throw or whatever, to get up off the floor and get in again. You must learn this yourself. You must expose yourself to circumstances where this is likely to happen, i.e. hard, punishing, contact training. You can't actually be taught this. You can theoretically but it is not the same thing.

You mean you have to go through the pain.

Yes, definitely and decidedly. I have taken some good injuries in the course of learning my trade and whilst I certainly did not like it at the time, the experience of being hurt and of knowing I can still keep on performing has given me a lot of confidence. Nowadays I'm very into pain – avoiding it myself and putting other people through it rather than me.

So you feel that this avoidance of pain is a negative factor in karate training?

Yes I do, at least once you are out of the beginner and inter-mediate stages of learning the art. Don't you agree?

To a certain extent of course I do. But being realistic, you can't teach that stuff to people, they won't stand for it. Start dishing out that kind of training and you lose them even quicker than most of them would normally quit. It's a rarity to find people who are willing to put up with the harsher forms of training.

Well there you go, Digger. Fighting is a tough game and karate, done properly, is a hard strenuous thing in which to earn your qualifications.

Do you not think that karate serves any purpose other than teaching people how to fight?

Now hold on, I didn't say that. The determination to achieve a perfect technique, as in, say, winning a kata tournament, where you have no opposition apart from yourself, I think that this is bloody marvellous for your self-control and your physical ability. And for the average person who just wants to spend four or five hours a week going up through a curriculum of learning the art, I think karate is just great. Also, by doing this, the average man or woman will reach a certain level of defensive ability. But if you are talking about someone putting himself on the line, as in entering the field of protective security in any shape or form, then it's a different matter. I firmly believe that they should expose themselves to as many forms of physical jeopardy as they possibly can, from boxing and kickboxing with the head-gear on, and then with it off, to aikido, ju-jitsu and the like, which will twist your joints and throw you in every conceivable way, to the rough-housing you get in judo and wrestling. What's more, I think it an absolute necessity that anyone who sets himself up as a self-defence teacher should be able to do the business himself.

I love kata and I think they are excellent methods of teaching you maximum mobility, providing they are taught in a combative manner. Which means that you are taught, along with the moves, exactly what they are for. And then you have to learn to use them correctly in all the hundreds of different ways that are possible. I have used a lot of movements that are direct *bunkai* (applications) from the Goju kata in my time. In fact not too long ago I was very grateful to my teacher in Japan, who taught me this one particular application from a movement in a kata called 'seiyanchin'.

How long ago did this one happen?

Well, it wasn't that long ago actually. Now before we start, I considered this to be a real vicious and unprovoked attack and so I'm not at all sorry about the end result. I was standing in this area that I look after – it's an outdoor arcade actually, part of a big entertainment complex – and these two big blokes walked straight up to me. As they got to within a few feet of me, one of them sticks out his hand for a handshake, smiles and says, 'Hi, Gary, how are you mate?' They almost had me! I halfway reached out to take his hand, then realized that the other one was sliding around to my side. I started to move and the one in front quickly grabbed both of my arms above the elbows, pinning them to my sides. Meanwhile his colleague had whipped a sizeable piece of iron scaffolding out from under his raincoat and promptly swung it at my head. I'm telling you, it would have taken my head off had it landed. It was a nice, well-rehearsed double act, from the friendly direct approach to the arm grab – which is a good one, I have used it myself many times.

Fortunately I saw it coming and was able to pivot and twist into the blow, jerking the one who had hold of me around as well. The tube missed because I'd moved in close to the one who was swinging it and his arms – it was a two-handed job – hit my shoulder, which made him drop the weapon. I was then able to use this particular double-arm disengagement to break free of the grip and finished the kata movement off perfectly by jamming both of my thumbs into his eyeballs – and that 'cured' him completely. The other was that close to me, he had no other option but to grab me, which he did. He tried to put a silly head-lock on. Well, I love people getting affectionate like that. I butted him that hard in the side of his head that I saw stars myself and then I bit him right through the cheekbone.

I should really have picked up what they had brought along to do me in with, to keep as a memento, but at the time my major concern was in vacating the area. I wish I'd got it though, it was a beauty, quite thin iron tubing but heavy, about three feet long with a big jutting-out piece like a construction joint or something. It would have definitely crushed anything it hit; this was a really serious attempt to give me a 'permanent' headache. So if I hadn't done my homework on *seiyunchin*, I might have been flicking my bottom lip up and down now instead of doing this interview.

Well, I'm certainly glad you made it. Apart from any other consideration, I think it's a really interesting and entertaining story. Let's move on to your best techniques, the ones that you have developed over your many years of 'field-testing'.

Okay. However, some of the stuff I do and the way I do it works for me because of my size and because of the hard physical work I used to do. Remember, I spent a lot of my early life slaughtering and butchering in the meat works. Now in the course of a day you have to push, drag and wrestle up to one hundred animals into a position to kill them. Sometimes when you were working with sheep, you'd have to cut and then punch the fleece off the sheep's body with your bare hands. Your knuckles get skinned and your hands and forearms get ripped from all the bone splinters. The pain tells you to stop, but if you want to get paid that day and keep the job, you have to continue. So that sort of gruelling work, if you stick at it, has a tendency to toughen you up considerably and it made me very powerful for close-in fighting.

I like to start, given the choice, from a totally negative posture, hands down by my sides and in the Goju parallel stance. No build-up, no talking, no threatening, just right into it, as explosive a movement as I can possibly make. Now I personally like to charge in on my opponents rather than use long-range kicks. I can kick, and I have kicked people and put them away in the past, but I just don't feel as comfortable with kicks as I'd like to. I like to close in with people fast and tie up their hands to prevent them using a weapon on me. I always assume they have one and that way I'm not taken by surprise. More and more people are tooled-up nowadays. I must say here that I have got nothing against long-range kicks or high kicks, I know that performed well by the right person, they work fine, it's just that I find them risky. When I was in Japan, in Mr Yamaguchi's dojo and then Mr Higaonna's dojo, it took me years before I had the confidence to try and pull off a roundhouse kick to the head. I'd always stick to front kicks if they were in front of me and side kicks if they moved to my left or right. But really, when you are training in Asia, you learn to defend against really good kickers but you have a difficult time becoming a good kicker yourself. Because from the *rei* (bow), they nearly always attack immediately, so therefore you are always defending. At least that's how I found it to be. The Japanese are fast, they are supple, super-fluid with their legs and so consequently they use lots of kicking techniques to get in on you. The only way that I could effectively stop them was to beat them off the mark, charge in on them as soon as the bow was over and get them on the ground. And that tactic of charging in has, in practical situations of violence over the last twelve years or so, proved to be one of the most effective things that I learnt in Japan. Believe me, I'd have been glassed and bottled and stabbed a lot more times than I have been, had it not been for my ability to instantly dash in close to opponents and polish them off at close quarters.

If I need to get hold of them, I prefer catching them on their left side because most people are right-handed. Of course, all of this depends on the particular situation, but once I have hold I inevitably spin them off-balance or to an unfavourable body angle. I can use all sides of my body, most people can't. See, when I work on a bag – I use a full-length, eight-foot kickboxing bag – I don't just hit it, I grapple with it as well, lifting it, pulling, pushing, as well as, of course, punching, kicking and butting it. I just attack the bag as if it were a giant person and I get into it with everything. You name it and I use it on the bag: shoulders, shins, knees, forearms, even my arse. I have my students move around me holding air-bags so that I can practise putting good solid shots and combinations into them from every conceivable angle. I also have them doing the same thing.

Now I have never had much success at locking wrists and applying aikido-style holds on people in fast, 'live' situations. Maybe some people can, after years and years of practice, I don't know. For me, I have to stick to elbows and knees. I can hook strongly with either hand. I like palm-heel strikes. I instinctively headbutt opponents in the face or body as soon as the distance is right. I use the elbow against head butts coming at me, or finger strikes for the 'peepers' (eyes). I have already told you that I often use stamp-kicks against the leading knee. I'll sometimes footsweep them and, when they are down, I often find myself stomping on their elbows and knees before dropping a knee, or two, into them. In my dojo I will often have my students just trying to block and stay out of my way whilst I chase after them trying to kick, punch, sweep and grab them. It's good training for both them and me. Sometimes I have had four or five of them leap on me in a totally non-prearranged fashion, so that I can tune in my body to getting out of situations like that, which I am quite likely to find myself in, during any night of the week.

Any final suggestions on how you feel a karateka can improve his chances of surviving in the street, the sort of advice you give to your students?

Only to recap on what I have just said. If you don't already do bag-work, start right away. Get yourself a super-large kick bag and practise all your techniques on it from ranges of one foot away to eight feet away. Learn to apply the techniques slowly and rhythmically with correct footwork that takes you around the bag in both directions. As you get more conversant with it, begin giving it some real stick whilst at the same time protecting your ribs and lungs by keeping your elbows tucked in close to your body, and protect your groin and stomach by lifting your knees. Another good training tool is the *makiwara* which you should hit with everything from the long-range lunge punch to *ura-zuki* (short punch) from very close. You should condition your arms and legs to the reality of being bruised and hurt by strenuous blocking practice. A *wing chun* dummy would be great for that, if you were working alone. As a final comment on this, I'd say that going into the dojo with the correct, serious attitude is vitally important. If you are not careful, there will be a lack of realism in training. Students are generally very co-operative in the dojo whereas, outside, nobody is. I make my students really put the techniques in if their opponents forget to move or block, or do whatever is called for in that situation. They have to be made to understand that they may lose half their face at one shot.

Do you have any specific advice on dealing with a person coming at you with a weapon, a knife for example?

My personal thing is, if you can't hit him with anything – a chair, a table, a lampstand – then as he comes at you, charge in and trap his weapon hand. Half-turn him away from you and take the opportunity, if it's possible, to push him down anything, like a flight of stairs; out of anything, like a window; or under something, like a passing vehicle. I teach my students a particular method that was taught to me by the two Korean teachers I told you about earlier in which you have to get control of the weapon hand and concentrate, no matter what, on holding that weapon in the opponent's own hand, even if it means getting your own hand cut in the process. You do it by locking his thumb against the knife. You then bend his elbow in a circular motion and plunge the weapon back into him. In other words, you can give him what he intended to give you. Nice, instant justice, don't you think? You obviously don't agree because you have gone quiet, for a change.

No, it's not that, I'm in complete agreement with you that anybody who tries to stick a knife in you, deserves a taste of it themselves. I'm all for 'an eye for an eye'. I'm just thinking about the follow-up problems – like explaining these tactics and the 'kill or get killed' attitude to a judge and jury, and perhaps even a coroner.

Well that's a consideration of course but I'm not going to lose sleep over it. If I take the time to think about all that might happen to me afterwards, I'd be unable to do the job I'm doing as effectively as I now do it. Nobody in their right mind wants that type of aggravation in their lives. But as I have told you before, if it is a situation of them or me then I have no hesitation whatsoever. When somebody tries to stick a blade in me or cave my skull in with an iron bar, and they fail to complete the job, then they are in for the most savage retaliation that I can possibly dish out. And that's a promise.

What would you say to someone who accused you of setting a bad example of a martial artist by the work that you do and the life that you lead?

Bullshit, that's what I'd say to them. To my understanding, the original Asian concept of the martial arts was for defence against unwarranted attack, right? And the epitome of a martial artist was the Japanese samurai. And what were they employed as? Fighters, that's what. What were the best Chinese fighters doing to earn their living? Working as caravan guards for the Emperor and for rich merchants. The best-trained warriors were hired for their fighting abilities to protect the welfare of people who couldn't do it themselves, and I have made a living out of doing exactly the same thing. I give a perfectly legitimate service to the best of my ability to my employers and I believe that, over the years, I have saved an untold number of people from injury. And I bet that I have discouraged quite a few idiots who, had they been successful on the night I ran into them, would probably have gone on to cause a lot of trouble for other people who would have been unable to cure them as well as I did.

Would you describe yourself as a violent man?

No, I would not. You see, I have gone through the last ten years of personal private life and travel without getting involved in one silly, even harsh, verbal incident outside of my professional working time. And during my work, remember, I am only reacting to the actions of other people. I was brought up correctly in a civilized, disciplined environment and I would never dream of sticking a broken glass in someone's face. The concepts that are subscribed to in the dojo – purity of thought and development of the self – are all well and good but reality is somewhat different. My place is the street and the type of people that I come up against, the scum that I have been describing, do change your outlook somewhat. You have to adapt to the society that you are in. So I do not see myself as a violent person, no.

Gary, thank you for a very interesting interview. I wish you continued success in staying on top.

Thanks, Digger, I fully intend to do just that.

* * *

POSTSCRIPT. Gary passed away in 2001. Here's what I wrote in *Combat* magazine at the time:

> The fond farewells have been said, the tears wiped, the lumps in the throat swallowed. Gary, the great fighting man, has gone. We are all still in shock. As I write this, I

still can't believe that 'The Digger' has died. Logically, we understand that everyone dies, but as I gave the sad news to those who knew Gary, both here in Liverpool and further afield, the universal reaction was shock. Gary was larger than life and his death was totally unexpected. Gary had been rushed to hospital, in the early hours of Saturday, February 17, where he died from pancreatitis. We were all terribly upset, but Terry O'Neill was devastated. Gary had stayed with Terry for his first couple of years in England, and they were close friends. I trained and worked with Gary quite a bit during that time, and remained a mate ever since.

Gary was always surrounded by myth and rumour: he served in Vietnam, worked for the CIA, was a mercenary soldier, a Triad enforcer. All nonsense, and irrelevant because the truth was impressive enough. For over thirty-five years Gary was involved in professional violence, more precisely, in the profession of stopping violence, in some of the most dangerous places around. Over the years he established himself as a legend in a business where we are not easily impressed. Alongside this 'frontline' work, Gary also taught others how to look after themselves in a violent confrontation. Again, his work in this field was acknowledged by his peers as being top rate.

I asked Simon James, my training partner, to set down his memory of meeting Gary, because I think you will find it shows a side of Gary which those of us who knew him well remember.

One Christmas Day in the early Eighties, my Mum was terminally ill in Fazakerly Hospital, Liverpool. I called a cab to take me down there and Gary Spiers turned up. At the time he used to drive a cab occasionally as well as working the doors. I recognised him – he was already a hero of mine in the martial arts – but this was the first time I'd ever met him. I felt dwarfed sitting next to this huge man and I was in awe of his reputation, both as a martial artist and as the most fearsome streetfighter around. Everyone knew his name. I wasn't really sure what to expect but Gary was friendly and warm.

The drive down to the hospital took about forty-five minutes, and Gary talked non-stop about cars, travel, taxi-driving; he had decided to work Christmas Day because it was double or triple rate and he was after buying a new car. Eventually the subject turned to martial arts, which of course Gary was passionate about. When we got to the hospital he asked me how I was getting home, because cabs were hard to get that day. I said that since it was Xmas Day I'd be about three hours, so I'd just have to hope I'd be able get a cab later. Gary said, 'Don't worry about that, Digger. I've got a mate round the corner, I'll go round there and pick you up later.'

I stayed more than three-and-a-half hours, but sure enough, when I left the hospital Gary was waiting there, looking like a huge bear jammed into this old Austin Princess. He'd been there half an hour. I was amazed he'd waited and told him I was very grateful. He dismissed the thanks and carried on the conversation about martial arts as if we'd never had a break. When we got back to my house he pulled into the drive and we talked for another hour or more in the car. As anyone who knew Gary will tell you, he was a great storyteller. I listened in awe of the great man as he recounted many tales about training abroad and violence in the pubs and clubs of the north-west.

I asked Gary why he worked doors, why he would put himself in such situations. He told me about an incident which had occurred recently. He'd had a big fight in the town centre with a gang of blokes who were harassing a young girl. She was trying to get away and Gary pulled her into the doorway of the pub where he was working, trying to shut the doors behind her. The gang pushed through, though – nine of them. Luckily Gary was able to 'put them away'. Gary was known as a violent man because of these kinds of incidents, but few people saw the full picture. Not many men would risk fighting nine men to protect a young girl they didn't even know.

Gary then told me something that has always stuck with me. He said that it was a shame that so many people train to a high level in martial arts but never use those skills to protect other, less able people.

I learned a lot on that day, and I saw a side of Gary I guess a lot of people didn't see. What he told me shaped my attitude towards martial arts and towards people, and it was a prime motivation when I began door work myself many years later. You see I was only a kid at the time, maybe fourteen or fifteen years old, and I hadn't been training long. Yet here was a guy who'd travelled the world, a personal student of Yamaguchi himself, a legendary fighter and martial artist, and he still took the time to talk to me and cheer me up. He'd spent the whole of his Christmas Day, when he could have been out earning money, talking to me.

In this book I have assembled many of the memories and the experiences that I have of working with Gary. Amongst those who knew him in the door business, as well as the fighting arts, his name still rings out.

Mark from the Gutterfighters delivers a textbook tiger's claw as Si Squires
attacks in a protective suit during a seminar. *(Photo by Richie Owens)*

CHAPTER 17

THE GUTTERFIGHTERS

WHEN WE STARTED training bodyguards, we needed to develop a syllabus for their close-combat skills. Traditional karate, which takes years to learn, would not fit the bill, so I looked to other sources. I had investigated World War Two Combatives, a US military term for hand-to-hand combat, in the Seventies, mainly through the various training manuals, and was, to be frank, unimpressed. That was because I was looking through the prism of Asian martial arts. Re-evaluating the WW2 material later, I found it actually ideal for our bodyguard training purposes because it was designed to be taught to previously inexperienced personnel in a short period of time. As I trained various government BG teams from 1980 onwards, I gradually developed a compressed syllabus which the guys could learn within the time limits of the course, yet apply on demand in an attack situation.

Terry asked me to write a regular column for *Fighting Arts*, based on the realities of self-protection. I called this the 'On Guard' column and it became a hit with the lads who wanted to train for street reality. When we got together for the first open BG course in 1985, Lofty Wiseman based his Unarmed Combatives on the WW2 syllabus. He told me that for SAS unarmed combat, *Kill Or Get Killed* by Colonel Applegate was their bible. However, perhaps the most important figure in combatives was an Englishman. William Ewart Fairbain joined the Shanghai Municipal Police (SMP) after serving with the Royal Marines. At the time, Shanghai was perhaps the world's most dangerous city, equivalent to Johannesburg today. A year later, patrolling a foot-beat in the red-light district, he was evidently attacked, because he had the unnerving experience of waking to find himself in hospital. While recovering from the assault, he noticed an advert for 'Professor Okada, Ju-jutsu and Bonesetting'. Fairbairn started training in Japanese martial arts, eventually gaining black belt second-dan from the Kodokan. I have known several people who took up training as the result of a violent attack. Every one trained with an extra degree of commitment, knowing that violence was a grim reality. Fairbairn expanded his training to include Chinese boxing under Master Cui Jindong.

In 1910, Fairbairn was promoted to sergeant and began his long career as an instructor in close-quarter combatives, firstly on the pistol range. Over the years he developed and expanded police training to new levels. For example, he introduced the Mystery House, a multi-room shooting facility later adopted by the SAS as the famed Killing House. As he rose through the ranks, his influence spread and he was able to introduce more innovations. He created the first SWAT team, the SMP Reserve Unit, fully equipped and heavily armed as a mobile reaction force. Whenever they went on a callout, Fairbairn was there gaining first hand experience in the alleys and slums of Shanghai. It is estimated that Fairbairn was involved in over 600 armed encounters during this period.

The name of Fairbairn is often linked with Eric Anthony Sykes. A somewhat mysterious figure, it is now believed that Sykes may have been a member of the Secret Intelligence Service (SIS). What is known is that he worked for an estate agent, and also organized hunting expeditions. He also acted for US companies, importing firearms and ammunition into Shanghai. In about 1926, Sykes joined the Sniper Unit, a section of the Reserve Riot Unit, and took part in numerous callouts.

In 1939, Fairbairn retired as assistant commissioner of the SMP, and together with Sykes travelled to England, where they were accepted by the War Office as Captains. Fairbairn first trained the Home Guard, whose highly secret auxiliary units had a covert role far removed from the popular 'Dad's Army' image. They were to act as stay-behind parties to become in effect the British resistance movement following the expected Nazi invasion. He also trained the Commandos, the raiding force that was to be Britain's offensive arm, striking at vital enemy targets.

Fairbairn produced his classic manual *All-In Fighting* during this period. Published in the USA as *Get Tough!*, this shows marked changes from the Shanghai phase. Police need to handle drunks, handcuff resisting suspects, and disperse crowds. Military/infiltrators need a stripped-down system to instantly subdue an enemy, with or without weapons. Fairbairn and Sykes gathered together a select group of twelve men, who were put through a twelve-week instructors programme, and then sent out to spread the system through the forces. Included in this group were Bill Pilkington, who was already experienced in ju-jutsu and Indian *lathi* stick fighting, and Gerald Carr, from Liverpool, whose preferred weapon was the docker's hook. It was during this period that Fairbairn and Sykes produced their famed 'F-S dagger', which became the badge of the Commandos and the emblem of many special units worldwide.

Following success training the Commandos, Fairbairn and Sykes were recruited by the Special Operations Executive, the secret agency tasked by Churchill to 'set Europe ablaze'. SOE agents needed to blend in while operating in occupied territory, so relied on a variety of covert weapons as well as unarmed skills. This became known as 'silent killing', the final evolution of the Fairbairn system. *Get Tough!* was further revised and only the most aggressive, potentially lethal, techniques retained. America started a counterpart of the SOE, the Office of Strategic Services (OSS), and such was the fame of Fairbairn that he was requested by the OSS to provide instruction in silent killing to their personnel. He stayed in America until the war ended, finishing with the rank of lieutenant colonel, and was decorated for his invaluable contribution.

Meanwhile Eric A. Sykes stayed in Great Britain training the SOE and other secret agencies, including the Secret Intelligence Service (SIS). Sykes was an intriguing character and it has been speculated that he was himself an agent of SIS while in the Far East. Besides being a superb shot, he was a master in the use of arcane covert weapons, such as sleeve and lapel daggers, killing needles and disguised firearms. Sykes refined the *Get Tough!*-era syllabus and, like Fairbairn, eliminated all but the most effective stuff. He died in 1945.

It is important to note that Fairbairn taught a total system, including the use of impact weapons, edged weapons and firearms as well as hand-to-hand methods. This all-in system is known by many terms. The SOE called it silent killing. Current military terminology prefers CQB, or close-quarter battle. American instructors refer to CQC, close-quarter combatives. Fairbairn called it 'gutterfighting'. To quote Fairbairn: 'You're interested only in disabling or killing your enemy. That's why I teach what I call Gutterfighting. There's no fair play; no rules except one: kill or be killed.'

Combatives is not a martial art, like karate, ju-jutsu, aikido or wing chun. Nor is it a style, like Shotokan or Goju-ryu. In articles and Internet forum threads we sometimes see people discussing the merits of a style or system and comparing them to combatives as if it was another similar activity. It's not. Combatives could be described as 'what works in a fight', and as such transcends such comparative discussions; because if you use this definition the question then becomes, 'What do you think is best for self-protection, wing chun, or what works in a fight?' It becomes a ridiculous question.So, how can we justify the claim that we are emphasising 'what works in a fight'? The primary instructors of combatives teach from their own direct experience. When Fairbairn and Sykes were appointed as the staff for Britain's wartime close-combat training it wasn't because they had cups, trophies, or even because of the black-belt grades. It was because they had used their methods in countless violent confrontations on the streets of Shanghai, the world's most dangerous city. Experience was further gathered as trainees returned from wartime operations, so by 1945 the Shanghai foundation was laminated by even more direct application, making the methods taught by Fairbairn, Sykes and their associates highly tested under combat.

Since the War, other instructors have offered the results of experience working in the frontline security industry, notably Geoff Thompson and Peter Consterdine in the UK. All the instructors mentioned teach from 'what works in the street'. They all teach different techniques, because we are all individuals and have our own preferences, but the concepts they teach all have a commonality. Everything is simple, direct, aggressive. Pre-emptive where possible, counter-offensive where not. From this we can extend the definition of combatives to 'what works in the street for the majority of people'.

* * *

One of the things I did with the bodyguards was to buy a number of kick-shields and striking mitts, in order for them to accelerate the training experience by getting feedback from striking an impact target. One of the surprising things I found was that many of the guys with previous martial arts experience couldn't deliver impact power. I've held the pads for guys with black belts and felt nothing when they hit. Then the next guy in line, with no previous training, would rock me with really powerful, natural strikes. We did have some superb martial artists on the course, guys like Peter Consterdine and Nick Hughes, who could perform under pressure and deliver massive impact. They had both worked the doors and were using impact pads in their regular training.

Training the guys was a real revelation for me and I immediately saw the utility of the WW2 methods, allied with modern situational control tactics and other concepts from our experience on the doors. Since then I have researched, refined and reviewed the programme, and have used it for the self-protection training of police, security and civilians ever since.

* * *

Simon James, a keen martial artist, attended the course with Marcus Wynne in 1996. We kept in touch and eventually started a training group in Prescot, Merseyside, in 1997. Many of the first members had trained in Filipino martial arts, Jeet Kune Do and similar systems. Tony Da Costa and Ian Davies started right at the beginning and are still training today, as instructors in their own right.

Training was based on the above concepts, plus lots of heavy, anaerobic fitness work, again of the type used in bodyguard training. Combative conditioning training includes such drills as ton-ups and Tabata protocols, really intensive work. We utilise kettlebells, medicine balls, sandbags and plyometric equipment. Fitness is essential, to us it's the mirror image to fighting. 'Toughness' is being tough on yourself, pushing the limits, never giving up, because the scum you confront are likely to be hyped on speed or coke, or in a drunken rage, or just working on sheer, natural viciousness. You must have willpower as a weapon, and that is developed in arduous training.

Several years ago, Si Squires approached us for some training and he and his guys became part of our group. Si has pioneered high-stress scenario training, especially involving fighting against an opponent in a padded suit, which allows full-on responses. Through Si we have been able to include this essential aspect into our seminars.

Gradually the demand for this training spread, at first within the UK, then overseas. In 2003 we held our first international training seminar in Merseyside with participants from all over the world. This has become an annual event. We were also asked by a number of our regulars to start an instructional training programme, similar to what we have done in RSA. We now have three generations of instructors certified here.

There has never been a better time to train for self-protection. There are good, experienced instructors teaching highly effective, proven methods, in most areas of the country. Just make sure they emphasise 'self-protection' rather than 'self-defence', as there is a difference! I once saw a quote, which really impressed me. I added a bit on the end and had it printed on cards for friends and training course members. I think it says a lot.

> Somewhere, right now, your enemy is training
> so that when he meets you,
> he beats you.
> Train hard,
> Stay ON GUARD!

Dennis stops an attack with a stab-kick to the knee at a demo in 1982.

CHAPTER 18

REALITY CHECK

AFTER *FIGHTING ARTS International* terminated, I was asked to write a monthly column for another UK martial arts magazine. To launch the series, my then training partner Si James interviewed me. I have included it here because it encapsulates many of my thoughts on reality-based fight training. The questions are Si's, the answers are mine.

You would mix and match skills, for example introducing grappling into your regular training. In the pre-Bruce Lee era, was it unusual for traditional martial artists to do this?

On a formal level it was. The traditional systems were very insular, and didn't really encourage much experimenting between different styles or schools. Having said that, on an individual basis, I'm sure many other people besides us were doing this. It's the pragmatic approach, adapting what works. Probably Bruce Lee's main contribution was that he encouraged people to do this.

A point on grappling. I just want to make this very clear, because everyone and his dog is teaching grappling now: I don't like it. I think it's boring, I don't like watching it, I don't really like doing it anymore – but you've got to do it. It's like eating your greens as a kid. As a martial artist you have got to know it. People are teaching it as a complete fighting system: it's not. It has big problems when you get into the street with it. The biggest downfall of grappling is that it can be defeated by biting, eye-gouging, blades and multiple opponents, methods forbidden in the systems which promote grappling. It has those weaknesses, but then every system has weaknesses, you've just got to know as many options as you can to take care of as many problems as you can.

Terry and I used to do a lot of grappling. Terry had practised quite a bit of wrestling, I'd done a little bit of judo. We used to practise breaking holds, groundwork and things like that, because as everyone knows, a lot of fights end up on the ground unintentionally. You've got to know how to survive down there, but no one would ever voluntarily go to the ground. The idea of using your grappling offensively never occurred to us, we used it defensively to get out of a situation. Our offensive battery was karate-type techniques. Generally speaking, you were in a crowd situation where you'd definitely want to avoid grappling. We used to do it for fun. Terry and I would wrestle in the foyer of the clubs. You would get customers arriving for their office party having to step over two characters in tuxedos rolling around on the carpet.

One time, Terry, Gary Spiers, the late Steve Cattle and I were on a train going to Denmark. We spent most of the journey grappling. Steve was a very good judo man, Gary had done ju-jutsu and wrestling, so we paired up and exchanged techniques, rolling around in the corridors. We looked up at one stage and we were in a station, with people running round pointing at the 'mad English' and calling, 'Polizei!' Fortunately the train moved off before we got locked up.

I've also found that in the places where you're most likely to experience violence – pubs, clubs, outside in the street – the environment itself is unsafe for grappling, and apart from the broken glass, tables, chairs and other obstacles which hinder/hurt you, you're being kicked by his mates.

Yeah, without a doubt. You and I have both worked in places where you don't even like to put your boots on the floor, never mind the rest of your body! And there are always plenty of volunteers willing to dive in if you're on the floor. You've got to know it, but avoid it – avoid grappling, particularly ground grappling, as much as you can. It is definitely not where you want to be.

You've described how you've moved away from traditional systems, yet many people maintain that traditional martial arts hold all the answers to modern problems. After all, the reasoning is that if it worked hundreds of years ago, it must still work today. What do you think of this argument, and what gives you the right to question arts which have been practised for centuries?

Well, to answer the last bit first, what gives me the right is that the martial arts were all created by people, they were adapted by people over the years, and I am a person as well. We all have the right to ask these questions and to work out solutions for ourselves.

I base what I do on outcomes: what is your outcome, what do you want from your training? Now, in the martial arts, particularly the traditional martial arts, a lot of the training is process orientated, in other words the outcome is the training. You are training for the enjoyment, for the fitness, or, for the kinaesthetic performance of the art. You enjoy the actual performance, and that's fine, I don't have any argument with it. However, you can get that same feeling of performance from many other activities, it's not unique to the martial arts, you don't have to study a fighting art to get that. So that's the process, now what of other outcomes?

If your outcome is to compete, to enter and possibly win tournaments, trophies, medals and titles, then obviously the sport systems are the way to go, and the training in those systems is very useful for that aim. If you want to master an art, its kata and all the traditional aspects, again that's fine, and there are lots of systems that offer that. However, if your outcome is self-protection, and I would suggest that the majority of people initially take up martial arts for self-protection, then if you look at the traditional arts, they don't actually offer solutions to this problem, the reason being that they don't handle the attacks that actually happen on the street, in the way they happen on the street. They learn to handle a theoretical attack, and it's usually part of a loop, in other words you learn to fight your own system. Karate people learn to fight against karate punches and kicks, judo people fight from a grip and so on, they don't mix and match and they don't look at how people actually attack in reality spontaneously on the street.

If you want to train for sport, art, or health, that's fine, but since most people take up martial arts for self-protection, this should be made clear. How many sport instructors tell prospective students that they don't really teach protection? We are all a product of our experience, and my experience, from my own encounters and also based on the experience of people I respect, such as Terry, Gary, Tommy Mac and other good doormen, leads me to believe that you have to adapt and modify to a very great degree, to the point where it's no longer recognisable as a traditional martial art.

If we take the four requirements of a fighting system – mindset, tactics, skills and equipment – we find that the skill side in the martial arts is okay, there is a library of skills that we can take, modify and adapt. They don't, however, offer us much in the way of tactics or mindset. Traditional arts profess to teach the mental aspect, but you have to really dig in to get it. There are sayings and aphorisms that you can interpret and finally work something out. It's not taught overtly, it's not taught explicitly and usefully. The mindset and the tactics are the most important parts, so the things that are lacking are the things that you need most.

Mindset is composed of a couple of factors. One is preparedness, which means that you've assessed your tactical situation. We are not living in peaceful times and we are all impacted by violent crime. Your assessment rates the probability of attack: if not a likelihood of an attack, at least a possibility. That then is a spur to situational awareness, the second aspect, which is like a mental radar which you keep on at all times when you're in a public area. This then detects any signs of an attack or preparations for an attack, or, the very subtle behavioural indicators that could lead you to know you should be elsewhere. In this way you can avoid an attack or avoid a situation, which is obviously always the best thing to do. Then, at that time, you don't need the other parts... you don't need the skills, you don't need the tactics.

So mindset, particularly for people who haven't had the time to train extensively in systems, or are physically weak or infirm, for them mindset is a must, but it's also important for the rest of us too because it's always better to avoid a problem than confront it. This avoidance is obviously something which is very important in the world of close protection because you don't want to be dragging your VIP through a fight. You want to avoid it. The whole of bodyguarding is based on avoidance. Become extremely avoidant.

How can you train to acquire the correct mindset ?

It's a secret [laughs].... you go into a cave in the mountains and thirty years later come out with the correct mindset, as long as you've taken the right herbs as well.

Mindset is something we cover in detail on our Combatives courses, and the great thing about it is it's actually one of the easiest aspects to learn, you've then just got to do it for the rest of your life. Situational awareness is a matter of staying at the right level according to the particular threat environment at the time. As humans we're not naturally very aware because we're predators, and predators don't tend to be as 'switched on' as prey animals. Prey animals are always looking around wondering if they're going to get eaten by one of the predators. As the supreme predator on the planet we tend to mentally switch off, think about other things, so we do have to inculcate this to make sure that that mental radar is switched on. We have a systematised way of teaching this, explaining all of the principles and concepts. The best way to elicit the mindset is in scenario training. That's the best tool.

The training field is often dominated by people who have a system to sell, or a blinkered 'wasn't invented here, not interested' attitude. Have you met with much resistance when trying to introduce new concepts to trainees? For example, you have increasingly integrated a lot of cutting edge mental training technologies into your teaching.

To expand on the mental training technologies, I fundamentally use NLP [Neuro-Linguistic Programming]. What NLP does is either allow you to do more in the training time span, or to cut down the training time taken to achieve the same level. This is a proven and demonstrable fact. It's a kind of accelerated learning. It is the study of excellence in any particular field. So if we use NLP, in the instructional side if you're teaching or in the learning side if you're a student, you will achieve more, faster, to a better level.

As for people being resistant to new ideas, well of course this is a people problem, not unique to this field at all. People like to operate in a comfort zone. They are familiar with it and are unwilling to change. They will only change if you provide the motivation. What you offer must be clearly to their advantage. That's the job of the instructor, to provide that motivation to change.

Even the newest stuff coming out now, in five years time people will be set in their ways with that. We'll be trying to break the complacency again. It is a continually evolving subject. In this business, if you think you've got it down pat then you're already starting to fossilise.

So that would explain why you don't teach a set and structured system?

Yes. The idea is to offer as many options as possible because options give you flexibility of behaviour. In terms of evolution, the organisms with the most flexibility of behaviour have triumphed. That doesn't mean that the individual should have hundreds of different options, it just means that the system should offer many options. He can then adopt the options which best suit his particular purpose. That's why what we do is systemised, but it's not a system. It will continue to evolve. It keeps me really busy, revising lesson plans and so on, but it's got to be done. Material that's ten years out of date is no use to anyone. It must be continually evolving, continually growing, added to from many different sources. I would say I learn something from every course I teach. That goes in the pot. I am constantly open to ideas from anyone. I believe that's how good instructors are made. I've been in classes next to the most famous instructors in the business and there they are joining in, on the firing range or in the gym. They don't stop learning. That's the lesson for the rest of us.

I understand that these advanced learning technologies, such as NLP, emphasise 'state-based' training. Can you explain what this involves?

State-based training is simply aggression. It's accessing the ideal fighting state, that state where we use our mental and physical resources to the utmost, where everything is welded together to fight to the utmost in a survival situation and to win. Not just to survive but to win.

I understand what you're saying here, but many people find it difficult to access the kind of controlled rage you utilise in this fighting state. How can decent, law-abiding people who spend their lives controlling anger, avoiding conflict, who indeed may never have experienced conflict, learn to access and control this fighting state.

Good question. By the way, some of those people who have never experienced conflict are teaching martial arts! How do you learn to access and control aggression at will? Well, the answer is in the question because accessing and controlling aggression involves controlling anger. Anger is negative for us; we need to convert anger into controlled aggression, which is the 'turbo booster' for the fight. I want to emphasise though, that avoiding conflict is the priority. But when the conflict is unavoidable, the only option is to win. We avoid the fight if we can, but if we must fight we must win. A good friend of mine, a colonel in the South African police, has that as his motto.

What if you can't access the anger in the first place, is there a danger that, in controlling anger, you could slip back into fear instead of channelling forwards into controlled aggression?

Fear and anger are mirror images of the same emotion. There is a danger of slipping into or being paralysed by fear. This is the panic state. Everyone talks about 'fight or flight', well the third aspect is freeze. The Three F's: flight, fight or freeze. Flight is okay; if you can avoid, as I've said, off you go. Fighting is okay. If you have to fight, you've got to learn to do it real well. Freezing, obviously, is the bad one. It's what some people call hyper-vigilance, or the human-factors people in aviation call 'negative-panic'.

Can you tell us more of this process?

Fear conversion is part of the state-based training and it's a process that you can learn from reading about it, in theory, but you must have experienced it in practice. We have a series of drills to do this. For the people who tell us they've never experienced anger, what we usually do is argue with them about this till they get real angry about it and then, in NLP terms, we anchor it. They can then use that in the scenarios and in the training, but that's just the start; anger is just the spark to ignite the controlled aggression. This is the crux: controlled aggression. It's like the attack dog which can be made to attack or switch off with just a simple word of command. So you are totally under self-control. It's directed and it's forceful. The state we're trying to access is a state of ferocious resolve. This has two aspects: the ferocity is the raw, animal fighting instinct, and the resolve is the determination to do whatever it takes to win the fight. That is the state instilled in our people in the training. Ferocious resolve.

A lot of people are teaching self protection these days, covering aspects such as awareness, verbal conflict management, fear control, pre-emptive striking and so on. All important aspects, but somewhere in-between there has to be the willingness to act.

Yeah, excellent question. Willingness is one of the 'Ness brothers'. A good friend of mine, Lieutenant Dave Spaulding, of Montgomery County Sheriff's Office, came up with the Ness brothers idea for his lectures on the subject. The Ness brothers, readiNESS, which we've already talked about – that situational awareness – and also willingNESS. Willingness is vital. There are many cases where people have had situational awareness, they've detected the threat, but they weren't ready and willing, particularly willing, to do something about it.

People have been killed or seriously injured because of that. I know a lot of switched-on people who haven't made the conscious mental decision to act. Again I go back to what we talked about before, that determination to do whatever it takes to win the fight.

Today I had the chance to see many of these training principles in action on your very successful Edged Weapon Defence course here in Liverpool. What are the realities of the knife threat and why do you feel that traditional methods do not effectively address the problem?

The main problem is that they don't train against the knife in the way it is actually used in real attacks. For example, karate teaches knife as an extension of the hand. Knife *randori*, as seen in some aikido systems, can again be quite unrealistic. The knife used in the street is very seldom locked out, never stops moving, is very fast and comes in at a variety of angles. In fact, most of the time the victim seldom knows he's in a knife fight. It's only afterwards he realises he's been stabbed.

This happened to a friend of mine. He was in a fight, and he thought he was winning. They were pounding each other good style, but the other guy had a balisong knife in each hand. My mate only realised he was in trouble when everything went black and he slipped into a coma. There just happened to be someone highly trained in first aid nearby who saved his life. Every major internal organ was punctured, and it took many, many hours of surgery to save his life. Happily he recovered.

That is quite typical, it is not the exception. A lot of the time you are not even aware a knife is there, so your defence has got to be based on that. There again the martial arts don't offer much in the way of solutions.

Is situational awareness a valuable tool in alerting you to the presence of edged weapons?

Very much so. To get back to something I mentioned earlier, one of the things that you learn in that line of work is reading people, the behavioural cues. On a subconscious level you're processing what you're seeing all the time and sometimes you just know something's out of place.

You check it out, and you find out the guy's carrying a weapon. Sometimes it's actually a physical cue – his body posture shows you he's nervous about something, he's trying to hide something or cover something up. This is a whole subject in itself. When we train people how to carry weapons in countries where it's legal, we cover this –how not to give yourself away if you're legally carrying a concealed weapon – and this is the flip side of learning how to recognise someone who is carrying an illegal weapon, oris uncomfortable carrying a weapon. Being able to size someone up quickly is a big part of it. I guess it's a product of experience. Anyone coming into this business should definitely try to work with experienced people to learn this.

Dennis, you are renowned as a world class instructor in many different fields, from firearms to empty hand, how can you stay on top of all the latest developments, maintain your skills, in so many different areas?

Obviously this is a must. One of the ways I do it is by attending training events, conferences, conventions and so on, particularly in the USA. ASLET and IALEFI hold international and regional training conferences where you can train with the world's top use-of-force instructors. For many years I've attended these events, which offer both hands-on skills as well as the theoretical side. I've also been honoured to be invited to teach at these prestigious events too.

There is a tremendous exchange of information and direct skills at these events. You learn so much: formally, in the set classes, and informally, in-between and after classes, networking with the instructors, both the famous and not-so-famous ones. You've got to be out there to seek out the information. Basically you've got to be a student, and that's what I regard myself as. I am a serious student of this subject.

What motivates you to continue to train and study at such a high level?

Because I still go to various parts of the world, frequently travel to the most dangerous city in the world to train and operate there. So my motivation is very high. We tend to become complacent in our own situation. Where we live we tend to accept what the politicians once called 'the accepted level of violence', but violence is never acceptable, and we must always remember that time is going to change things. We're not always going to be young, we're not always going to be as fit, but we still want to survive our natural lifespan. Training is very important, your motivation should be the future.

Is there a vast difference between the various skills you teach, not only in terms of the physical training, but also the psychological and tactical aspects?

Basically the subject I teach is CQB, close-quarter battle, which is a completely integrated system. It is all fighting, all combat, whether you are using weapons, including firearms, edged weapons, impact weapons, chemical weapons, or you are unarmed, it is all the same.

When you take that as the basis, you are training yourself. YOU are the weapon, you are the fighter. When we train people in firearms, the man is more important than the gun. It's the same through all the different aspects of CQB. So basically we're training the individual. We are training the person to be a fighter. That's why unarmed combat is so important, it is the basis of everything else. That's why even some of the special operations forces in various places still emphasise hand-to-hand combat, even though they're equipped with high-tech weaponry. In a way, you are never then unarmed. Physically, mentally, there's no distinction in the training. It's all integrated together because the mind has to operate under the physical stress.

How do you see the current state of reality-based training? What are the trends, both good and bad?

Reality-based training is an interesting term. Let's make it clear: whose reality? We are all products of our own experience. I teach according to my own experience, but my experience is necessarily limited. So you have to access as much reality as you can from many, many sources and add it to your training. For example, the skills you need as a doorman are not always that applicable to what you need for normal, civilian self-protection, because doormen have a different role. Police officers: self-protection and arrest techniques for the police officer are task specific. Again the ordinary man doesn't need the same type of training. But he does need a particular type of training, and it must be based on reality – the reality of what may happen to him in the street. Scenario training is vital. What we need is fidelity of simulation, in other words the simulation must replicate reality as closely as possible. It must be in the same environment, the same type of attack, with the same levels of force and aggression. This is where we get into training equipment and the use of environmental simulators. This is another field where a lot of progress is going to be made.

You have worked, trained, and been friends with some of the world's very best martial arts, military and police experts. Who has influenced or impressed you the most?

I have been influenced by everybody I've trained with, either positively or negatively. Most of the people I would name would not be familiar to the readers, except for Lofty Wiseman, who is a legend. His knowledge and ability are just awesome. And working with Lofty has been a tremendous experience.

Overall, the person who has most influenced me in this field, without a doubt, is Terry O'Neill. He gave me the first advice on it, he started me in this business, and he continues to be my best friend. He really is the 'boss' in this business.

Terry O'Neill launching one of his trademark kicks in a karate competition in 1972. He could pull off these moves in the street too.

CHAPTER 19

FIGHT-WINNING TECHNIQUES

TERRY, GARY AND I used a variety of martial arts and other fighting methods in our many confrontations. This chapter discusses the main techniques favoured by each of us.

TERRY

Working with Terry was, at times, like being in a martial arts movie. I've never worked with anyone else who handled situations with such mastery. My old mate Tommy McNally once put it this way: 'If there was just you and Terry working, it was like working with a gang.'

The epitome of karate is the *ippon*, the 'one-strike kill'. When Terry was competing he won the majority of his fights with *ippons*, clean one-hit victories. Photos of him competing in national and world championships show perfect form; you could use them to illustrate a technical manual. Well, he was the same in work. The vast majority of his fights were over with one kick. He would be in the middle of a melee delivering textbook kicks. What a learning experience!

Terry had a long competitive career, during which he won the Shotokan National Championship numerous times (in both *kumite* and *kata*) as well as captaining the British national team and winning the World Championships. Those who saw Terry compete will remember his classic form and his willingness to use new and spectacular techniques. He could use his techniques in the street just as easily as he used them in competition. I once saw it written that Terry had fifty knockouts with head kicks on the door. Well, from personal experience I can tell you that it would be well into the thousand, or more. He used to knock people out so regularly it was boring.

Working with Terry, I found out how he was able to pull off so many wins. He was always practising. He would get the karate-trained doormen to act sparring partners during quiet periods, and he'd go over some sweep or high kick again and again. For many of us this was a bonus to our working life. Terry then had less willing sparring partners when he would use those same techniques against troublemakers, of which there was always a ready supply.

I have seen him use spinning leg sweeps to put guys down, especially if he only wanted to quieten them, rather than kayo them. Head-high back roundhouse kicks were common too. As I've said before, some nights it was like working in a martial arts movie. Watching Terry score *ippon* with a new technique in a tournament, I've often thought, 'Hmm, where have I seen that before?' When it comes to high kicks, Terry is the exception that proves the rule. All self-protection instructors, myself included, advise you to avoid high kicks and the advice is valid. Yet Terry could make them work. I've worked with other good karate lads who couldn't.

According to Tommy Mac, who knew Terry before I did, he wasn't a 'natural'. He worked very hard at his techniques and his flexibility. Terry could drop down into a full splits, then lean forward with his chest flat on the floor. To kick, he would raise his knee up level with his ear. This flexibility gave a fantastic surprise element to his kicks, they came in at you from unexpected angles.

In competition, Terry was beating top international karate men who were expecting his kicks. So you can imagine the effect in the street, when his opponents were not expecting it. I've seen him kayo three guys with head kicks, then when they woke up number three, who had seen his mates hit first, he had no idea what happened. Before 1973, when the Bruce Lee movie boom made the martial arts popular, most people had no idea about how kicks could be used in a fight. The height and distance of karate kicks were totally alien, even to experienced street fighters.

Terry used the classic roundhouse kick for most of his victories, in the arena and in the street. Everyone in self-protection says you shouldn't use them in the street, they are too risky, but Terry was the exception because he was so skilful, so fast and so powerful that he could do it. He later added more unorthodox kicks, and these were equally devastating. The 'reverse roundhouse kick' was especially effective for the following reason. I'll explain from Terry's point of view. To throw the kick, he would start by raising his right knee high as he turned his body anticlockwise. Now, the opponent might pick this up and instinctively react by moving away, to his own right. However, Terry's leg would cross the centre line and he would hook back with his heel, striking the opponent on the right side of his head as he moved right into the kick. A conventional right roundhouse hits the guy on his left, the reverse kick hits on his right, and this is a very deceptive attack.

Terry also used other techniques. He kept a diary (that would be some read!) and noted what he used each time. I'm sure he eventually used every strike in the book. I've seen him use ridge-hands, slaps, hammerfists. The only thing I've never seen him use was a headbutt. With neither of us being football players, it wasn't in Terry's or my toolbox. I've told already about the time at the Top Rank when Terry, Richie Molyneaux and I all went down under weight of numbers. We all fought our way back up. We had a karate function in the upstairs room, and a whole load of the top guys joined in with us. Those were the days! Apart from that, I recall Terry grappling from standing to ground with a guy because he wanted to. Terry told the rest of us to stay back and he had a good 'pull' with this guy. Guess who won?

Terry's feet are deformed, not only from slamming them into pads, kickbags and people, but from the flexed positions he puts them in to get the perfect kick. He could bend his toes back further than anyone else, and seemed to have an extra joint in the middle of his foot. Often after putting a gang to sleep, Terry would worry about legal consequences and, if arrested, that his shoes could be submitted to forensic science exam. So he would swap shoes with me. I once mentioned that I was also likely to be arrested and accused, but he countered that nobody would believe that I could kick to the head so that was OK. His shoes were awful, all lumps and bumps, while he always said my shoes felt great, very comfy.

In these fights Terry was never under any stress, any pressure. He was brimming with confidence and would often deliver some funny quip as he delivered the bad news with his foot. We were expected to award him *ippon* just like a karate referee. Terry did a lot of pure basic repetition of his techniques. Tommy Mac told me that when Terry lived on about the twelfth floor of a tower block when a young man, he would run down the stairs, stopping at every landing to do a combination of techniques. Specifically for sweeps, he would get a training partner and work on the entry, contact and follow through, over and over again. Some of this was done in personal training, in the gym, park, or even on nightclubs during quiet nights. I was his partner quite a bit for this and still have the scars to prove it! In application Terry generally used the sweep at long range, no grabbing. I have the feeling that Terry mainly used sweeps in the street as practice for competition, but I could be wrong, and maybe he just liked a change from routinely sending people asleep with kicks. The karate guys weren't very open to experimentation in the dojo, so Terry would use aggressors in the clubs to perfect his new techniques.

Specifically regarding the footsweep, Tommy recalled that Terry told him that at first he would sweep at ankle height, then he gradually worked higher, until he could hit a guy just under the hip and still down him. His object was to make the guy flip a 180° through the air. What a player. I've seen him do variations such as reverse-sweeps too.

Terry is still at it. He's still on the front line doors in Liverpool and he has lost none of his skill. There was a major kick-off, I wasn't there but a guy who was working with Terry on the night in question gave an eyewitness account, in which Terry basically took on a gang and put them all to sleep. He side-kicked the first, propelling him right out of the door and across the pavement. Another was downed with a finger-jab to the eyes. He swept the next and continued the action with a stamp. While doing this, he was holding the other doormen back, saying, 'It's all right lads, I'll handle this, there's only a few of them.'

I was talking to one of his black belt students once and he said he'd never seen Terry compete. Terry had retired from competition before the student began. It struck me then how lucky I was to have seen Terry not only compete at national level but also to work with him when he was doing it for real on the doors. It was a unique education.

GARY

Tommy Mac summed up Gary's fighting technique as 'impact'. And, really, that's it: he specialized in delivering massive impact. As a big man he was obviously powerful, but what impressed was his speed. He could deliver a series of devastating attacks in a fast flurry, and get them on target, usually with fight-finishing effect. He would also use elbows and headbutts mixed in with the punches, often by grabbing and hitting. He liked to maul and brawl and, with his wrestling background, was happy to grapple. He folded guys up like a deckchair. He considered grip strength important, and had a special set of weights made with handles that fitted around his thumbs. He'd press these to strengthen his thumbs and grip.

Gary had probably the best fighting brain for unarmed combat of anyone I've ever met. His techniques were somewhat less classical than Terry's, for example he would use headbutts. At the Top Rank, I saw him knock out someone with a rear headbutt (see Chapter 6). His knee strikes were also highly effective. 'Grab his head and deliver the biscuits and cheese,' he said, using the Aussie rhyming slang for 'knees'. Up close he got personal, and would rip, gouge and bite. 'I launched myself at him and bit him like a Mako shark,' he told me after one tussle.

Gary had encounters with numerous guys, including two of the most feared men in Liverpool. He had only been here a short time when he was visiting a mate who worked as a bouncer at an after-hours drinking club. A fight erupted and Gary picked up one of the guys, a heavyweight bloke, and simply carried him up the stairs and right outside. It turned out he was one of the most respected doormen in the town, who said, 'I'll be back to continue this.' Gary replied, 'Bring a few mates with you to make it more interesting.' They actually became friends later.

Gary used various kicks, but never to the head like Terry. Goju-kai specialised in whippy instep kicks to the groin, usually delivered from a cat stance. Gary taught us to bounce the foot off the floor, as if you'd stepped on a nail, to add speed to the strike. It was very effective. He would also drive his huge feet into the belly in a crippling front kick. Not many people use front kicks effectively, but Gary did. He had these enormous feet, we used to say they were like kids' drawings of feet, and he would go into the middle of a big crowd fight and just scoop people into the centre and kick them broken with these huge feet, which were usually bare. Side thrust-kicks to the belly were also favourites. He once used the side-kick in a more unorthodox way. Scamps disco was above the Bier Keller, and when that huge hall emptied most punters would go upstairs to continue the festivities at Scamps. The reception area was tiny, so there would be a large queue outside waiting to be allowed in to the foyer to pay. One busy Friday, a punter started banging on the door. Gary opened it and told him to hang on, he'd be let in as soon as possible. He banged again and was told again, in more forceful language. When he banged the third time, Gary had had enough. He quietly slid back the bolts, took a run up and blasted the door with a full-weight thrust-kick, then went outside, ignoring the unconscious punter, streaming with blood, and asked if everything was all right.

Gary had picked up the Thai-style scything kick while training with the famed kickboxer Ray Edler in Tokyo. In matches, the Thais employ the shin in a scything smash to the opponent's thigh, like an 80mph baseball bat, gradually inducing a 'mobility kill'. Gary adapted the kick for street use. Firstly, in the ring you pivot on the ball of your foot, turning the entire body like a flywheel as you deliver the kick with a rigid leg. For the street, wearing shoes on uneven surfaces, this can be problematic, so Gary preferred to use more of a karate action, planting the support foot firmly and utilising hip torque to deliver the kick. He changed the target area too; he would grab his opponent and apply his shin across the bladder and belly in a fight-finishing cruncher. In his final years Gary returned to his first love, wrestling, and regularly worked out with the great Tony Buck.

Naturally when Gary arrived I was eager to train with him. Straightaway I realised that what he taught was not Goju-kai. I later found it was not the Okinawa style either. Gary really taught his own system, based on what he'd learned in Australia and Japan and heavily influenced by his considerable practical experience. I called it 'Ga-ryu'. Later it became known as Applied Karate and looking back it was better for the street than any strictly traditional style. Recently Gary characterised his system in the clerihew 'Do-it-ryu...before they do it to you!'

DENNIS

While doing judo I had a friendly tussle with a friend at college and laid him out with a chop to the neck. That was the first time I used what we now call the axehand, and I've used it several times since. When I was heavily into karate I used the *zizami-tsuki*, a lead-hand punch similar to the boxing jab. I found I could hit fast with it. However, it usually splattered the nose, sending blood everywhere, so wasn't really a good 'witness friendly' technique. While working at the Blue Angel in Liverpool, a large guy tried to grapple with me and I put him on his knees with a short *ura-tsuki* (close-punch) to the floating ribs. That was the first time I used a body shot and I can't remember having much luck with them since.

So when I started doing CQB work, the bodyguard role, one of the things is the weapons transition: you've got to keep your hands available; it's not a good idea to punch. Even Mike Tyson damaged his hand punching Mitch Green in a street fight – that's the example we all use. So I'd been closed-fist punching, but then with the rise of Aids, it didn't seem like a good example to get infected off someone's teeth or blood. I had used slaps for a long time. I'd started using open hand slaps, backhand and forehand slaps, and was getting good results with them, knockouts.

My mainstay became the elbow strike. I found it easy to generate impact, causing a knockout without blood or damage. I also added slaps, mainly because we used them in Goju karate and they seemed effective. Testing them at work I found they were, indeed, highly effective and I have used them ever since. The type of slap I favour is a fast, whipping action, in contrast to the powerslap taught and used so effectively by people like Peter Consterdine. Either the palm or the backhand can be used.

Another Goju technique was a thrust kick to the knee or shin. We now call this by the wartime term stab kick. This is a devastating technique, and I've seen it used to break a leg in the street. It can also compromise the balance. You get a change of level: it brings your opponent down at a funny angle and the follow up is usually very easy. It works partly because it's unusual, like the sweep. A chap I worked with swept a guy who was threatening him. The guy went down, he scrambled up, was looking, thinking, 'I haven't been punched, but I was on my back.' He got swept again, the other way, went down, got up, and after the third sweep, he said, 'That's it,' and he went off, because he just didn't know what was happening. That full sweep, it's a beautiful technique. You couldn't use it all the time, but when you could, it was great.

Working with Terry and seeing him deliver head-high roundhouse kicks eventually rubbed off on me and I tried them out myself, with various levels of success. Eventually I started getting the desired kayo, which is fairly amazing, as my high kicks are pathetic. The fact that I'm tall, that often I was standing on a step helped a lot. Also, when you kick to an actual target you don't have the balance/recovery problems associated with kicking thin air. This is telling testament to the power of what NLP calls modelling, and in Terry you had the ultimate model for performance. Later at Ruperts, Don modelled my performance, and actually started getting KOs with high kicks too!

Gary taught me the Thai kick. I liked his variation to the belly, but I developed my own variation by slamming my shin across both of my opponent's shins, scything his legs and dropping him face down. I also used the kick as originally taught by the Thais – to the thigh muscle – usually in intervention situations. Like Terry I worked on foot sweeps and had good results bringing guys down with this unexpected action. I never did the spectacular variations, such as the reverse spin, that Terry could pull off.

Over the years I've used numerous techniques: chin jabs,

hammerfists, webhands (to the throat), but the one which has been the favourite in the past fifteen years has been the choke. Actually, this is a misnomer, because technically a choke attacks the air supply, while the method we use cuts off the blood supply to/from the brain. It really should be called a strangle, but since I taught it to numerous doormen, they all call it the choke. I used the strangle for years as an intervention technique, running in to deal with a fight already underway. With a rear approach it's easy to snake your arms around the throat and squeeze. It was Nick Hughes who showed us how to apply this as a pre-emptive while facing a potential assailant. A very fast push/pull action and you have him wrapped up and asleep in quick time.

It's a great technique and relatively non-threatening. They don't feel pain, they just feel pressure, so they don't panic. If you start choking somebody, compressing the larynx, and they start panicking, they get an adrenalin rush and you've got a berserker on your hands. But with the neck restraint, they feel something and they usually grab your elbow, and then that's about as far as they get. Then they go unconscious, they have a bit of a spasm, and they wake up disorientated with the fight gone out of them. You see, even with knockouts, if they're on drugs, they'll get up again. They get up again after being knocked unconscious, just bounce up again. And that's from a good, heavy doorman – whack! – sparked out. Bang, up again. It's fearsome, Terminator stuff. It's changed the whole game. You get a guy who's been out for three days on speed and cocaine; as you know, cocaine mimics the effects of adrenalin.

Tommy Mac always reckoned that if somebody tried to choke him, he'd have the guy's eyes with his thumbs. And he got into a discussion with Arthur Tansley, a judo man, who used the judo cross-lapel choke. So it came to, 'Okay, we'll try it.' The rules were that Arthur started with his hands ready on the lapels, and Tommy had his hands on top, ready to go for the eyes. And as soon as Arthur felt pressure on the eyeballs, he was to stop his choke. Terry was the referee. And Tommy himself told me, 'Terry said, "Go," and that's all I remember.' They did it again, and the same thing happened. Tommy told me, 'It wasn't dramatic, but nothing seemed to happen. I didn't get my thumbs up and I just couldn't do anything.' It was that fast, and I have to say that impressed me. That's faster than I can put people out.

WEAPONS

Terry was not much of a man for using weapons. At one time we had access to the entire inventory of US made 'Bucheimer' blackjacks and saps via the chap who imported them from America. After 'field testing', neither Terry nor I were impressed. I did once see Terry wield a length of broomstick that he picked up in a major brawl downstairs in the Victoriana. To be honest, he was doing the guys a favour because strikes with a light length of wood were a blessing compared to what he could do with his hands and feet!

At one time I was much taken with the *nunchaku*, or rice flail weapon, especially after Gary showed me how to swing them effectively. To be honest, they are far from the super-weapon shown in the martial arts movies, and you often end up hitting the doorframe, walls, your mates or yourself. The police in Birkenhead came to us after finding a lad unconscious in an alley with a pair of *nunchaku* beside him. It turned out he had knocked himself out while training. I have used the *nunchaku* as a restraint device, ensnaring and squeezing the throat. Looking back, it was taking a chance, as the risk of serious, even fatal, injury is high.

The highlight of my *nunchaku* career was when I'd bought a new pair of really beautiful, dense-wood sticks while on a trip to Paris. Back at the Top Rank there was a huge kick-off, with about 200 guys throwing tables, chairs and bottles. Gary and I ran into the mix and the Kiwi started kicking everyone in range, while grinning from ear to ear. I decided it was sticks time, whipped my new toys from my inside pocket and launched a classic swing at the nearest fighter. I hit him but the stick kept on going into the crowd, leaving me with the other end and a dangling bit of nylon cord. I never saw the other shaft again.

Gary was pretty adept with the sticks, and this being before Bruce Lee popularised them, no one knew what they were. One day Gary was driving his first UK car, a VW Beetle, and became involved in a road-rage incident, with the other driver swearing at him. I got the details from one of the lads who was in the car with Gary. The door of the Beetle opened and Gary came out – and just kept coming. The other driver was obviously unaware of just how much beef you can cram in a VW. Taking his *nunchaku*, he smashed the other car, caving in the bonnet until it buckled like a piece of foil. He got back in and drove the Beetle away, leaving the other guy wondering if his luck was good or bad.

Most compact impact weapons are, in my opinion, worthless for the skilled fighter. I remember when the expandable baton was first issued to Merseyside Police. I saw an officer whack a troublemaker on the leg, three times, full power. The guy just looked at the constable and said, 'What was that supposed to be?' The officer turned to me and said, 'I need a bigger stick!' The best impact weapon is the big Maglite. I started carrying one at the Quad, and soon many of the lads followed suit. After a few years, police pressure on the security companies stopped their guys carrying the big light.

Gary was very fond of knives, and having worked professionally as a butcher, was very adept at using them. When he first arrived in the UK, after about a week he went over to Paris for a week of R&R. While there he bought a flick-knife with a 10in blade. A while later we were going to Manchester and had bought our tickets at Lime Street station.

As he handed his ticket at the barrier Gary was sorting through a large wad of currency. The ticket collector, seeing the cash, asked, 'Where's my cut?' Gary produced his flick-knife, snicked open the blade, and replied, 'Anywhere you like, Digger.'

Years later he was working in a nightclub with a restaurant, when a punter objected to having to leave the premises just because the music had finished, the bar was closed and drinking-up time had expired. Passing a table, he grabbed a steak knife, brandishing it at Gary. In a precursor to the famous scene in *Crocodile Dundee*, Gary displayed his own blade and announced casually, 'Got one of those myself mate, and I love all that stuff.' The punter dropped the blade and legged it.

Obviously, carrying a knife is a no-no legally, but Gary often worked in extraordinarily risky places, often alone. He faced bats, blades, and machetes on numerous occasions, and that flick-knife probably saved his life more than once.

Gary was a natural with a knife in his hand. In our early training, Gary taught me some very practical knife techniques. In recent years I've done a lot of knife work under top instructors here and abroad, but that initial grounding has served me well. One favourite move is virtually unstoppable and is a good item in your trick-bag. Actually Gary's knife skill came not from the martial arts but from working as a butcher. As a young man he had travelled Australia in the migratory meat industry, cutting and boning large animals on a piece-rate basis. Commercial pressure was intense, your crew only made their bonus if every member pulled his weight, so speed, skill and dexterity were prerequisites. Also, in an all-male transient community, disputes were common and often settled with the tools to hand, the knives. Gary was knowledgeable about knives and could discuss Bowies and Fairbairns, but he always recommended butchers knives as they were quite cheap, easily available and were designed to cut meat.

Gary usually had a knife on him, which he routinely used

for cutting his steak and any other flesh that needed slicing. Brian Waites told me while at the Goju Kai he came into the dojo one day to find Gary practising 'stabbing the bag'. He was using a training knife to work slash/thrust combinations on the kick bag. Brian found this weird, but such training is now accepted in the blade-based systems. In many ways, Gary was ahead of his time.

SITUATIONAL CONTROL

Winning fights is much more than a collection of strikes. For example, the pre-conflict phase, comprising proxemics (the distances between people as they interact), unobtrusive readiness positions, assault cues, verbalization and tactical positioning is where the fight is often won, or, lost. Use of deception and distraction leading to destruction is another vital aspect. As Gary once announced, 'I battered a gang of six of them last night. Mind you, I cheated a bit.' All experienced doormen learn this stuff, usually subconsciously. However, nothing in combat is ever guaranteed. A karate doorman was arguing with a drunken Irishman, and it was rapidly going bad, so the doorman decided to go pre-emptive and attempted a distraction. The punter was offering to fight, so the lad said 'Okay mate, I'll fight you as soon as that copper goes past,' while pointing over the drunk's shoulder in the oldest trick in the book. It worked, though, and as the drunk turned to look the doorman hit him full whack across the side of the head with the *nunchaku* he'd been holding behind his back. The Irishman just turned back and said, 'I don't see any fecken' copper.' Time for Plan B!

I was tremendously fortunate in working with Terry, Gary, Tommy and others, who were terrific role models for this kind of knowledge. Some 'self-defence' instructors teach from a background of sport or theory and have never been in a real fight since they left school. They are to be avoided like the plague.

All the top self-protection instructors – Geoff Thompson, Nick Hughes, John Brawn, Peter Consterdine, Jamie O'Keefe and John Skillen – have a background in martial arts honed and distilled by years on frontline door security. We all pass this material on to the trainees on our self-protection programmes. Situational awareness is arguably the most important aspect. With good situational awareness, you can avoid the fight; which is usually the best option. I first learned this concept from Terry. We were walking down Church Street in Liverpool city centre on a crowded Saturday morning, following a hectic night working on the Vic, and I asked Terry how it was possible to remember all the guys we'd had confrontations with, so as to recognize them if we encountered them in the street. Terry replied that it's impossible to remember so many guys, and that we should be on our guard all the time. That was the first inkling of a subject I have studied in detail ever since. With Colonel Cooper I learned the Colour Code, to key the level of alertness with the threat level. From Marcus Wynne I learned the OODA-loop, to mentally outmanoeuvre an enemy by making decisions faster. But it was Terry who summed it all up with that first, simple advice. Although this chapter has emphasised the techniques, the hard skills, on our seminars we make mindset the most important topic.

Q & A

I have regular correspondence with a variety of interested people about working in security, training with Terry and Gary, and so on. Here are some of those questions, with my replies:

Did Terry fire most of his kicks from the right or left leg?

Terry's favourite side was his right, but he was equally adept with the left.

Does he have any problems with his knees because the amount of kicks he throws puts enormous stress on the knees?

When Terry was thirteen years of age he had TB in his knees and was told by the doctor that he'd never play any sport. Many years later he met the doctor and reminded him of his prognosis, then told him he was captain of the British karate team. The doc just shrugged. Terry also suffered a bad knee injury in a team match against the Italians. He was last to fight, and the Brit team had the match already won, so Mr Enoeda told Terry to 'make a show' because the previous fights had been over quickly. Terry opened up with spinning kicks, and was entertaining the crowd when his supporting foot tangled in the canvas – they were, unusually, competing on mats – and couldn't pivot. The left knee joint burst under the torque of Terry's hip rotation. That left him with a weakness in that knee.

I think his number one target is the head but did he also score knockouts with body shots?

Yes, he has dropped guys for several minutes with thrust-kicks to the body. He would do this if the guy was especially obnoxious and needed 'punishment'. Terry also embraced the Thai-style kick to the thigh, which he picked up at the Meguro gym in 1970. However he tended to use this 'playfully' on his mates (it still hurt, though, as I can confirm).

Terry used a special elbow variation a lot, can you explain this?

I find describing techniques difficult. It was a type of spin elbow. From face to face he would pretend to break off the confrontation by turning away, but would continue into a forceful spin, raking the elbow up vertically under the chin. I include it in our training on the elbow strike.

How did he keep the right distance to fire a head-kick? Because in the regular talking distance that is pretty hard to do – or is his flexibility superb?

Terry's control of distance was superb. He could head kick from 'too close'. Chatting to Tommy Mac recently he mentioned a case where Terry was escorting one guy out of the club and was attacked by another. Without releasing the first Terry head kicked the other from a great distance, stretching across in a way Tommy said was sheer athletic brilliance. In that same conversation with Tommy, I reflected that it's difficult to write about working with Terry without being accused of exaggeration. You really had to see Terry in action to understand what we are talking about. I was greatly privileged to have spent those years working with him.

Did he ever use closed fist punches? Or did he prefer open hand strikes?

Terry used punches, as well as open-hand strikes. But I'd say eighty per cent of the time he used kicks. Terry kept a diary, and noted which techniques he used each night. He also tried out new techniques. I remember the first time he used the ridge-hand strike, because he discussed the effect afterwards.

Did he never use nasty techniques like knee-break or groin kicks?

He used various groin strikes, both kicking (with the instep) and striking (fast flick with the backhand). I have seen him grab the testicles in a grappling situation. Regarding the knee-break, I have done this with a stab-kick at the Banyan Tree.

Did he ever get punched before he could fire his pre-emptive strike?

I have never seen Terry hit before he could strike, but when I started working with him he already had about eight years door experience. His techniques are well known, whip-tip quick kicks and strikes, but his mindset was equally expert. I've never seen anyone go through the OODA cycle as quickly as Terry. So his pre-emptives were always a fight-finisher. I've been in a situation where Terry, another doorman and myself were swarmed by a massive crowd, in the Top Rank in about 1971. We all went down, and all fought our way back to our feet. That was an interesting event.

When Terry kicked pre-emptively in the street, you claimed he did so off his lead/right leg. Did Terry usually fight in a southpaw stance?

Really he mixed and matched. He kicked with either leg, and with front or rear, as the situation dictated. If he took a fighting stance it was normal, left foot forward, then kicked with the right. But usually he worked from however he happened to be standing. The 'interview' process didn't last long with Terry. Part of his efficiency was his really quick OODA-loop processing. He knew when violence was imminent, usually long before the guy he was facing.

What kind of repetition training did he do? Air punching or/and kicking or with resistance? Because I always heard the air punching/ kicking isn't good for your joints.

At first Terry, like all karate-ka, did his reps in the air. And you're right, it's not good for the joints. However Terry was an early advocate of hitting resistance. He brought a kick-shield back from a visit to the LAPD Academy, and started using it. This was before any were available in martial arts shops here. He told me he used to take it to classes and hold it in front of guys as they kicked, but stopped, because it was embarrassing just how lacking in impact they were.

What was his tactic against especially tall guys? Was he that flexible to kick them still in the head?

Terry is fairly tall at six foot one and could easily kick taller guys in the head.

You said the only one that could make the front-kick work was Gary. Didn't Terry use thrust kicks for punishment? Or were these side thrust kicks? Because I thought Terry could make every kick work.

Yes it was side thrust kicks that he used. Terry used front kick as a feint in sparring, but really didn't use it as a scoring technique, in either the arena or street. He always praised Gary for his use in the street, and Bill Christall for being able to front-kick in the dojo. By the way, Terry was one of the few people who could use *yoko-geri keage* (side snap-kick) successfully.

I have special interest in his close roundhouse kick. Did he pull his knee very near to his body to pull it off? Because this is the only way I could think they could work.

Terry brought his knee close to his ear when kicking. I've said it a thousand times, his kicks were amazing. They came at you from a strange angle. I'm the same height as Terry, but his foot would come down at me.

Did he usually kick to the side of the head or the chin/jaw?

Regarding target, it is a function of the weapon. At first he used a very classical kick, flexing his foot to strike with the ball of the foot. He would be very precise in his targeting. Later, at the suggestion of Ticky Donovan, he adopted the competition ploy of slapping with the instep, which is a bit quicker. So he mainly struck the face, using the instep like a super-slap. If the guy turned his head, then the kick would land elsewhere on the head, but nevertheless achieve kayo. Sometimes he'd use the old ball-of-foot kick, or, when side-kicking, the welt of the boot.

I know he hurled a barbell into a stack of mats for punching power. But my question is how did he get his kicking power?

That barbell throw was an early drill, I never saw him do it. He told me about it when we were sitting in the gym of the YMCA where he used to train. I'd say he developed most of his power, punching and kicking, from repetition training and from using weights. I once asked Terry which he favoured, *kata* or *kumite*, and he answered, 'Kihon,' which means 'basics'.

You said his flexibility is lesser now due injury. Is he still able to perform head-high kicks? Like on the incident you told where he had to move fifty yards to another door because the police thought there was a trained killer. Or would he kick someone in the groin so the head is in a better position?

He can still kick high, but he himself believes his flexibility is less. He rarely kicked the groin, mainly the head, sometimes (as punishment) the body.

Did he ever break his ankle, because on pictures I saw of him his ankle is really thick like mine and I had broken it in the past? And also how did he get back to his kicks even with his really damaged knee. But I think I can answer the questions on my own: it's probably his willpower.

I don't know if he broke his ankle, however he had lots of foot/ankle/knee injuries from hard sparring. Yes, willpower was the key.

What types of punches did he use? Karate reverse punches?

Reverse punches and lead hand jabs, but rarely. I was talking to a guy who does karate and he was surprised when I showed him how close Terry would kick. He'd kick them in the head at the range where I'd use a chinjab!

One of the most important questions. How is he even able to knock out multiple opponents with kicks? Would he roundhouse kick one then maybe sidekick one, or would he use the same kick to multiple persons?

I have seen him use roundhouse to the first, then straighten the same leg into a head-high side kick to the second, then sort of hop in and roundhouse the third, all with the same leg.

Were his spinning-back kicks also head-high or to the body?

When he started using spin kicks they were usually to the head but sometimes he'd use them as a sweep to drop the guy. That would often stun them.

Can you recall if he ever used knee strikes?

He used knee strikes, but again, not frequently. He knew that roundhouse worked 100 per cent and used it. He tried out just about every technique in the book, but just as 'research'. His staple was the kick.

He never used a headbutt? What would he use instead in close-quarters? Chinjabs?

He used the chinjab on one notable instance on the door of the Banyan Tree, a bar attached to a well-known city centre hotel. Terry is confronted by three guys who are refused entry. Terry is actually standing outside the club, getting some fresh air, thumbs hooked in his lapels. Anyway the 'mouth' steps forward and starts being abusive. Terry, always one to know when the fight has started, delivers a chinjab, just a short blow travelling less than twelve inches. As his hand retracted back to his lapel, the guy dropped, out cold. His mates became apologetic and dragged him to one side. The thing that makes this stand out from the hundreds of similar knockouts is that when the mouth recovered he accused one of his mates of hitting him from behind. He hadn't seen Terry move at all. He was rubbing his chin and complaining about being bottled from behind.

Usually, however, as described above, he'd kick from very close range to a guy right across the pavement. I never used the headbutt even once, and I can't recall Terry ever using it either. I did see him bite a guy once, but I put it down to playing with his dogs so much!

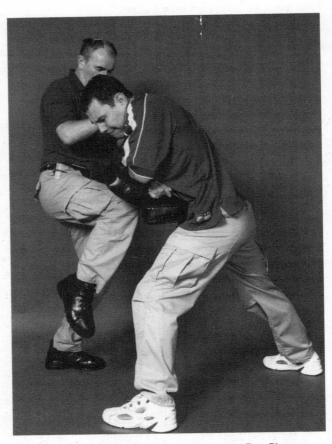
Den fires a knee into the pads with training partner Tony Rimmer.

CHAPTER 20

OLD SCHOOL, NEW RULES

HAVING STARTED ON doors in 1969, I have seen many changes, both in the way we work and in life in general. Liverpool has always been a violent city, but the type and level of violence was very different when I started working. Men were still likely to favour a fair fight, and even let a downed opponent back to his feet until he'd had enough. That was then, this is now.

One major change is gang culture. The last time I sat down for a brew of tea with Gary, he said, 'Dig, every bastard is in a gang.' Ordinary guys with decent jobs have adopted the culture of the gang. Fashion – shaved head, goatee beard, bulked-up physique, what I call 'doorman chic' – reinforces this behaviour. Previously, if you lashed a guy out, he may threaten to come back team-handed, but generally he'd wake up the next day with a hangover, time would have lent distance to the memory of being thrown out, and if he did try to recruit his mates, he'd have to hunt all over the place to get them together and they would also have hangovers and tell him to forget it. Now, the guy is on his mobile phone and can quickly assemble a crew, who will be likely full of 'beak' and raring to go. Back then, shop windows were brightly lit showcases rather than a steel mesh barricade. Taxis, too, had no protective grilles. Now, the signs of increased crime are everywhere and the professional security staff are in the front line of facing it.

Back then, let's be frank, doormen ruled by dishing out a hiding. If you crossed the line you got a smack, at the minimum, and everyone knew the rules. There was no CCTV, and if the police did eventually turn up to investigate a complaint the management denied all knowledge. They would literally not even know the full names, let alone addresses, of the doormen. I'm not fully condoning what went on then, but I believe that the pendulum has swung too far the other way. Now we work under constant CCTV scrutiny; at one place we had twenty-six cameras on us. The SIA licence scheme means that all details are held centrally and you can be identified by your badge, and it's an offence not to display it openly.

In the old days, if a gang tried it on we'd chase them all over the town and give them severe discouragement. We once chased a few into the Mersey Tunnel. Now, you daren't step off your door. I'm not calling for a return to the old days, but the threat facing doorstaff is far heavier than back then and they are working with their hands tied behind their backs.

Remember, the job of the door crew is to provide a safe environment for customers to enjoy themselves, and in the current climate doorstaff are not able to do that. I've often said that if you replaced the crew on a major city centre venue with a police team, how long would it be before the officers used CS spray, batons and handcuffs on the punters? Doormen not only work unarmed, but can't even use unarmed methods without risking their badge.

Another of the biggest changes over the years has been the vast increase in armed violence. When I started on doors there was a guy called Jimmy on the club scene who was infamous for having stabbed a guy. This guy lived on this reputation for years, so rare was it. Now, of course, everyone seems to carry either a knife or a firearm. Since all legal handguns were banned in 1997, armed crime has increased by about 400 per cent: so the ban worked then! At the time of the ban there were an estimated million illegal firearms in Great Britain, and despite the many futile amnesties, this number has only increased. By the way, official statistics can only count the offences that are brought to the attention of the police. There are numerous shootings and threats with weapons that go unreported, so the true statistics are even worse.

One of our guys had a pistol shoved into his chest while working in the city centre. He managed to disarm the guy, a drug dealer, and during the subsequent case it was found that the pistol was one of sixteen Glocks stolen from Merseyside Police at Altcar Range Training Area.

But by far the biggest change over the years has been the proliferation of drug taking. I was talking to one of the Drug Squad in about 1981 and he mentioned a heroin haul in Birkenhead. I expressed surprise, as previously addicts could get their heroin legally by prescription and there was virtually no widespread problem. The officer told me that the Government had scrapped the legal medical supply of heroin and since then the illegal trade had flourished, with Birkenhead being known as 'Smack City'. Why the Government, armed with the experience of illegal drug crime in America, would take a measure guaranteed to introduce the same problems here is beyond my simple brain. Whatever the logic, we all pay the price for the habit, and police and security have to now face drug-fuelled violence.

Liverpool has always been a hard-drinking city. The various psychoactive drugs have just added a pint of bat's blood to the witches' brew. 'Beak' (cocaine), 'speed' (amphetamine) and 'tablets' (Ecstasy) are so widely available they may as well be on offer at Tesco. Let's face facts, a substantial proportion of the population regard a 'line' or a 'tablet' as a normal part of the night out. Prices have fallen. When we were at the Quad, an Ecstasy tablet sold for up to £25. Currently, they are about £2 each. Everyone and his dog is involved in either taking, dealing or importing drugs, and they all think they're gangsters. They all think they can fight because they're drug dealers; and when they are out of their skulls on their own products, that reinforces the belief.

Without going into the science too much, cocaine and amphetamine mimic the effects of adrenaline, causing dramatic changes in the internal chemistry of the brain. On such stimulants, a guy becomes fearless, with pain tolerance through the roof and brimming with aggression. These are the exact attributes required for winning a fight, and a few chemicals can match years of training. I've seen many guys punch a brick wall, full power, again and again. I've seen a guy headbutt a solid wooden door, then do it again, with a grin on his face. I've seen two doormen take it in turns to choke out a skinny cokehead, who, despite losing bowel and bladder control, never went to sleep. I've seen a guy unconscious, totally out, recover in the blink of an eye and, from being on his back, was up and over a head-high fence in one motion. I've seen the 'jack-in-the-box' effect where a guy pops back up again and again after being felled by a heavyweight doorman. I've seen a slender woman thrown out only to come instantly back through the doorway with a head-high, two-footed kick. Of course the next day, when the drug wears off, they will probably need to go to the hospital, but we face them while they are roaring with chemical turbo charge.

There is a whole generation out there on every drug known to man. People with respectable day jobs take drugs while out at night. I once confiscated a bag of coke off a crewman from a nuclear submarine. Nice if he went into a rage while manning the missile switch.

* * *

Back in the day, we all worked individually for a particular nightclub; each club would have its own door team. Then Gary told us about how Bobby Jones in Australia had put door work on an organized footing by having a company with contracts with the various venues. Eventually, this system took hold here in the mid-Eighties and Gary was one of the prime movers in getting the different guys together. Door security companies were launched, some good, many bad. The better companies have definitely improved the security scene. Merseyside's Premier Security, for example, has a strict code of conduct, with no smoking, drinking or eating on the door and smart appearance and punctuality being emphasised. Many old school guys found it hard to adapt but eventually they all fell into line, and the result is a far more professional standard of service.

The licence system has also improved door work. Every local authority introduced its own scheme, with the guys being required to pass a training course and a criminal record check. This worked and for several years we had good, professional lads working who had been checked out as clean. Then the Government stepped in with the Security Industry Authority, or SIA, which it set up to 'manage the licensing of the private security industry'. This had been planned as the solution to the door wars of the Eighties, when various firms struggled violently for power, but, like all government projects, was years too late. Meanwhile the local councils had actually solved the problem. What the SIA has done is to introduce a bureaucratic mess into the process. The criminal record checks are still exactly the same and it is difficult to see just what the SIA has achieved. The training course is pathetic. As a professional instructor myself, I'm baffled how they expect to train doormen in a two-day classroom lecture presentation, then give them a written test which any member of the public could pass easily. You can learn the legal side, you can learn the medical side, and you can learn things like fire safety, but you can't learn to be a doorman on a course. There is a guy who used to come into one of the clubs and decided he wanted to become a doorman. He got a grant to pay for the course, passed the written test, and was badged by the SIA. He turned up at the club looking for work. The only problem is that he has no legs, is wheelchair-bound, has a colostomy bag and catheter and only one eye. No one in the entire process told him that he lacked the basic physical requirement to work on a door.

Then the licensing laws in this area specify that there will be video cameras everywhere on the doors. So everything you do is on TV. People can take your badge number and report you. So you have to be able to stay within the law, whereas before you could be very violent and get away with it. It's still a violent job and there are still a lot of people who will start fights in clubs and pubs. So in that way the doorman's job is a lot harder than it ever was. Having said that, it's also become a lot more professional. The big companies who run the leisure business want to deal with decent security companies. There are bad ones out there, but there are some good ones, and the level of professionalism now is higher than it ever was before. And that's good for the people who go out to the clubs.

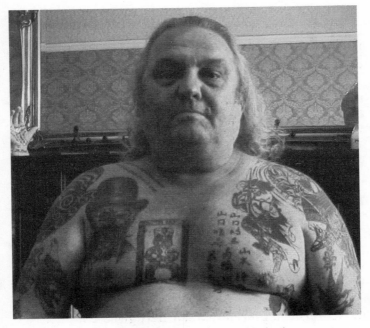

The last picture of Gary Spiers, taken shortly before his death.

CHAPTER 21

GARY THE GYNAECOLOGIST

WORKING AND HANGING out with the lads was always a real laugh. Here are a few memories.

Liverpool has the oldest Chinatown in Europe, with numerous restaurants serving genuine Cantonese food. I developed a taste for it about the same time as I started karate. When I was eighteen I had a girlfriend, Lin, of Chinese descent, and her grandfather cooked some tasty, simple dishes. At that time the restaurants wouldn't serve dim sum to Westerners, but going there with Lin opened the door to delicious shumai, ham-bau and other snacks.

Terry and I were regulars in Chinatown from about 1970 onwards. Eating on Sundays, after working up an appetite training, was especially memorable. Often the dim sum bowls were piled so high we couldn't see each other. Terry and I always fought to pay the bill, none of this 'whose turn is it?', each of us would try to grab the check and pay it. One day we were grappling for the bill and Terry grabbed my arm and ripped the entire sleeve off my new leather jacket. I said, 'You can pay the freakin' bill then!'

As much as we ate, we were novices compared to Gary. He could scoff for England. However, he never fought to pay the bill; quite the reverse, he would disappear, or fall asleep, then promise to get it next time. He arrived in 1971 and 'next time' happened in about 1999, when he bought Terry and me dinner in Chinatown, after a movie, then sulked about it. Gary would eat in the cheapest noodle shop and consume several of the largest bowls. The first time he did this, the cook came out to see who could eat so many bowls.

Together with his 'soldiers', Gary frequented an all-night Indian gaff in Bold Street. Gary would sample everyone's meal, dipping in with his French flick-knife (I suggested he should buy a flick-fork and spoon too). Then, when everyone was sated, he'd order his own huge scoff and eat it solo. Once, after falling out of there at about 3am, the guys were chatting on the pavement when one of the waiters ran out brandishing a knife. Gary side-thrust-kicked him into a heap and the guys piled in on him, only to find that Gary had left his flick-knife on the table and the hapless waiter was trying to return it.

Owners of all-you-can-eat buffets would groan when they saw Gary walk in. He would stay there all day, eating enough for six ordinary men. My good friend John Mon tells of passing a greasy spoon café in Lime Street and, seeing Gary seated, entered to have a chat to him. Since Gary was eating, John ordered a breakfast too, and then called for the bill, telling Gary, 'I'll get these mate.' To his shock the bill came to £34. Gary had been there all morning, consuming nine breakfasts.

* * *

Gary used to collect debts. He once left a message on a debtor's car roof by spraying a pound sign and a question mark with paint stripper. One another occasion, he turned up to collect ten grand from a businessman only to be told that he had a cash flow problem. 'You're living in a two-hundred-grand house, driving two thirty-grand cars, you owe my boss ten grand and you have a cash flow problem?' said Gary. 'I can help. The Criminal Compensation Board will pay you a grand for each broken rib, another couple of grand for a broken jaw, five grand for each leg – you'll make a profit.' The businessman paid up.

Terry was in dispute about payments on his Shogun and the finance company sent two heavies to repossess it. As far as Terry was concerned, all he saw was two men trying to steal his car, so he ran over to them. The first bailiff took a step towards the lad and was immediately felled with a head-kick. His partner became rooted to the spot in shock, babbling, so Terry gave him a mighty push, propelling him right across the roadway. They never tried again.

* * *

Terry always had at least one dog and Gary also owned a dog for a while. This was a huge Great Dane called Rangy. Now Danes are a passive breed, but Gary trained Rangy to be savage. Hammer Films would have been delighted to cast Rangy in *The Hound of the Baskervilles*. He would sometimes take it to work, and you would think that a twenty-stone, scar-faced Maori with a twelve-stone, slavering dog would be a bit of a deterrent. Not so. Gary was standing near the bar one evening, minding his own business, when he turned round to find a grinning idiot winding the dog's tail like a starting handle. 'I'll never understand this town, Dig,' Gary told me afterwards.

I've mentioned elsewhere about Gary smashing a car with *nunchaku* in a road rage incident. Another time he was in his car with John Clark (who told me the tale) when a parked truck blocked the street. Unable to pass, and in a hurry, Gary sprang into the cab, dropped his strides and parked a turd on the driver's seat, then wiped his bum on the delivery notes. He then got back into his car to wait. After a couple of minutes the driver returned and, after seeing his 'present', went ballistic. He asked Gary if he had seen who'd done it. Gary nonchalantly told him, 'You must have upset someone by blocking the road, mate.'

Before Terry learned to drive, he was a terror as a passenger. Once, when driving to Manchester with John Kerruish, Terry, who had been eating fruit, quickly pulled the empty paper bag over John's head. Suddenly blinded while doing seventy on the East Lancs Road, John had a sharp intake of breath, gluing the bag to his face. In a panic to rip the bag off, he poked himself in the eye, so that even after the bag was shredded he couldn't see properly through streaming eyes. Terry thought this was hilarious and later did the same to Tommy. It was only when he learned to drive that he realised how frightening this was.

* * *

Because the three of us had trained in karate styles, which heavily used Japanese terminology, we used this as a kind of code, or shorthand. If one of us was having a discussion with a group of guys he would tell the approaching others either *daijobu*, meaning everything was okay, this is not going to kick off; or, conversely, *dame*, it's going bad. This was fine, but Terry would often speak to the punters in Japanese, or using the stilted English that many karate instructors copy from their Japanese seniors. The bewildered punters would have no idea what Terry was telling them to do, and I've often wondered how many guys were knocked out because they didn't speak Japanese.

Gary was a joker. The Japanese term for the standard block to a kick is *gedan-barai*. Once, during a confrontation which was rapidly going bad, Gary asked his antagonist, 'Do you know how to do gedan-barai?' and when the guy answered in the negative, Gary said, 'This is going to be easy then,' and kicked him in the groin.

That fast, snappy instep-kick to the groin is a favourite of Japanese Goju-kai karate and Gary used it a lot. When we went to London to have a meet with Brian Waites, we were on the platform of the Underground during rush hour. As we went to board our train, a city gent barged into Gary, who instantly whipped a kick right into the bollocks. As the doors closed I saw the gent, bowler hat askew, writhing on the platform. What a start to his day. Gary explained that it wasn't being pushed that annoyed him but that the guy hadn't apologised.

While Terry was baffling the punters with his mixture of Japanese and broken-English, Gary would either use obscure Aussie rhyming slang or a series of very ornate locutions. When Gary first came to England, if he wanted to read your newspaper he'd ask, 'Can I peruse your periodical?' Eventually he stopped using this ornate language, but I remember when he told a staggering punter, 'Your present level of inebriation prevents me from permitting you admission to this establishment.'

* * *

Back when it was still legal Gary, Terry and I were pistol shooters. Like many martial artists, Gary and Terry were good shots, but they were always at it, always joking. At one session on an outdoor range, the three of us got lumbered with target changing duty in the butts. You are in a trench, with the shots going over your heads. Terry threw Gary's ear defenders onto the backstop, then, as Gary bent to retrieve them, pushed him onto the impact area. Gary was scrabbling his legs like a cartoon dog as bullets hit the sand all around him. Terry was laughing like a drain. I could only shake my head.

At a pistol competition we watched as one shooter, a police officer repeatedly, fumbled and dropped his pistol. Gary approached him. 'You're a policemen aren't you, in London, right? Jeez, the next time I'm in trouble down there I'll call a postman!'

* * *

Anyone who has had any dealings with Terry will no doubt be wondering why I haven't so far mentioned an aspect of him every bit as characteristic as his head-high kicks. This is his punctuality, or, rather, his total lack of it. As long as I've known him he's always been late for meetings and appointments; not just a few minutes late, but hours late. Whenever we arranged to meet in a coffee shop I'd always bring a book.

I read a lot of books waiting for the lad.

Sometimes on my night off we'd be in the movies or Chinatown and I'd warn Terry he'd be late for work. He would phone in some far-fetched excuse, usually involving breaking down on the motorway. A club manager told me that wherever Terry was supposed to be when phoning his excuses, he could always hear Chinese music in the background.

When we were in Japan he really surpassed himself in making people wait. One day we had a series of meetings, all with people who were doing us favours, and were late for every one. Firstly we had arranged to meet Master Higaonna, to book our tickets to Okinawa. We were an hour late. Then we had arranged to link up with Howard Alexander, a Canadian martial arts student, who was going to take us to meet Donn Draeger. Now this meet with the legendary Draeger was to be a highlight of our trip, so you'd think Terry would have been on time. No chance. We pitched up at the statue of a dog outside Shibuya station, a well-known meeting point, over an hour late, and Terry fully expected Alexander, who didn't know us, he was just a friend of a friend, to be there. I had some inkling where the Shimizu Jodo dojo was, so we made our own way there and eventually got to meet Donn, and met him several more times after that.

Finally, we were to meet Master Kanazawa, who had very kindly invited us to dinner. On the way we bumped in to Frank Hargrove, an American resident in Japan and Okinawa, who was highly graded in Shorin-ryu Karate, and who spoke fluent Japanese. Frank was a great guy, and we went for a coffee with him. So, when we turned up at the station to meet Master Kanazawa we were only a couple of hours late. We managed to find Ebisu dojo, and, when asked where we'd been Terry blatantly said we'd waited at the station, but didn't see anyone waiting for us. Apparently, they'd had all the troops out looking for us, so that was a bit thin.

Gary was just as bad, especially if you arranged to meet him in the morning. When Gary was in Tokyo, an American guy had arranged to meet him at a subway platform. Standing waiting, the American noticed another *gaijin*, a Belgian priest who sorted language-teaching jobs for the lads. They struck up a conversation and found that they were both waiting for Gary, who had arranged to meet both of them, at the same time and place, to do completely different things – and he didn't turn up for either of them!

When Terry and Gary arranged to meet each other it must have been epic. Glaciers would flow and species evolve during the wait. The first to arrive – late, of course – wouldn't know if the other had been and gone, or was even later.

I estimate that Terry only spent about two thirds of the time in work that he should have. Even so he knocked out several hundreds of guys. God knows how many he would have stiffened if he'd been on time. You might wonder why anyone would put up with such tardiness. All I can say, from my point of view, spending time with Terry was always worth the wait.

* * *

During the early Seventies, Terry was always trying on new clothes. He had very conservative tastes back then, and wore either sports jackets or blazers, with slacks. Trying on trousers was always a laugh because he would always check whether he could kick freely in them, and would whip a series of head-high thrust-kicks, to the amazement of the are-you-being-served shop staff. He would often argue about the size of his jackets. The outfitter would typically assess Terry as forty-two-inch chest, whereas the bulk of his lats muscles added a few significant inches to the dimensions. With a knowing smirk they'd bring a size 42 jacket. Terry would do a lats spread and split the seam, then walk out saying he didn't like the colour.

* * *

I bumped into Gary in town once. He immediately took off about the quality of doormen he was recruiting. 'It's not like our day, Den, these no-hopers want the money, but they don't want to do the job. I had one front the door last night looking for work. "Okay, you want to be a doorman, move me out of this club." He didn't want to try that Den, so I set him an easier problem: "The local Chief Inspector is in, he's pissed and he's groping the manager's wife. How would you sort this out?"' All this was told, with appropriate gestures and colourful Aussie profanity, to the consternation of the punters buying the *Daily Sport*.

Finally, the title of this chapter? It comes from Gary's business card.

> **Gary Spiers**
>
> **Gynaecologist**

On the back…

> **Awkward Cunts**
>
> **my speciality**

ACKNOWLEDGEMENTS

Numerous friends and colleagues contributed to this book. Graham Noble and Si James allowed me to use their interviews with me. Tommy McNally encouraged me to write the book, gave great advice, devoted many hours to giving me background of his experience, as well as consenting to a formal interview.

John Clark, who was my first firearms instructor, shared his memories of working with us on VIP protection, as well as working with Gary.

Marcus Wynne has been a source of inspiration to me as an instructor and writer. He always urged me to write a book; well, mate, this is it.

Nick Hughes kindly contributed material on the Aussie connection, as well as his experiences on the doors, in bodyguarding and in being a top fighting man.

Many thanks to Geoff Thompson for his very kind foreword, and for being such a positive inspiration to all those involved in the self-protection community.

Finally, thanks to Terry O'Neill, for permission to use material from *Fighting Arts*, for the interview, and for the most valuable thing of all, his friendship over the years.